More praise for

The COSMOPOLITAN CANOPY

"We know that the modern world-system has a major built-in contradiction. We profess loudly a normative universalism. But we practice deep racial and ethnic divides. How do we as individuals navigate this social anomaly? Elijah Anderson uncovers the ambiguous ways we do this in this exciting ethnography." —Immanuel Wallerstein, Yale University

"Once I began reading this brilliant book I could not put it down. Anderson provides an incredibly rich narrative of the interactions of city dwellers from different segregated neighborhoods—ghettos, ethnic enclaves, and suburbs—in public places. By revealing hidden social and racial dynamics, Anderson explains not only the conditions that ease racial tensions and promote interracial harmony but those that reinforce traditional racial boundaries as well. This book is a must-read." —William Julius Wilson, Lewis P. and Linda L. Geyser University Professor, Harvard University

"Elijah Anderson has devoted his life to documenting the racial divide in inner-city America. In this new, artfully personal ethnography, he dares to hope for an expansion of the space for human civility, while confronting us soberly with the immense ongoing toll of racism in everyday relationships in our nation." —Philippe Bourgois, author of *Righteous Dopefiend* and *In Search of Respect: Selling Crack in El Barrio*

"Elijah Anderson's *The Cosmopolitan Canopy* is an amazing achievement. His keenly observed and richly rendered portraits of life in Philadelphia's public spaces consistently yield insights so original and so perceptive that they leave you saying, 'Wow.' " —Ellis Cose, author, *The Rage of a Privileged Class* and *The End of Anger*

"This is the most important book on race relations in many years. Elijah Anderson, skilled ethnographer of the black community, takes us behind the statistics into the scenes of everyday life. We witness front-stage performances of integration and backstage racial ethnocentrism, as well as the venues where interracial cosmopolitan civility is constructed. *The Cosmopolitan Canopy* is a report on today's African American elite that long updates E. Franklin Frazier's classic *Black Bourgeoisie*. It offers a gift for our pessimistic times: a book of realistic optimism." —Randall Collins, president, American Sociological Association

"Elijah Anderson is a master ethnographer. Field research is a way of life for him, a medium through which, unceasingly, over the course of many years, he has courageously explored the innermost recesses of life in an American city, especially the social worlds and the experiences of black Americans. Once again, in *The Cosmopolitan Canopy*, he moves from one area of Philadelphia to another, exploring the patterns of social interaction and behavior in various public places. Anderson calls these urban spaces 'cosmopolitan canopies'—a concept likely to evoke lively, illuminating discussion." —Renée C. Fox, Annenberg Professor Emerita of the Social Sciences, University of Pennsylvania

"*The Cosmopolitan Canopy* is a richly detailed account of how the public spaces we all share can either separate or help bring us together. I strongly recommend it."

—Marian Wright Edelman, president, Children's Defense Fund

"A rich narrative. . . . Anderson's observations are keen but not distant as he offers journal pages and interviews, showing his own full engagement in interactions with a cross section of Philadelphians. Anderson also offers singular insight into the social machinations of blacks in professional versus social settings. Fascinating sociology and people-watching at its profound best." —Vanessa Bush, *Booklist*

"Anecdotes abound, and the author includes excerpts from his own journal of his perambulations and observations, giving his account immediacy and verisimilitude. The writing is generally crisp and clear, free of sociological jargon, and thus accessible to most readers." —*Kirkus Reviews*

"Anderson's nuanced treatment of 'the social dynamics of racial inequality' and his precise observations (the politics of eye contact, for example), . . . offer immediate pleasure."

—*Publishers Weekly*, starred review

"Elijah Anderson . . . might be the nation's leading people-watcher." —Dan Rodricks, *Baltimore Sun*

"Yale sociologist Anderson is a skilled, experienced ethnographer of urban race relations, and his observations are insightful. . . . The sheer wealth of perception and shrewd commentary makes this book very accessible and intriguing for students and others interested in the state of U.S. race relations in the early 21st century. . . . Highly recommended." —W. Griswold, *Choice*

"Philadelphia plays the starring role as Anderson shows how, in real life, we really do get along—with overlapping 'canopies' that combine to make a cosmopolis. A much-needed study of how boundaries disappear, assert themselves, and melt." —*Herald Review*

"Best of all is the author's relaxed and inspiring enjoyment of the city as a place of constant surprise, a multiplicity of pleasures, and wonder-inducing urban spaces." —Frederic and Mary Ann Brussat, *Spirituality Practice*

The
COSMOPOLITAN CANOPY

Race and Civility
in Everyday Life

ELIJAH ANDERSON

 W. W. Norton & Company   New York · London

For my friend and teacher, Howie
aka Howard S. Becker

Copyright © 2011 by Elijah Anderson

For information about permission to reproduce
selections from this book, write to Permissions,
W. W. Norton & Company, Inc.,
500 Fifth Avenue, New York, NY 10110

For information about special discounts for
bulk purchases, please contact W. W. Norton Special Sales
at specialsales@wwnorton.com or 800-233-4830

Frontispiece photograph by Elijah Anderson.
Map of Philadelphia created by Tom Gavin.

Manufacturing by Courier Westford
Book design by Dana Sloan
Production manager: Devon Zahn

Library of Congress Cataloging-in-Publication Data

Anderson, Elijah.
The cosmopolitan canopy : race and civility in
everyday life / Elijah Anderson — 1st ed.
        p. cm.
Includes bibliographical references and index.
ISBN 978-0-393-07163-4 (hardcover)
1. City and town life—Pennsylvania—Philadelphia.
2. Gentrification—Pennsylvania—Philadelphia.
3. United States—Race relations. 4. United States—Ethnic
relations. 5. African Americans—Social conditions—1975–
I. Title.
HT153.A53 2011
307.7609748'11—dc22   2010044411

ISBN 978-0-393-34051-8 pbk.

W. W. Norton & Company, Inc.
500 Fifth Avenue, New York, N.Y. 10110
www.wwnorton.com

W. W. Norton & Company Ltd.
Castle House, 75/76 Wells Street, London W1T 3QT

1 2 3 4 5 6 7 8 9 0

CONTENTS

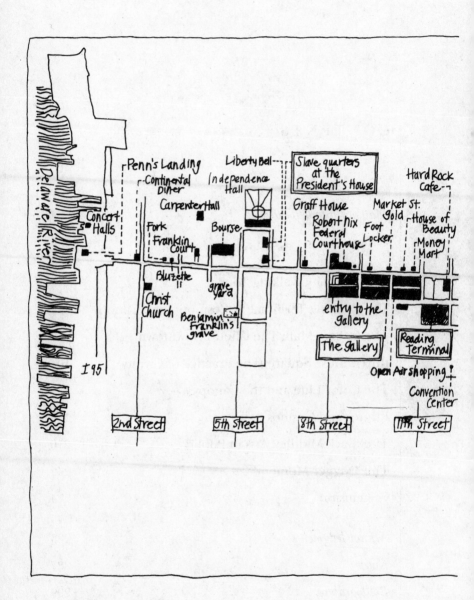

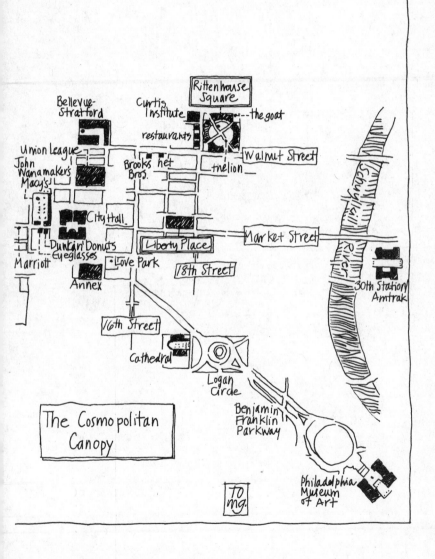

Rittenhouse
Square

Bellevue-
Stratford

Curtis
Institute

----the goat

restaurants

Walnut Street

Union League

Brooks
Bros.

het

the lion

John Wanamaker's
Macy's

City Hall

Market Street

Dunkin' Donuts
Eyeglasses

Liberty Place

Marriott

18th Street

Love Park

Schuylkill River

Annex

30th Station
Amtrak

16th Street

Cathedral

Logan
Circle

The Cosmopolitan
Canopy

Benjamin
Franklin
Parkway

TO
mg.

Philadelphia
Museum
of Art

PREFACE

I have long been fascinated by the lived experience of race in America, especially through my home city of Philadelphia. How do ordinary people in this diverse city interact across and along racial lines? From early morning through late at night, downtown streets are crowded with an ever-changing kaleidoscope of people, not only rushing past one another in dizzying swirls but also mixing and mingling for a moment or two amid the busyness of everyday life. Working people, shoppers, commuters, students, tourists, pleasure seekers, municipal service employees—whole hosts of strangers, a myriad of acquaintances, and intersecting groups of friends—all share public space, more or less peacefully. When and how do racial identities figure into these everyday encounters? When and how do city dwellers set aside their own and others' particular racial and ethnic identities to communicate in more cosmopolitan ways? What conditions enable people in some urban places to consort with others with such civility? These questions arise as we observe public life in almost any contemporary American city.

Over the last half-century a wide array of civil rights legislation, court decisions, and presidential actions, including affirmative action, has made black people full citizens under the law. In these decades a process of incorporation began, opening doors for future generations of African Americans to positions of power, privilege, and prestige. Support for these policies was strong but by no means unanimous; debate about them has intensified even as they have been successful in transforming race relations. The extension of affirmative action to various other underrepresented groups, including women, created more visible diversity in American institutional and cultural life, particularly in urban centers. Social tensions and racial polarization notwithstanding, this process pushed us inexorably toward racial peace, with a public embrace of diversity.

This ethos of getting along, as well as the tremendous growth in immigration, has given rise to the emergence of what I call cosmopolitan canopies[1]—settings that offer a respite from the lingering tensions of urban life and an opportunity for diverse peoples to come together. Canopies are in essence pluralistic spaces where people engage one another in a spirit of civility, or even comity and goodwill.[2] Through personal observation, they may come casually to appreciate one another's differences and empathize with the other in a spirit of shared humanity. Under the canopy this sense of familiarity often breeds comfort and encourages all to be on their best behavior, promoting peaceful relations. Here racially, ethnically, and socially diverse peoples spend casual and purposeful time together, coming to know one another through what I call folk ethnography, a form of people watching that allows individuals informally to gather evidence in social interactions that supports their own viewpoints or transforms their commonsense understandings of social life. In this context of diversity and cosmopolitanism, a cognitive and cultural basis for trust is established that often leads to the emergence of more civil behavior. At present, this emerging phenomenon can be observed in Center City Philadelphia, where I have lived and conducted ethnographic fieldwork for more than thirty years.[3]

During that time I resided for extended periods in three quite different urban neighborhoods: West Philadelphia, where universities rub elbows with the poor; historic Rittenhouse Square and less prestigious parts of Center City; and Chestnut Hill, an upper-middle-class area toward the northwest. Over the long term I have done fieldwork in many other neighborhoods and followed my subjects into places outsiders seldom enter even by accident. Engaged as a citizen, as well as a disciplined sociologist, I have partaken of the broad spectrum of social life, becoming an "observing participant" in Philadelphia.[4] This account conveys what I have seen and heard and presents what sense I have been able to make of interactions occurring in public. My primary concern in this book is with the ways in which Philadelphians live race and how this helps to explain how race is lived in contemporary America.

This work grows out of ongoing ethnographic work in Philadelphia—a study of how people go about meeting the demands of everyday life, develop commonsense understandings of their social world, and share these ideas and practices with others in their culture. Local knowledge arises from these concrete experiences and interpersonal interactions.[5] The ethnographer tries to apprehend and represent this local knowledge in a form that others can comprehend. No ethnography presents exact truths; all accounts of social experience are renderings.

In deference to the privacy of my subjects, who deserve respectful treatment, I have disguised individual identities and actual occurrences while describing social processes and interaction patterns in public. I am most concerned with understanding and portraying the behavior I have observed. In the spirit of the *flâneur*, the wanderer in the city originally described by the French poet Baudelaire,[6] this work begins with a walking tour of Center City Philadelphia that stops and lingers at the cosmopolitan canopies. After describing several of these iconic spaces, I move inside to the semipublic setting of the workplace. There I take up the issue of the color line, the instances of racial discrimination that are most problematic for the canopy, rending the fabric of civility for a time but not overwhelming or destroying it.

The public spaces of the city are more racially, ethnically, and socially diverse than ever. In many impersonal spaces, social distance and tension as expressed by a wariness of strangers appear to be the order of the day. But the cosmopolitan canopy offers a respite as well as an opportunity for urban denizens to come together to do their business and to engage in "people watching," or a distinctive folk ethnography that serves as a cultural and cognitive base on which people construct behavior in public. In such settings, city dwellers are encouraged to express their cosmopolitan sides while keeping their ethnocentric feelings in check. Here, ethnic and racial borders are deemphasized, and opportunities for diverse strangers to encounter one another in a relaxed context are created. The cosmopolitan canopy and its lessons contribute to the civility of the increasingly diverse city.

1. | A CENTER CITY WALKING TOUR

In 1938 the sociologist Louis Wirth published his seminal essay called "Urbanism as a Way of Life," based on his observations of city life in Chicago and drawing on the German sociologist Georg Simmel's earlier work on European cities, "The Metropolis and Mental Life."[1] What mainly concerned Wirth were the qualities that for him defined the city, particularly size, density, and heterogeneity. Especially striking to him was people's blasé orientation as they traversed urban spaces with an impersonal bearing that suggested an attitude of indifference. In the seventy-four years since Wirth's formulations on urbanism, much has happened to big-city life.[2] Of course, some conditions have remained constant, but many have changed profoundly. Strongly affected by the forces of industrialism, immigration, and globalization, the American city of today is more racially, ethnically, and socially diverse than ever, with profound cleavages dividing one social group from another.

As anonymous pedestrians actively "see but don't see" one another, skin color becomes a social border[3] that complicates public observations of city life. Today what Wirth described as urbanites' blasé indifference seems to have given way to a pervasive wariness toward strangers, particularly anonymous black males. In places such as bus stations, parking garages, and sidewalks, many pedestrians move about guardedly, dealing with strangers by employing elaborate facial and eye work, replete with smiles, nods, and gestures designed to carve out an impersonal but private zone for themselves. Increasingly, pedestrians are required to contend publicly with the casualties of modern urban society, not just the persistently poor who at times beg aggressively but also homeless people, street criminals, and the mentally disturbed. Fearful of crime, many are prepared to defend themselves or to quickly summon help—if not from fellow pedestrians, then from the police. In navigating such spaces, people often divert their gazes, looking up, looking down, or looking away, and feign ignorance of the diverse mix of strangers they encounter. Defensively, they "look past" or "look through" the next person, distancing themselves from strangers and effectively consigning their counterparts to a form of social oblivion.

In public, stereotypically, white skin color is most often associated with respectability, civility, and trust, and black skin color is associated with poverty, danger, and distrust—above all, with regard to anonymous young males.[4] Many ordinary pedestrians feel at ease with others they deem to be most like themselves; the more threatening the "other" is judged to be, the greater the distance displayed. And mainly because of the persistence of what I call the "iconic black ghetto"—the large, "unfathomable but dangerous place" in the city where poor black people are concentrated—black people, especially males, bear close scrutiny by virtually everyone else in public.[5] Black strangers more often greet and otherwise acknowledge other strangers, particularly other blacks. But most other pedestrians, in an effort to remain impersonal, appear simply to follow their noses, at times barely avoiding collisions with other strangers. If they speak at all, they may utter a polite "excuse me" or "I'm sorry," and, if it seems appropriate, they scowl. In effect, people work to shape and guard their own public space.

Yet there are heterogeneous and densely populated bounded public spaces within cities that offer a respite from this wariness, settings where a mix of people can feel comfortable enough to relax their guard and go about their business more casually. In these areas people display a degree of cosmopolitanism, by which I mean acceptance of the space as belonging to all kinds of people.[6] In Philadelphia this cosmopolitan zone is known as Center City. Here we find cosmopolitan canopies where the display of public acceptance by all of all is especially intense, becoming one of the defining characteristics of the place.

Having come to know these cosmopolitan canopies, as well as other spaces that seem to defy this spirit of cosmopolitanism, I invite you to take a virtual walk with me from

Philadelphia's eastern border at the Delaware River, along its central axis, Market Street, all the way to the core's western boundary, the Schuylkill River and Thirtieth Street Station, which connects Philadelphia by rail to its surrounding suburbs and the rest of the country.

A good place to begin is Penn's Landing, as it is locally known, which commemorates the arrival of William Penn, Philadelphia's founder, in the late seventeenth century. Today Penn's Landing contains various attractions, including eateries, a concert hall, a floating restaurant, and the Independence Seaport Museum. The area draws large crowds of people who indulge in exotic cuisines, tour the museum, attend a performance, walk their dogs, or simply sit along the banks of the river and watch the boats go by.

As we move west from Penn's Landing, we cross I-95 and reach the beginning of Market Street. Walking up Market, a wide boulevard heading west away from the Delaware River, we encounter buildings and establishments from many periods of Philadelphia's history. Immediately on the right at Second Street is the old Christ Church, where George Washington, Benjamin Franklin, and other founding fathers worshipped. Franklin is buried in the graveyard behind the church, and the pew where he used to sit has been roped off. Between Third and Fourth streets along Market is the original brick-and-wood post office, with the site of Franklin's house just behind it.

The area is a hodgepodge now. A few inexpensive stores, left over from the days before outlet malls, sell men's suits

and shirts, ladies' accessories, and Army-Navy surplus merchandise. Interspersed among these stores are popular restaurants and watering holes such as the Continental Bar and
Restaurant; Fork, an upscale eatery; and Bluezette, a black-
oriented nightclub. Some local nightspots offer dancing.
These places draw a mix of people, but a young and hip crowd
from the city and the suburbs predominates. In the evening,
especially on weekends, the area is crowded. It attracts different types of people at different times of the day and the year.
Its social neutrality is remarkable. Diverse people converge,
defining the setting as belonging to everyone and deempha-
sizing race and other particularities. No one group claims
priority, a hallmark of the cosmopolitan canopy.

Beginning around 5:30 in the evening on weekend
nights, the spaces around Second and Market transition to
a nightspot. What earlier was a somewhat tame business district serving the local neighborhood changes abruptly. Its
more ethnic, even sleepy public face comes alive and turns
cosmopolitan. Every other establishment has become a destination for young adults from South Jersey, the Philadelphia
suburbs, and local colleges and universities. Here young people dance with all kinds of others, including those from the
North Philadelphia ghettos and the river wards of Kensington and Northern Liberties. White, black, Latino, and others
from all over the city, and the world, mingle to the sounds of
salsa at Cuba Libre.

The area just north of this section of Market, called Old
City in an effort to appeal to tourists, is the heart of the local

art scene. In order to draw a crowd, most galleries coordinate their openings on the first Friday of each month. The galleries attract an upscale but laid-back and mature clientele that adds a certain mix to the nightlife. The site of much recent investment and new and rehabbed construction, the neighborhood has become vibrant, even "hot," drawing many young students, professionals, families and singles alike. In nice weather a festive atmosphere prevails on first Fridays as crowds wander from one gallery to another, sharing the sidewalks with informal outdoor exhibits and the occasional street performer or musician playing for tips.

Not everyone, however, is welcome there. I have seen black vendors spread out their wares of incense, bootleg music and videos, ties and scarves, as well as African beads, statuettes, and other ornamental items in this area, only to have a policeman come along and tell them they must leave. These street vendors are tolerated farther up Market, but not on Second Street. The black vendor here is viewed as "out of place," a renegade and not an artist, and a potential danger, a threat. If he didn't know it before, he is quickly made aware that he does not belong.

As we walk up Market and approach Fourth Street, the Bourse is on the left. Opened in 1895, this commodities exchange, modeled after a mercantile exchange in the German port city of Hamburg, was the first in the United States. The building was strikingly modern in its time, with its steel frame, multilevel design, and skylights; now a mall, it still seems contemporary. Originally it housed grain dealers, export agents, steamship lines, and telephone and telegraph companies, as well as the commercial, maritime, and stock exchanges. From its inception it was a kind of canopy, facilitating cooperation among its business tenants and allowing customers to feel enclosed in its open interior. Today the Bourse holds retail and food stores, as well as dozens of other types of small businesses. It is still an urban gathering place where people come to do business, shop, and people watch.

Continuing west along Market, we cross Independence Mall, with its view of Carpenters' Hall, where the first Continental Congress met. Nearby is the site of George Washington's house, which served as his office and residence through the 1790s, while the new nation's capital was under construction. Although Pennsylvania had passed a gradual emancipation law in 1780, the president and his family were attended by at least eight slaves they brought from Mount Vernon. Two managed to escape to freedom. Years later John Adams, an opponent of slavery, occupied the same dwelling. When the site for the new Liberty Bell Center was being excavated in 2006, archaeologists discovered remains of the slave quarters behind the stables, and controversy swirled about how Washington's slaves should be represented here. Facing the mall is the Federal District courthouse, and a few blocks up sits the house where Thomas Jefferson wrote the Declaration of Independence. And in the distance is Congress Hall, the relatively small building, still intact and open to visitors, that housed the Constitutional Convention.

We continue our tour up Market to Ninth Street. Anchored

by the Gallery, an urban mall built in the 1970s that currently includes a Big Kmart and a Burlington Coat Factory as its major tenants, this area has been home to discount stores for decades. A downtown destination for people from the city's poorer neighborhoods, particularly blacks and other people of color, the Gallery gives serious pause to members of the typical suburban crowd. The grand main entrance is at Ninth and Market streets, where a large sign above wide steps leads directly to the lower level. All sorts of decidedly nonsuburban people occupy the stairs; homeboys, young black men in their twenties, and other black, brown, and white members of the underemployed and working poor are scattered around. The Gallery sits near the bus and subway transit lines that connect several black ghetto communities to this part of the city, providing the black poor with a degree of access that enables them to congregate here. Here they shop, hang out, or gather to socialize, talking and laughing out loud among their friends, their presence staking a claim on the Gallery and advertising what is to be encountered inside.

By noon on warm summer days, black religious proselytizers in front of the building often preach on a microphone and offer fliers to passersby, many of whom try to ignore them. There is always a certain hustle and bustle throughout the day, although at midmorning it is relatively quiet. To enter the Gallery, we must make our way past this phalanx of people and descend the steps, which is rather daunting to would-be shoppers from the suburban middle class.

Just west of the Gallery, at Market and Eleventh, is an

open-air street market with a large and visible black presence. Licensed vendors selling T-shirts, incense, jewelry, scarves, African garb, and other items share sidewalk space with hustlers plying passersby with drugs, bootleg videos, and other illicit goods. Middle Eastern men sell cheap jewelry to African Americans. Their demeanor is usually one of tolerance, but occasionally blacks receive defensive stares. Black people interpret what they call "the look" as intolerance or, at worst, "the hostile gaze" of racism; yet they continue to patronize these shops. In this block the legal meets the illegal; depending on the time of day, or day of the week, either legitimate or underground sellers predominate.

On Saturdays, the whole area is transformed into a carnival-like setting. Low-income people shop, stroll, or simply watch others, staring, meeting, talking, and looking to see and to be seen; some watch those who are watching them. Vendors find customers, drug dealers make deals, friends encounter friends by happenstance and habit, and young people organize evenings together. This area near the Gallery qualifies as an outdoor social center, an informal setting where leisurely inner-city working-class black people give face time to one another, mixing among themselves and with Latinos and some working-class whites, and all enjoy themselves. However, the vagaries of the weather and the open presence of criminal activity at times make this an edgy scene, which leaves completely comfortable only those who possess ghetto-honed street smarts. Usually the scene is pleasant and relatively relaxed.

Across Market Street, next to the Robert Nix Federal Building and the William Penn Annex of the U.S. Post Office, a group of stores competes for the same low-income, mostly black clientele that frequents the informal street market. At the House of Beauty, which sells low-priced items such as barrettes, combs, perfume, and wigs and extensions using real human hair, women and children trickle in and out. Next door is Market Street Gold, a bling-filled jewelry store, and then a Foot Locker with its big red sign. A bold yellow Money Mart sign promises check-cashing services, catering to those who barely manage from one payday to another. Adjacent is Philly's Kids, a children's clothing and shoe store. Along this stretch, vacant storefronts advertise for new tenants. In fact, the whole block between Eighth and Ninth streets signals its perennial status as "development in waiting." West of Eleventh Street, establishments drawing business from the Convention Center, one block north on Arch Street, begin to dominate, including two major hotels. The centerpiece is the Reading Terminal Market, a Philadelphia landmark that has benefited from the upsurge in tourists and particularly convention-goers in the city.

Always a place where many different types of people came together, the Reading Terminal today serves as a major cosmopolitan canopy. Its denizens represent a diverse lot who come here to shop while becoming exposed to various kinds of people getting along quite well together. Indeed, this setting epitomizes the cosmopolitan canopy, for it represents not only the great racial, ethnic, and class diversity of the city of Philadelphia but also the goodwill that is expressed and experienced by most who enter these premises. The friendly attitude that prevails here is infectious. Established and reinforced by old-timers, it spreads to newcomers as they enter. People here model comity and civility for one another, contributing profoundly to the definition of the local situation. In these circumstances people observe one another, becoming ever more urban by learning through their interactions the parameters of behavior allowed here and at the same time making sense of one another. Here they engage in the intense form of people watching I call folk ethnography, a peculiar way of making cultural sense of strangers in public places.

A Hard Rock Café, identified by its trademark huge guitar hanging over the entrance, occupies a corner of the Reading Terminal building. Pedestrians stop and look around, being careful not to bump into others as they take in the sights. Meanwhile, city buses roar by. Cars and taxis are everywhere. The mass of pedestrians moves about, seeing but not seeing, paying what Erving Goffman called "civil inattention"[7] as they move along the sidewalks and cross at the lights, or occasionally jaywalk. The setting hustles and bustles with life.

Farther up the street are a Dunkin' Donuts and an Eyeglass Emporium; up to the corner and down the way is a Marriott Residence Hotel. Not long ago moderately priced electronics stores and strip joints lined these streets, and boom boxes, their sounds, and their devotees were ubiquitous. But these establishments and their clientele were pushed out to make

11

way for the new Convention Center. Facing City Hall on the other side of Market, the Wanamaker Building, which once housed the original Philadelphia department store, now houses a Macy's, the only true department store remaining of the original four in Center City; it serves as a reminder that the heyday of urban retail has long passed. Yet, the recent history of this streetscape points to the possibility that those smaller, upscale businesses may expand. This area is in flux as the new competes to establish itself amid remnants of the old.

One interesting bridge between the old and new is the Wanamaker's Organ (Macy's) Christmas Light Show, a tradition in Philadelphia since 1956. A few weeks before Christmas, the department store is transformed into a community space where residents from all over the city gather to see the annual spectacle of lights and hear carols played on the famous Wanamaker's organ, the largest functioning pipe organ in the world. A spacious corner section of the store is given over for this event, and all kinds of children are in attendance with their parents in tow. It is a high time for the holiday expression of "goodwill toward men," taking place under the canopy that was long known as "John Wanamaker's," but which continues this distinctive tradition as Macy's.

Historically, City Hall has served as a giant, ongoing public works project that sits astride the intersection of Market and Broad streets at the center of the "greene Country Towne" originally laid out by William Penn. It is still the official central point of the expanded city, connecting all four directions and offering impressive views. This massive Second Empire–

style building has provided jobs for many of the city's residents, starting with Irish and Italian immigrant construction workers. Designed to be the world's tallest office building, it was begun in 1871, but the task took thirty years, during which time skyscrapers in New York City and Chicago surpassed its 549 feet. Maintaining the vast structure, with its profusion of intricate decorative detail, continues to occupy city workers and contractors. Thousands of municipal employees staff its many offices, where citizens come to do business large and small. Traffic must circle around it, but pedestrians can walk straight through on both Market and Broad. On most days only a few people sit in the courtyard.

To the south are the Union League and the old Bellevue Hotel, two Philadelphia institutions long associated with the elite, whom Leonard Richards called "gentlemen of property and standing."[8] In profound contrast, not far to the north lie some of Philadelphia's poorest black ghettos. On the west side Market Street becomes a corridor of residential and office high-rises; on the other corner the Benjamin Franklin Parkway leads past luxury apartments, large office buildings, and various public institutions to the Art Museum. Here, catty-corner to City Hall, is Love Park. Like most public spaces, it has been used for purposes not intended by its designers and hotly contested over the decades. Originally, the park was planned as a fitting terminus to the Benjamin Franklin Parkway. Built in the late 1960s atop an underground parking garage, it was dedicated as a memorial to the late President John F. Kennedy. The plaza gets its name from the sculpture *LOVE*, by Robert

Indiana, which was placed there for the U.S. bicentennial in 1976. Its removal in 1978 provoked such public outcry that the chairman of the Philadelphia Art Commission bought and reinstalled it that same year as a "gift to the city."

The place flourished for a decade or more, but then went through ups and downs as the fortunes of Center City fluctuated, despite the high hopes of urban developers. Adjacent to Suburban Station, it is a space where streetwise urban dwellers would not venture at night, as reports of murders, muggings, and incivility are all too common there, in what is essentially a kind of no-man's land in the middle of Philadelphia's downtown. Originally, black children from the local neighborhoods came there to play the game of double Dutch jump rope. In the 1980s skateboarders frequented the plaza's attractive smooth surfaces and curving steps, and in the 1990s some of its stars made it famous by winning professional skateboarding competitions. In 2001–2002, the park hosted the X Games, which were televised internationally. When the games ended, Mayor John Street tried to enforce the existing ban on skateboarding on public property and had the park renovated to be less hospitable to skateboarders. When this policy became an issue in his reelection campaign, he promised to build an alternative skate park, but nothing seems to have been done.

An organization and website, Free LOVE Park, advocates its restoration for skateboarders. Its website asks, "Where has the LOVE gone?" The park still plays a civic role on occasion. It is the main site for political rallies in the city, and every four years the Democratic Party's presidential candidates speak to large and diverse crowds. The water in the fountain is often dyed to mark special occasions: pink for breast cancer awareness month; blue for police officers killed in the line of duty; red for the Phillies' 2008 World Series victory. On nice days it functions as a cosmopolitan canopy. People pursue their own particular pastimes, from youthful skateboarders to chess players young and old. Interracial groups of people eat lunch and engage in urban sociability. No one group claims this public space; the urbanites who congregate here understand that they and others are always welcome.

At lunchtime on weekdays, small groups of white corporate types walk around, apparently on their way to a restaurant or back to their offices, often with a lone black person among them. This phenomenon is common, but not the reverse; I have never observed a group of black professionals with a lone white one. The social interactions that involve these well-educated, well-heeled, and often sharply dressed black men are especially interesting ethnographically. Black professionals and executives in white-dominated corporations are at once members of an elite class and of a historically stigmatized group. They occupy an in-between position, incorporated into the professional class but not entirely at home there. Many are expected to "represent the race" to the elite and represent management to black subordinates. Yet they are sometimes mistaken for their poor and marginalized cousins from the ghetto. Awareness of this common predicament links anonymous black professionals in predominantly white public settings. When I pass by a black man alone among his white colleagues, he gives me a knowing look, or even greets me; the others are unaware that we've just had a privileged ethnic communication.

In other intimate interior spaces that range from quasi-public to semiprivate, the canopy effect is a matter of degree. At Broad and Chestnut streets, for a long time, a jazz bar exhibited qualities at once intimate and public. Here's how I described it in my journal:

> After descending the steps off Broad Street down into Zanzibar Blue, you feel as though you have entered a dark inner sanctum, an underground world of live music, food, liquor, and a cosmopolitan mix of people who have in common a certain appreciation of jazz. On the left is a bar with a few people sitting around, sipping their drinks and nodding to the smooth beat. As your eyes slowly adjust to the gloom, little candlelit lamps become visible atop neat rows of four-top tables with blood-red tablecloths. You then encounter two hefty black bouncers in dark suits. They engage the visitor with small talk while checking him out to see what his business is, especially if he is a stranger dressed in dark clothes, though here everything has a dark hue.
>
> Over in the corner sits a dark-skinned black man engaging his brown-skinned honey; his gold-rimmed glasses sparkle, capturing and reflecting the scarce light. Nearer the bandstand, nine black women gather to honor a friend on her birthday—as becomes apparent later on when the

waiter delivers a small cake with two candles on top. On the other side, facing the bandstand, another black couple enjoys a meal while waiting for the set to begin. The maitre d' shows another black man and me to a table, first a two-top but then a four-top that we accept more happily. We both order Delta catfish, Cokes, and bread to keep us until the meal arrives. We talk. More people slowly appear. A young, white, professional-looking couple sits behind us. In a while, to our right, another; and in fifteen minutes, still another. The place seems to be filling up, though it has a long way to go. This is Sunday night in downtown Philly. Our Cokes and bread arrive, and we sip and nibble and talk, taking in more of the scene.

The band is now set up: a cool-looking white man on guitar, a black Muslim with a coofee (cap) on sax, a small brown-skinned man on drums, and the leader, a muscular, baldheaded black man, on bass. The leader opens with the usual introductions. To start the first set, he makes fun of straying black men and their family responsibilities while pleading for the audience not to be too judgmental—"give a brother some slack because he always comes home." Chuckles come from the audience, the blacks perhaps "getting it" more than the whites. The combo plays. Naturally, the sounds are smooth, melodious, stark, and loud. People go into conscious listening and watching mode, as they are here to see the show—and it's quite a show.

A show is being put on by the clientele as well as by the combo. People observe one another, watching how others

17

react to the sounds. When a player works especially hard to bring out an unusual or seemingly difficult but appealing sound, the audience collectively agrees to give the player some recognition—applause, that is. And when the guitar player makes a sound not commonly associated with the guitar, members of the audience clap spontaneously, almost on cue. It is particularly interesting when the blacks clap enthusiastically for the white player. Everyone notices. People here are aware of each other but at the same time anonymous. They feel a sense of community while they are here, and then they move on.

Another intimate setting is the off-track betting establishment, located on Market, near Seventeenth.

Here a diversity of people gathers, for the ostensible purpose of betting on the horses. Located in the center of downtown, the setting is quite accessible to the various ethnic neighborhoods of the city, by car or by public transportation. Upon approaching this space, you must make your way through a throng of pedestrians, your progress depending on the time of day and, of course, the weather. As might be expected, the crowd that gathers in this parlor is a diverse collection of people reminiscent of a Damon Runyon short story.

After entering one Saturday afternoon, Acel, a black friend of mine, and I make our way downstairs to find the betting emporium. The air is dank and heavy with smoke, from both cigars and cigarettes, and leaves even nonsmok-

ers' clothing reeking, especially on summer days. The space underground is in marked contrast to the bright sunlight of the street. The arrangement is unique: TV monitors line the walls, and the clientele sits transfixed, all eyes on the monitors, as they track the horses and their bets in the comfort of a space they have made their own. Here they can sit back and enjoy a cold one or a smoke without worrying about offending anyone. While betting is supposedly the main purpose for coming here, the atmosphere itself is a significant draw. All kinds of people are present, including characters who appear to have come through the school of hard knocks as well as others who seem more genteel. It is a racially and ethnically mixed crowd of people who hail from the nearby Irish, Italian, and African American neighborhoods. Throughout the afternoon men and women sit in their seats against the wall or at the bar, smoking and drinking, talking and laughing with other regulars, or making fast friends of people they've just met. Here people bet on possibility, and the charge they get from the visit is most often deemed to be worth the cost.

Moving on south down to Sixteenth Street, we enter the heart of the Center City business district. Here the crowds of executives and office workers ebb and flow with the time of day. The streets are rather narrow and the high-rises shoot straight up, forming deep urban canyons. At 9:00 a.m. these streets are teeming with people who scurry about Center City from their parking garages, from public transportation, or, increasingly, straight from their in-town homes. After the initial surge things quiet down for the rest of the morning. At noon they rev up again, as people spill out of the office buildings and converge on the eateries, or venture into the parks and squares to enjoy their lunch with friends and colleagues. The pattern is repeated in the afternoon; the sidewalks are relatively unpopulated until 4:00 p.m., when they begin to fill with people on their way home or to evening engagements. On weekends these streets are quiet, and many of the otherwise bustling lunch places are closed.

Four blocks west and two blocks south of City Hall is the prestigious Rittenhouse Square area, with its hotels, boutiques, and upscale restaurants. Purveyors of gourmet meals and luxury goods are interspersed with establishments offering moderately priced necessities. Sidewalk cafés have come into vogue. Some draw a tony clientele, others an assortment ranging from university students to young professionals and office workers of all races. Here lunch is a more leisurely affair that includes a sizable helping of socializing. People congregate here after work, too, often drawn by the promise of encounters with members of the opposite sex. This attractive young crowd contributes to the interesting mix of street life. So do the nannies and the well-heeled homeboys who shop at NET, an expensive retailer whose clothes appeal to young hipsters, including drug dealers.

Just down the street is Brooks Brothers, a long-established, conservative clothier catering to professionals, black as well as white. Tweeter, an electronics store, was also on this stretch and attracted a mixed group of customers. Street life in and around Rittenhouse Square includes the occasional homeless person, although some who look homeless on closer inspection are found not to be; they may be mentally ill and have a place of residence, but present themselves on the street in the seemingly aimless manner of the homeless. Easily confused with the destitute, they wander about the streets alongside the homeboys, professionals, and suburbanites. Immigrants are also in evidence. Traversing these public spaces, we overhear many different languages—including Spanish, Russian, Polish, Hebrew, Chinese, and Somali—as people speak to one another or to someone near or far away via cell phone. Everyone takes these conversations for granted as part of ordinary life. Paying "civil inattention,"[9] pedestrians may pretend not to notice what others say, but in reality they consciously people watch and enjoy eavesdropping and taking in whatever snippets of conversations they can understand.

Around the corner from Rittenhouse Square between Seventeenth and Eighteenth, a McDonald's frequented by locals is nestled between two buildings in the middle of the block. Like other establishments in the area, it experiences periodic surges of patrons who use this space in ways peculiar to their needs. On most mornings it serves as a gathering spot for the elderly of the neighborhood, at least some of whom are well-heeled. They congregate for breakfast, or sometimes just for coffee, but mainly they socialize. Many are proud regulars whose conversations feature the doings of their children and grandchildren. After sitting around for a couple of hours, they leave just before the lunch rush and are replaced by noisy young students from the nearby schools. Through the morning these elders sometimes vie for space with the homeless, as the staff works to figure out who is who.

Such goings-on peg this place as a hybrid institution, whose ostensible purpose is providing fast food but which also serves as a site for slow-paced sociability. The Barnes & Noble bookstore up the street in the next block serves a similar hybrid purpose. The homeless and mentally ill are present there, too, although they may try to pass themselves off as normal. They sit at the tables in the café for hours, engrossed in books and magazines, hoping to pass the inspection of employees charged with keeping an eye on everyone, but especially on the homeless. In inclement weather employees may tolerate these unwanted visitors, whom they are able to spot in a minute by citing their appearance and, at times, their odor. The staff acknowledges that a game is going on, as the store serves as a hangout for people who sometimes buy little or nothing; they opt to enforce the rules sporadically, in response to problems they observe among customers.

Rittenhouse Square occupies a slightly enlarged city block from Eighteenth to Nineteenth and Walnut to Locust. The most successful and prestigious of William Penn's original squares, Rittenhouse Square boasts old shade trees, exotic plantings, elegant entrances, and self-consciously civilized behavior. The park itself has many uses; the activities carried on there are as varied as the people who engage in them. This urban green space not only serves as a backyard for the

high-rise apartment buildings in the surrounding neighborhood but attracts people from all over Center City and various other parts of Philadelphia.

On nice days people from all walks of life inhabit the park.
Old men of any color or ethnicity play chess or checkers;
elderly white women and men promenade, some escorted
by their black home health aides. Young people play Frisbee,
lounge on park benches, and sunbathe or nap on the grass.
One or two students from the Curtis Institute of Music across
the street are playing music, their instrument cases open on
the pavement in front of them as people cock their heads to
listen or simply stop for a while, sometimes throwing coins or
even bills into the cases. Dogs, with their owners in tow, have
a field day. The homeless, the mentally ill, the well-to-do, students, black homeboys, bicycle messengers, office workers,
and businesspeople are all here, observing the show and, for
the most part, not only getting along but thriving on one
another's energy.

In the square, children are ever present. After decades
of losing families to the suburbs, over the past ten or fifteen
years Center City has been attracting them. Increased investment, ten-year tax abatements on new homes, and improve-
ments to the infrastructure drew suburbanites, especially
younger families, back into the city, producing a more varied
mix of people who make use of the square. "Billy" the goat, a
small metal sculpture located in the southwest corner of the
park, attracts young children and their parents. Many simply
hang out, whiling away the afternoon. Some make a daily pil-

grimage to this spot, allowing their charges access to the goat and a chance to socialize with other children. The children squeal and climb all over the structure, while their parents chat. The goat has become a gathering place for families who meet as strangers and may strike up conversations and eventually friendships. Today a wide range of people call Center City home: affluent immigrants, the urban middle class, empty nesters, African Americans formerly of North Philadelphia, ethnic whites from South Philadelphia and other nearby neighborhoods, and students who attend the University of Pennsylvania, Temple University, the Curtis Institute, the University of the Arts, or the Academy of Fine Arts.

Here they find a sense of community as they go about their business, talking, eating, sitting on the benches, or strolling about. The park is also home to hustlers of legal and illegal wares and to spiritual proselytizers. Some carry on group activities and may try to recruit people to join them. As on Market Street, a battle for space is going on between the poorer people who used to frequent this place and the more affluent residents, new and old, with the police acting as their agents. In the days of decline the police were more tolerant of the homeless and other poor people who slept on benches or spent their days panhandling or just hanging out in and around the square. Now they discourage them, although not in an acrimonious way. It is significant that the affluent are prevailing here. Generally when the poor and homeless invade an area, the affluent give it up, but here the middle and upper classes, who are predominantly white, are standing firm and even taking back Center City from the black poor and the homeless who staked claims on steam vents and doorways throughout the downtown area. There is still, however, a residue of the former time in a peculiar turn taking that occurs in the use of space in the area. In the morning the crowd is quite diverse. By midday the white middle class becomes predominant. At night the area becomes darker in hue. These fluctuating tones might be seen simply as matters of degree, for the night also brings out white people. Increasingly restaurants that compete with eateries in Old City ring the square. On Eighteenth Street, Devon and Rouge serve lunch and dinner and are also hot spots for nightlife.

Leaving the square, we walk up Walnut Street to the Schuylkill River, the western boundary of William Penn's original city, and across the bridge to West Philadelphia. Facing the river on the other side and to the north along Market Street is the Thirtieth Street Station. The grand waiting room is filled with people from up and down the eastern seaboard. Many travel between Philadelphia and New York and Washington, some commuting regularly, others making the trip occasionally for business or pleasure. At the same time, the station handles a huge number of daily commuters from the Philadelphia suburbs. Most of these folks are white, but increasing numbers of them are black. Among them are lawyers, doctors, college students, and office workers bound for businesses located in Philadelphia proper.

When they arrive, many transit riders make their way to the coffee shops for a bite before work. The Thirtieth Street Station offers a few commercial amenities: a flower shop in the corner, a shoeshine stand against the wall, even a common area where tables invite coffee drinkers. Nearby is the bookstore and newsstand, where any number of regional and national newspapers can be found. All these people are thrown together and enjoy a kind of comity and goodwill, or at least civility for the moment, until they go on their way to work, to school, or to other appointments. If they choose to wait here, they must sit on one of the many smooth wooden benches alongside complete strangers. Choosing a seat requires observation and thought, so that you sit next to someone who won't be a bother. People read the paper or a book; some simply stare into space; others pay civil inattention. Many more are on the move toward a connecting trolley underground, and a few choose to walk to their local destination.

After we walk past the memorial angel statue and through the double doors at the east end of the station, we encounter the taxi queue outside. The line is populated predominantly by white, middle-class business and professional people who are headed to Center City or the university area.

Walking west, we pass through the area commonly known as University City. The University of Pennsylvania and Drexel University have become the predominant presences here. The cosmopolitan feel of Center City reaches into this neighborhood, but only as far as Fifty-Second Street, where you would be hard-pressed on any given day to find more than a handful of whites or others who are not African American. Residents and those using the streets and parks and businesses here are largely working class; many trace their ancestors to the plantations of the Deep South. Today the children and grandchildren of these southern migrants remember what West Philadelphia was like years ago. Theirs is a history of invasion and succession, the classic process first identified by the Chicago sociologists Robert Park and Ernest Burgess.[10] Essentially, as blacks moved into a neighborhood, the whites who predated them there moved out. The process was sometimes gradual, in other cases quite rapid, but the pattern and the result were almost always the same.

As these communities changed from white to black, city services declined, and the withdrawal of resources contributed to the deterioration of the neighborhood. Deindustrialization left in its wake widespread unemployment and service jobs that seldom paid a living wage. Banks and insurance companies redlined the black neighborhoods, and upwardly mobile blacks ultimately moved out. Then, from a malign combination of the decline in available employment and the persistence of racial discrimination, black poverty became ever more concentrated and entrenched. The underground economy of hustling and drug dealing was left to pick up the slack. The authorities, particularly the police, paid scant attention and sometimes abused the victims themselves. The criminal justice system came to be viewed as arbitrary, ineffective, and unworthy of trust. Street justice emerged in the place of civil law, and reputation and street credibility became increasingly important for feeling safe and secure in one's own community.[11] The use of weapons for self-protection spread from criminal perpetrators to potential victims, generating a self-reinforcing spiral of fear and mayhem and fueling the negative image of the iconic black ghetto.

Where Market Street intersects Fifty-Second Street is a classic strip found in every city with a black ghetto of any size. Colloquially referred to as "the Street" or "the Block," in Chicago it is Cottage Grove; in Gary it is Broadway; in Memphis it is Beale. The Street is famous and its reputation widespread. The historic bright-light district of the segregated black community, it is where things are "really happening," where those "in the know" know where to go, where the best nightlife in the city is reputed to be found. As the hippest street in town, it is derisively referred to as part of the chitlin' circuit, where authentic blues and jazz clubs operate with marginal, if any, white involvement with the presentation or proceeds.

At the end of Market Street, continuing west, we reach the city limits. A concentrated black presence spreads in both directions, north and south. The area to the south, formerly the site of heavy industry and manufacturing plants, is in the throes of deindustrialization; the nearby airport does not make up the difference. It had once been a working-class white area, but as whites fled, the district became black and poorer as well.

Most of Philadelphia's working-class neighborhoods have

particular racial-ethnic identities. The city remains, for the most part, a patchwork of racially distinct neighborhoods, and its residents have an exquisite sense of who does and who does not belong. When people hear that a man comes from Kensington, West Philly, or Chestnut Hill, for example, they will often classify him according to their cognitive map of local ethnic geography as Irish, African American, or WASP. The most powerfully imagined neighborhood is the iconic black ghetto, or "the 'hood," often associated in the minds of outsiders with poverty, crime, and violence. This icon is by definition a figment of the imagination of those with little or no direct experience with the ghetto or contact with those who live there, and yet, when a black person navigates spaces outside the ghetto, those he encounters very often make reference to this residential area in order to make sense of him, although their interpretation is often erroneous. Even middle-class African Americans outside of the helping professions may have limited knowledge of the texture and rhythms of life inside these isolated neighborhoods. Still, like that of whites and recent immigrants, their sense of group position is strongly affected by their perspective on the imagined ghetto.[12]

Nevertheless, as we have seen in this chapter's virtual walk from Philadelphia's eastern boundary at the Delaware River to as far west as the Thirtieth Street Station, racial separateness is not the city's only story. In some public spaces all kinds of people coexist and have learned to get along, at times unself-consciously. Along this central spine of Market

2. THE READING TERMINAL: A COSMOPOLITAN CANOPY

Occupying a full city block in Center City Philadelphia, the Reading Terminal Market is composed of numerous shops, restaurants, and kiosks that offer an array of goods and services. In this highly diverse setting all kinds of people shop, eat, and stroll. Adjacent to the new Convention Center, it is centrally located among downtown office buildings and upscale condominiums but not far from white, working-class Kensington and black North Philadelphia. The Terminal building itself, an enormous former train shed, has been part of Philadelphia for more than a century. In the 1990s, when the Convention Center complex was designed and built, the space for the market was kept more or less intact. Many longtime customers feared that it would become simply an upscale tourist attraction, a food court more than a market, but so far the look of the place has more or less stayed the same, and it continues to draw residents from local neighborhoods, including professionals from Center City as well as Irish, Italian, Asian, and African Americans from Philadelphia's ethnic enclaves. Virtually all racial groups are well represented at Reading Terminal, but not in even proportions. On average, about 35 percent of the people there are black, about 10 to 15 percent are Asian and other people of color, and the rest are white, whether WASP or ethnic. The visual, impressionistic makeup of the place is that it is mostly white and middle class with a healthy mixture of people of color.

The Terminal is a colorful place, full of hustle and bustle. Food is a major theme; its pervasive smells invite tasting. The shops are bright and clean, a few adorned with neon lights. Some of the craft shops have been carrying more expensive pieces aimed at tourists. But the grocery stalls still offer fresh produce and meat direct from Lancaster County farms, fish, seafood, and a wide array of fruits and vegetables; these stalls are interspersed with others selling flowers, health supplements, tea, coffee, spices, books, and crafts. A number of businesses are family owned. Amish farm families are a strong presence in the market; their traditional dress adds an exotic element, while their high-quality, home-grown meats and vegetables are affordable as well as delectable. Asian families are also well represented, selling all kinds of fresh fish and produce. Blacks own only a few businesses here, including an African crafts shop that sells masks, beads, and other adornments. Delilah's provides delicious African American cuisine, or "soul food." Among the other eateries are a Thai place, an oyster bar, a French bakery, a Jewish bakery, a juice bar, a beer garden, and a cookie company, making the Terminal a particularly busy place at lunchtime.

Equally striking is the diversity of workers and the general comity with which they interact. For example, black men work for the German butcher with apparent easygoing demeanor and attitude. Some of the white-owned businesses even have black cashiers, which would have been rare or nonexistent not too many years ago. The customers, too, seem to be on their best behavior. People appear relaxed and are often observed interacting across the color line. The clientele at the many food counters represents various classes, races, and ethnicities. A black businessman can be seen talking on his cell phone. Hispanic construction workers are relaxing on their lunch break. This is a calm environment of equivalent, symmetrical relationships—a respite from the streets outside.

The Terminal has always been known as a place where anyone could expect civility. In the days when blacks never knew what treatment they would be given in public, they could come to the Terminal and know they would not be hassled.[1] The ambience has always been comfortable and inviting. Perhaps the focus on food is a reason for this, suggesting a kind of multiethnic festival. On any given day, one might see a Chinese woman eating pizza, a white businessman enjoying collard greens and fried chicken, or an Italian family lunching on sushi. When diverse people are eating one another's food, a social good is performed for those observing. As people become intimate through such shared experiences, some barriers can be broken. The many lunch counters encourage strangers to interact, as they rub elbows while eating. At certain counters in particular, talking with strangers seems to be the norm. One woman told me, "You cannot get people to shut up." The Terminal is a neutral space in which people who behave civilly, whatever their ethnicity, usually will not be scrutinized, as would likely happen in the city's ethnic neighborhoods if an unknown person were to pass through. In those neighborhoods taking keen notice of strangers is the first line of defense, but the Terminal is not defended in this manner.

Multiple sets of doors on three sides of the market are used from morning to late afternoon, six days a week. Upon entering from any side, you are met by shoppers; diners; unobtrusive security guards, both black and white; retired people; teenagers who hang out with their friends; twenty-somethings who come to meet friends and potential romantic partners; homeless people who gravitate to the market for shelter, food, and the unhindered use of public bathrooms; and business executives and workers from nearby office buildings who make up the lunch crowd. Wholesome sandwiches or full-plate lunches can be bought at a reasonable price and consumed quickly on the premises or taken out. At one buffet, you can get a hot meal of collard greens, chicken, sausage, roast, and salad for around eight dollars. Working people and retirees on fixed incomes take advantage of this bargain, at times meeting their old friends and making new ones. For instance:

Maxine Little,[2] an eighty-four-year-old black woman who lives alone in Germantown, takes the bus down Germantown Avenue almost daily "just to see what's going on." She typically arrives and walks around the market, has her lunch at Tootsie's Salad Bar, sees what she can see. Sometimes she encounters a "friend" or someone to talk with. After lunch she catches the bus and heads back up the avenue. Mrs. Little is an invalid, who moves about the Terminal with the aid of a walker—for her, the Terminal is an important social center.

At this cafeteria-style diner located inside the Terminal, strangers sit at the counter and eat together, watching the passing Terminal traffic and goings-on. Often the people who come for lunch are elderly and living on fixed incomes. They hail from many different parts of Philadelphia, but come here to eat a hot meal and to socialize with whoever is available. For some, lunching here is a critical part of a daily routine. Some journey to the Terminal just for this one meal—a smorgasbord of eats presented in buffet style for eight dollars. That is sometimes the only meal of the day for Mrs. Little, though she may "pick up some fruit" from one of the green grocers. The workers at the various stalls all know her and look forward to her visits; when she fails to show up, they grow concerned. She knows they care for her and feels valued.

Along the market's back wall, near the restrooms, black shoeshine men work and socialize, keeping up with one another. They share personal stories and seem always ready for a good laugh. Italians, Jews, Asians, and blacks sit nearby, snacking on baked goods and coffee while enjoying melodious piano sounds played live for tips. The municipal courthouse is within a short walk, and occasionally people appear for lunch with "Juror" stickers affixed to their clothing. There is always a scene to be part of and to observe here.

Under the canopy people relax their guard, although not completely. They look more directly at others as they observe the goings-on, and they move about with a greater sense of security. As they stroll up and down the aisles, stopping at the shops and kiosks to examine what is for sale and perhaps make purchases, they experience other people up close, and they generally seem to extend their trust to others. There is little cause for worry or alarm. People stop and buy items or just walk around, "getting into the mix" and enjoying "being out and about." Sometimes they spontaneously greet one another, verbally or with gestures; some bump into friends, who may well hang out here on a regular basis. A feeling of being involved with the others who are present here emerges, creating a remarkable ambiance.

On a rainy Tuesday afternoon in October, I was enjoying a bowl of oyster soup at Pearl's Oyster Bar in the Reading Terminal Market. About eight people sat around the bar eating a late lunch, or having drinks with their friends. Seated across from the main entrance that looks out on a busy street of Center City, and glad to be out of the rain, by turns I sipped my soup, read the local paper, and observed the comings and goings of the clientele. Suddenly, a signature event occurred. An elderly black woman aided by a walker appeared at the entrance of the Terminal and began to negotiate the heavy double doors. Clearly she was having trouble. At noontime, when the heavy traffic flows in and out, she would have had little trouble entering the building, but in the late afternoon things are quieter, the traffic is settled down, and the doors are often closed. Before I could offer assistance, a young white man with strawberry-blond hair and dressed in construction clothes who was dining with a friend sprang to his feet and offered the old woman a hand, helping her though the large doors. Once she and her bags were safely inside, I overheard him ask, "Are you alright? You OK?" He wondered whether he could be of further assistance. "Yes, son, thank you," she murmured, as she ambled off down one of the aisles of the Terminal. As I looked around, I saw that everyone's eyes were on this interaction, a model of public race relations characteristic of the Reading Terminal. The young man seemed to know that all eyes were on them, as he looked back at the woman a few times, completing his "performance." Then, as quickly as this incident began, it was over. But it likely made an impression on observers and, for the moment, reinforced the public definition of affairs in this space: kindness and civility were the order of the day, regardless of color, gender, or age.

The cosmopolitan canopy that seems to extend over the Reading Terminal Market can be divided into large, imper-

sonal zones and more intimate ones, the former being somewhat off-putting and the latter socially more encouraging.
In the more intimate settings within the canopy, such as the
Down Home Diner counter, people often feel welcome and
secure enough to relax, even to the point of engaging complete strangers in conversation. In these circumstances people
carry on their business but also formulate or reformulate their
ideas about others with whom they share this public space.

When taking a seat at the Down Home Diner, indeed
at any coffee bar or lunch counter, people feel they have
a license to speak with others and others have a license to
speak with them.[3] On occasion strangers engage in spontaneous conversation, getting to know one another. Testing
others and trying things out on them, people want to find
out whether those different from themselves are sincere;
happily, many discover that they are. People generally leave
these encounters with a good feeling about one another, as
though recognizing that they have experienced something
profound. Indeed, they have—they have made human contact across the assumed barriers of race, ethnicity, and other
differences. Some sense a bit of an edge to the setting, which
may be underscored by race and ethnicity, though most often
such borders appear salient but understated. In my journal I
recorded these encounters.

*At around eleven on a warm but overcast Sunday morn-
ing in March, Arthur, an African American buddy, and I
walked into the Down Home Diner, just inside the Read-*

ing Terminal Market. The place always seems to be crowded on Sundays with locals and out-of-towners, because the Terminal caters to both the Convention Center crowd and people from Philadelphia neighborhoods. The crowd that morning buzzed with small talk, resulting in a low-level conversational din. The overall tone was friendly. We took our seats at the counter, perused the menu, and ordered. He requested ham and eggs, and I ordered pancakes, ham, and milk. We caught up with each other over coffee while waiting for our food, occasionally looking around and checking out the scene. After a few bites of my pancakes and a drink of my milk, I felt a tap on my shoulder. I looked up to see an Irishman about forty-five years old. "Who won the game last night?" he asked expectantly. Without missing a beat, I replied, "The Sixers, 98–79." I shot him a smile, and he said, "Thanks," and moved on.

I was struck by the way this man assumed he could approach me about the ball game. He probably would not have done so on the street. But here, in the friendly atmosphere, he thought he could touch my shoulder, make such a request, and likely get an answer. Did he presume that, because I am a black male, I might be especially interested in basketball, would have followed the Sixers game the preceding evening, and would not mind sharing the score with him? He related to me as an individual, but also as a Philadelphia sports fan. At least he expected that I would be agreeable, and I did not disappoint him.

On Saturday, I was supposed to meet Alice at the Down Home Diner at ten for breakfast. I arrived at the Terminal about ten minutes early and walked around the area. The Terminal was busy as usual, full of a diversity of people. Some seemed to be from the nearby Convention Center, where a trade show was in progress. Others looked more like residents of upscale areas of Center City and the suburbs, and from the local Irish, Italian, and African American neighborhoods, along with Asians from nearby Chinatown and other parts of the city. This was the typical mix, but Saturday morning at the Terminal is special. On Saturdays people seem particularly relaxed, lazing about or doing their shopping in an unhurried way. The Down Home Diner was quite crowded. A line of people waited to be seated for the home-made pancakes, grits, eggs, sausages, and ham the place is known for; the delightful smells wafting through the air made them even hungrier. The seating consists of four- and six-top tables, booths, and a counter for ten to twelve people. I waited for a bit, and when a seat at the counter became available, I took it. The stools are spaced quite close together, creating a certain coziness that makes it impossible not to rub shoulders with those seated on either side.

As a result, upon sitting down, you are almost obliged to say "good morning" to your neighbor. The waitstaff is exclusively female and racially mixed. The kitchen is visible through the pass-through, and the cooks, who are black as well as white, are busy. Now and then a black dishwasher emerges to replenish the silverware or dish racks under the counter. The place hums, giving the impression of people going about their work with few other concerns. Food is presented, dirty plates are cleared, money changes hands, and diners come and go. While waiting for Alice, I ordered my coffee; it arrived quickly. In about five minutes the stool next to mine became empty. I quickly covered it with my leather jacket and cap to reserve it. A white man of about forty was seated next to the empty chair. After a few minutes another white man emerged and asked, of no one in particular, whether he could get breakfast here, revealing that he was new to the place. I answered, "Sure." He was really asking for the seat I was saving, the only one available. He stood there behind the seat and soon asked me more directly, "Is this seat taken?" I said that I was saving it for someone and that she should be here soon. Feeling some pressure to order my food, when the waitress appeared, I asked for pancakes, bacon, and milk. After taking my order, she looked over at the man standing up and asked whether she could help him. "I'd like to order some breakfast, but he's saving the seat," he tattled, nodding at me, as if the waitress would make me remove my coat and give him the place.

But the young Italian waitress simply looked at me, looked at the man, and moved on to another task, implicitly endorsing my right to save the seat. After a few minutes, noticing his frustration, I offered, "If she's not here in five minutes, you can have the seat." He nodded his acceptance. Then the man on the other side of the seat asked, "First date?" "No, no," I said. "It's not like that. I'm her professor."

41

"Yeah, right," he replied, smiling. Minutes passed and still no sign of Alice. So I removed my coat and offered the man the seat. "Thanks. If she comes, I'll move," he said. When the waitress came over he ordered eggs and oatmeal. As my food arrived, he commented, "Those look good." "Yeah, the food is pretty good here," I replied as I ate. Soon his food arrived, and he too began to eat.

We sat there elbow to elbow, shoulder to shoulder. I gathered that he was not from Philadelphia, and I asked him outright where he was from. "I'm from Sacramento. I've got a booth over at the Convention Center, and nobody's there to watch it." He was in town for an exhibition of farm implements and equipment, and he ran a manufacturing business. He noted how good his food was and how efficient the service was. He also commented on the diversity of people at the Terminal and added that this situation was unusual for him, as he had little opportunity for this kind of interaction in Sacramento.

Clearly, he was impressed. He revealed that he was from a pretty homogeneous background and that his water-skiing club was even more so. He said that the club was white and male and included a couple of white supremacists, though he didn't share their views. The man continued to tell me about his background, as I prompted him to talk about his work. It turned out that he employs a significant number of Mexicans in his business and that he is firmly in favor of allowing "illegal" immigrants to get driver's licenses: "They get licenses and Social Security cards anyway on the black

*market, so we may as well regulate them ourselves." Also, he
said, his business would fold without them. "I would not hire
a man of my own race—they ain't worth a shit!" As the conversation continued, he indicated that he assumed that I was
not supporting Bush in the upcoming election, while betray-
ing his own conservatism. He was concerned about terrorism.
He worried about "a rise in UPS uniforms being sold on the
internet" and, looking around the Terminal, observed that
the place was not protected and quite vulnerable to terrorist
attack. Soon he finished his breakfast, we said our goodbyes,
and he left for his exhibition at the Convention Center.*

What is so striking about this episode is that in this setting a white man with white-supremacist friends is able to
have a candid conversation with me, a black man, in which
he reveals his own feelings about race and diversity. Inside
the Terminal this generalized feeling of tolerance for others is infectious, spreading from person to person. This
ambiance allows people who go there to take leave of their
particularism and show a certain civility and even openness
toward strangers. The Down Home Diner is a miniature
cosmopolitan canopy under which denizens have opportunities to connect across ethnic and racial lines. Outside, in
a more impersonal public space, there is less of a chance
for such interaction. Of course, tension crops up occasionally everywhere, including the Reading Terminal. When
racial and ethnic tension does arise, it may stem from the
unease people experience as this diverse and intimate

context unsettles their preconceptions. Here people may find unexpected challenges to their sense of group position.[4] Most often, because of the apparent large store of comity and goodwill manifested here, tension remains on the individual level. People come to this neutral and cosmopolitan setting expecting people to get along.

SATURDAY AT THE TERMINAL

I arrived at the Reading Terminal on Saturday morning before eight. The intersection of Twelfth and Filbert, which frames the market's main entrance, is reasonably quiet this early: two or three passersby, a lonely car or two, a group of homeless males spewing "motherfucker" conversation—or at least, those are the snippets I hear.

Slowly the corner begins to come alive. Pedestrian and car traffic increase. A cop car speeds by. Now a middle-aged black man in a wheelchair appears, then a slightly older, unkempt white man, and both begin to beg, competing for handouts. Passersby rebuff them repeatedly. The man in the wheelchair moves on, maneuvering all about and navigating the sidewalk skillfully. After crossing Filbert Street back and forth numerous times, he plants himself at least temporarily on the southeast corner, ready to panhandle.

A well-dressed, middle-aged white man, cigarillo in hand, approaches and asks me whether I know what time the tour buses begin. He's an out-of-town tourist ready to take in the sights.

Now the wheelchair man makes his way across Filbert Street again and engages the city motorized-street-sweeper man, as though he knows him. But after just a few minutes, he moves back to his original spot, remains there for a few minutes, and then crosses the street a third time. It seems strange that he's always on the move, and when he appears ready to settle, he looks furtively about.

The large, red neon sign goes on: Reading Terminal Market. It is 8:15, fifteen minutes before the market officially opens. The trucks that have unloaded around the back on Race Street are now pulling away. In front the foot traffic suddenly picks up: a biracial couple, a white tourist couple with guidebook in hand, and a woman rolling a travel bag. The flow of car traffic becomes more constant, while the pedestrian traffic picks up, then ebbs. Three young black women appear and walk south toward Market Street. An Asian man appears seemingly out of nowhere. Outside, before they put their aprons and hats on, it's hard to distinguish the people who are going to work at the market from the people going there to shop.

Three white men walk toward me and are about to pass when one catches my eye, slows down, and steps over to engage me. "Hey buddy, you got a couple of bucks? Me and my friends got stranded in Atlantic City, and gotta get a train home. Can you help us out?" The others slow down and wait up, curious to see whether their friend's bid will work. Testing, I reach in one pocket and pull out a ten, then dig in my other pocket to see what I have. As the men watch intently, I

45

hand the man a dollar bill, then slowly disentangle another. The two onlookers are riveted, perhaps incredulous about the scene, but I give it up. The first man thanks me profusely, then rejoins his buddies, and they proceed on their journey. "Get that train," I yell after them. "Yeah, where do I catch it?" he responds gamely. I point east toward the Gallery, and they move on.

As the traffic picks up, I cross the street to join the man in the wheelchair, who has moved yet again. He engages passersby, some of whom he seems to know. What's his story? He says he needs to avoid a certain police officer. There's one policeman who doesn't like him, he says. "So I keep on moving. It is just him. He don't like me. He's always threatening me. I'm a panhandler. He is the only one who messes with me." A police cruiser with a white police officer drives by, and he points to it. "See, he don't bother me. Just this one guy, and he's black. And I been coming here for thirteen years— he been messing with me for seven. He just don't like me."

As a pedestrian appears, the wheelchair man says, "Good morning, sir. Can you spare a little change, sir?" The middle-aged white man reaches in his pocket, comes up with a dollar, and places it in the wheelchair man's plastic soda cup. "God bless you, sir." As soon as this transaction is over, the wheelchair man pivots to face another potential donor. "Good morning, sir. Can you spare a little change, sir?" Their eyes meet, but the man says nothing and moves on. The wheelchair man's eyes follow him as he moves off into the distance.

Undaunted, he speaks right up to the next person, who

has a quizzical look as he rolls his suitcase. "What you looking for? Where you want to go?" he asks the stranger.

"Where's the SEPTA line?"

"That way," the wheelchair man instructs, directing him toward the trains. The man with the suitcase accepts this as he passes on without donating anything. Unfazed, the wheelchair man continues, on a mission to get enough money for his breakfast.

Two Amish women approach. "Good morning to ya'll," he opens. "Can you spare a little change?" The women shake their heads and keep walking. As they pass, he says politely, "Ya'll have a good day, now."

Now an unkempt older white man appears. The wheelchair man greets him, "What's up, Red?" "Oh, just trying to wake up," he says, rubbing his eyes. "It's gon' be a great day," offers the wheelchair man. Red nods and then disappears into the Down Home Diner.

The wheelchair man now resumes his work, keeping up his routine for virtually everyone who approaches his corner. Those who don't contribute and are apparently in need of directions seem always to catch his eye. Part of his strategy is to appear polite, cheerful, and as helpful as possible.

In a few minutes a young white man approaches. "Hey, big guy!" the wheelchair man says, greeting the complete stranger. Now a family with small children approaches. "Hi, sweetie, how ya'll doing?" he says to the children. The parents draw back a bit, but then seem to humor him while encouraging the small tykes to greet the "nice" man. "Hi baby, how you doing?" he says. The children smile, as he engages the willing family before they move along.

By 8:45 the foot traffic has picked up considerably. Another man appears. "Good morning, sir. Spare a little change, sir?" He waves to everyone. "Good morning, ma'am. Can you spare a little change?" An elderly white woman stops and reaches into her purse. After digging for a minute, she comes up with some change and places it in his cup. "God bless you," he offers. She nods, smiles, and then disappears.

The panhandler acts as if he knows many of the passing pedestrians, or at least addresses them familiarly. "Thank you, sir. God bless you." After a while, he wheels himself across the street yet again, staying on the move. It is now 8:55, and he has collected about ten one-dollar bills. A surprising number of people contribute, or apologize to him for lacking the change to make a donation.

I cross the street and enter the Terminal. Right away, I bump into my old friend Maurice. I've known Maurice for almost as long as I've been in Philadelphia, but haven't seen him for about three years. He invites me to sit down at Pearl's Oyster Bar and offers to buy me a cup of coffee. I accept, go over to the coffee shop across the way, obtain my cup, and then return to Pearl's, where he was sitting with two other middle-aged black men. Maurice introduces me to Hal and Dave, and we all shake hands. Maurice and I begin to catch up.

Soon Ronny Blake stops by. He also knows Maurice, so we chitchat like classmates at a high school reunion. Then Olisteen, a middle-aged black woman I know, stops by. I make introductions, and we all hang out there for a while.

Then, as suddenly as this group formed, its members begin to depart. Now Maurice and I are left by ourselves. When the Puerto Rican waitress appears, he laughs with her for a few moments and then introduces us. We all laugh and chat for a time before the waitress has to move along to attend to her chores. Maurice and I return to our catching up. Suddenly the wheelchair man appears and passes on, a bag in hand; perhaps he's made enough money for his breakfast. I greet him, and he acknowledges me but hurries along.

By 10:30 the place has filled up more and is becoming busy. More young white families appear, people from Center City there to shop for groceries or to have breakfast at one of the many coffee shops. In a little while, Maurice and I split, but not before promising to get together again soon.

On my way to the bathroom, I pass by Leroy's shoeshine stand. Leroy is a man whom I've known for years but haven't seen in a while. So we catch up a bit. As we talk, his eyes wander down toward the sneakers on my feet. I notice his gaze and, catching him before he can say anything, promise that the next time I come by I'll wear shoes he can shine. We laugh. Business has been slow today; few people want their shoes shined on Saturday, their day off. With Jim, his co-worker, we engage in small talk, "talking trash" and listening to one another's latest, enjoying each other's company.

By noon the whole Terminal Market has filled and is

buzzing with shoppers, pedestrians, panhandlers, and workers. Outside on Twelfth Street the traffic has grown noisier.

I take a seat at the tables along the outside of the Terminal. After a short while a white man in his thirties and two Latino boys of six and eight sit down at the table next to mine. I eavesdrop as he begins to explain a map of local points of interest, and the boys look on attentively, often interrupting him with questions. It becomes apparent that they are waiting here for their mom, a thirtysomething white woman, who soon joins them to plan their day. Suddenly they're gone, but almost immediately two elderly white men take their place. They settle down for a smoke, with no pretense of a need to order food or drinks in order to occupy the space. They talk and watch the passing foot traffic; after finishing their cigarettes, they're off. Within a minute or two, a heavyset, middle-aged white man dressed in chinos and a pastel yellow shirt plops into a seat, resting his arms on the table. He watches the passing show of pedestrians, but about five minutes later he too leaves.

A steady throng of pedestrians marches by outside along Twelfth Street: a middle-aged couple speaking German, a middle-aged white couple with teenage boys in red Phillies baseball caps and colorful T-shirts, an elderly white woman. An Asian family appears with teenage children walking in front, the woman next, and the father bringing up the rear. Then a double date of two young white heterosexual couples; two Latino men speaking Spanish; young white women; a preppy-looking black teenager eating a donut with his white counterparts; a Mexican heterosexual couple with cold drinks; two older white men, apparently a same-sex couple; a middle-aged white man in a motorized wheelchair with a younger woman, who could be his daughter; a large black woman with her hefty sixteen-year-old son at her side; a couple of young white men in baseball caps; and a small clump of whites with pizza slices all file by—a cross section of today's foot traffic headed into the Terminal.

Inside, people mill about, talking and laughing, their faces aglow with smiles and pleasant expressions. The atmosphere is carnival-like, and they contribute to it as well as take it all in, shopping and eating, eating and shopping, while occasionally bumping into a friend or two.

I walk back to the shoeshine stand, and there Leroy sits, shouting out, "Shine 'em up! Shine 'em up!" Most people just pass on by, but Leroy and Jim continue to call out hopefully. On occasion a queue starts, and a few customers gather and wait, entertained by the men's bantering back and forth.

These various individuals generally get along well with one another in this space. They need not interact intimately; rather, they simply share the market with one another, interacting in the act of buying and selling. They give one another space, the "aura" referred to by Georg Simmel,[5] allowing each person to swim about in this sea of diversity while being largely left alone. They come, interact in a broad sense, obtain what they want, and return to the world outside this setting.

In the Reading Terminal, many of the blacks are relatively well off compared with most other local black people, particularly those who generally shop at the Gallery Mall (see chapter three). Many of the blacks who shop at the market avoid going to the downtown mall. At the same time, the Reading Terminal and the Gallery have different offerings; for example, few people would go to the Gallery for groceries. The Terminal serves the middle class, black as well as white. The blacks there know they are somewhat better off than average and appear to hold themselves in relatively high regard.

By 1:00 p.m. the din has turned into a moderately loud hum: small talk, occasional light laughter, and "What a Wonderful World" is played live and sung by a small band of white men dressed in red, white, and blue shirts and straw hats. They add to the Terminal's party-like atmosphere, which is being enjoyed by all sorts of people, but particularly by families with small children. The crowd is quite diverse—black, white, and foreign—and all appear to feel that they are welcome here or even that they belong. Some are visiting for the first time, but others are seasoned veterans who know just what to expect, clearly modeling this for all comers. Many come here every Saturday, at times from as far away as New Jersey or Allentown; they and other out-of-towners get a taste of Philadelphia from their experience here and take it back to their hometowns.

Now the place is crowded and amazingly busy, as waitresses at the various eating places run to and fro, busboys push carts along, and customers line up to be seated. I stop at the bookstore and find the clerk happy to chat. She's quick to smile and enthuses, "I *love* to come here to work. This is just a wonderful place to work. People are just *so* nice." We discuss the titles for sale, and she encourages me to return anytime. Meanwhile, people are passing by, occasionally stopping to browse, ask a question, or buy a book. The casual conversation that is common in many bookstores occurs elsewhere in the market as well, as customers and vendors trade ideas about food and the other wares on display. The confidence that everyone is "so nice" is contagious.

People enter and make their way to whatever shops offer what they desire—food and drink, an imported shirt or a hand-knit hat—or they simply hang out. A visit here is one of the most economical and entertaining outings in town. You get to watch a show simply by arriving and taking note. That may not be the main reason people come, but it is an important side benefit.

Pat, a middle-aged white woman and longtime patron of the Terminal, and a gourmand in her own right, swears that the market is the only place to buy fresh ingredients and pick up ideas.

To me, Reading Terminal Market is first and foremost a place for cooks. Cooks are in paradise here. Not only can a cook find excellent quality and variety, but also each specialized merchant is an invaluable resource. Harry Ochs can tell you which piece of meat at his counter is just right for your dinner party, how much to get, exactly how to cook it, what to serve with it, and where to find the other necessary ingredients. Not only that, the next time he sees you he wants to know how you made out. He knows you'll be able to find him if you're not happy. Cooks come from all cultures and walks of life. They are often curious about new ingredients. I frequently have spontaneous interchanges while shopping in the crowded produce stall, cheek by jowl with other cooks, picking up an unfamiliar vegetable and turning to the person next to me—"Have you ever cooked this?"—or telling someone which one of these bunches of greens is the Italian parsley. These conversations require no preliminary formalities: just ask the question, exclaim over the beautiful tomatoes, or catch a frown and whisper that the green beans at another stall are better. This exchange between food vendors and food lovers is the foundation of the atmosphere at the market.

In sharp contrast to that in the gourmet food stores featured in upscale malls, none of the food sold here is marked up so obviously that buying it is a display of conspicuous waste; nothing is packaged just for show.

The wondrous smells waft through the market, putting people at ease. The presence of food defines the place as a huge tent under which hospitality and satisfaction can be expected. This is not so obvious in the nearby streets, which attract many destitute people from local shelters. Outside the Reading Terminal almost any type of behavior might be expected, whereas inside the atmosphere is calm and reassuring. Occasionally the most compromised elements from the outside enter, but good behavior is the norm, and the security guards are seldom required to engage in active peacekeeping.

One telltale feature of the civility that defines the market is the ATM machine located right in the middle of the food court. The small kiosk stands alone, without walls or barriers, much less a locked door keyed by a bank card. Occasionally the guard, a young, heavyset black woman, wanders by or simply lingers around the machine; she has established herself as a presence. But there is no sign of surveillance cameras. Shoppers walk up, wait a moment for the machine to be free, get some cash, and stuff it into their wallets—all with a sense of security that is absent from most ATMs downtown or in neighborhood shopping centers. The very openness of the ATM, its placement within constant sight of others, seems a social guarantee of safety.

The cross-racial encounters that take place in this venue are generally pleasant, rather than anxious. Pat shares an anecdote about how ordinary interpersonal tensions are defused—in this case the tensions that arise as people jockey for position in long lines while waiting to be served.

I was shopping at the large produce stand on the Filbert Street side on a very busy Saturday afternoon. The stand was packed with shoppers. There were lines at all the cashiers. I had just put my heavy basket on the counter to check out. The cashier is an Indonesian woman with whom I'm friendly as a result of many Saturday shopping trips. She's pleasant and packs the vegetables very well, so I stand in her line whenever she's working. The scale was at my left hand, toward the line of people waiting behind me. As the cashier lifted some vegetables toward the scale, the woman behind me put something on the scale. I turned to see what that was about and saw an elderly but still able black woman standing quite close behind me. She offered no explanation. The cashier smiled and moved the stuff off the scale, gently putting it to one side. The woman remonstrated forcefully: "Don't move my things; if something of mine needs to be moved I will move it." The cashier smiled at the woman and at me, preserving an absolutely even manner. Had she, a white woman who looks decades younger, apologized or deferred to me, she might have offended the other woman. Because she knew me, she felt safe in apologizing sweetly to the older woman, reserving a private look for me by way of thanks in helping her overcome the risk of escalating unpleasantness.

Some fleeting cross-cultural exchanges, repeated over time, generate relationships that have unusual intimacy despite their near-anonymity. Pat, who loves to cook, tells this story:

I often buy fish at the EAT FISH LIVE LONGER counter. After many pleasant but uneventful transactions, I got to know a young Indonesian salesman better one day when I was choosing soft-shell crabs. I like them alive, apparently an unusual preference except where lobsters are concerned. He tickled the crabs to find the liveliest ones and took end-

less pains packing them in ice so that they would survive the long trip home on the trolley.

Now this man works at the sausage stand. Late on the day before Mother's Day, as the crowd was beginning to thin, he was helping me choose some sausage when he peeked over the high glass counter and suddenly told me, with tears in his eyes, that his mother had recently died and that he hadn't been able to go to Indonesia for her funeral. I realized I'm probably about his mother's age. I tried to console him, then bade him good night as he wished me a happy Mother's Day. A few weeks later, I encountered him at the market, this time in an aisle, not behind his big counter. We reached out to each other, putting our hands awkwardly on each other's shoulders, not knowing quite what to say but feeling a very real intimacy despite knowing very little about each other.

Few public places have an ambiance that generates such closeness and allows people to express themselves so openly. This ambiance is engendered at least in part by the physical closeness patrons experience in this space. The aisles are narrow and crowded; the dining tables are close to one another, creating a cafeteria feel, reminiscent of hundreds of high school students packed into a lunchroom. People literally rub elbows, overhear each other's conversations, and make eye contact despite any attempt at avoidance. Such physical proximity naturally yields a familiarity, an increased comfort level, and often direct engagement among diverse patrons of the market.

SYNERGY AMONG STALLS

The Reading Terminal's stalls and kiosks exist in close proximity, each adjacent to one or two others and across the aisle from still others. Concentrated as they are, these stores compete for passing customers, as different vendors offer goods to fill similar appetites or desires. The arrangement of stores seems random: stalls specializing in baked goods, meats, and cheeses are scattered among those offering dry goods, coffee and tea, and elaborate desserts. So the stalls complement one another, each playing off the others and enhancing the viability of all. Most importantly, together they generate a certain synergy, producing a cosmopolitan zone that attracts more and more people who come here and enjoy the pleasant atmosphere. Ethnic and other particularities are present, to be sure, but visitors get the persistent message that such particularities don't matter much.

Almost none of the stores in the interior belong to a national chain. This policy is a deliberate management decision, making the place resemble a local bazaar rather than a food court filled with the same fast-food eateries found in shopping malls. Pearl's Oyster Bar, Bassett's Ice Cream, the Down Home Diner, Delilah's Soul Food, the Shoe Shine Stand, the Beer Garden, the Pork Rind, Termini's, and the Candy Store—all are independent and locally owned, and most have been here for years. These shops, along with the Amish greengrocer, the Asian greengrocer, the Asian fish place, the bakery, the kitchen appliance store, and the two bookstores, attract regular customers who inspect the wares of other shops on the way to their favorite vendors and who may stop to buy something attractive. New vendors begin with carts in the aisles and then graduate to stalls as they grow successful and these sought-after spaces become available.

The constant comings and goings of people, including the shoppers, the loiterers, and the help, create a flux of foot traffic that filters in and out, here one minute, gone the next, roaming freely all about the premises. You can track a particular person as he moves from the Beer Garden to the restroom and then the Buffet, or out the side door, or as she takes in kiosks on her way to her favorite shop, where she buys a sandwich, then munches it slowly as she wanders through the bookstore to the door, probably headed back to work. The situation is quite fluid, as no set or even implicit path defines the circulation pattern. The sheer busyness and density of the place generates the energy that distinguishes the Terminal Market from more linear streetscapes with separate storefronts.

Anyone who lingers is impressed not only by the vastness and variety of goods found in the setting but also by the innumerable nooks and crannies you can find here. In these quiet corners conversation flourishes. Down this narrow alleyway an elderly man sits alone at a two-top eating a chicken dinner; next to him sit a young boy and his father finishing their cheesesteaks and fries. The collection of these distinct, yet interconnected, places has a synergistic effect that enhances the congeniality of the whole setting. People engage in a certain amount of face time with one another, meeting and holding one another's eyes or simply being civilly inattentive. Each space and its denizens play off against the others, producing a generalized body of good feeling that becomes infectious, extending throughout the Reading Terminal.

In the middle of the market is the large common court-like area surrounded by eateries that serve everything from pork sandwiches to pizzas. Large white Formica tables pushed together encourage strangers to sit and eat together. Between bites they look things over, perhaps staring in the face of a complete stranger or making casual, if accidental, eye contact with the next person. Whether they look down or away, an identity emerges to be established or truncated, depending on whether either party interprets the exchange of looks as an invitation to conversation. In this public place people can take up others' opening gambits or not, as they choose. In this setting strangers engage one another about the personal details of their lives. An anecdote from a regular customer illustrates this interaction:

At opening time on a weekday, I hurried into the market for my regular iced coffee. I stopped to hold the door for the man behind me, who said, "I love your scarf; where did you get it?" I answered that he had a very good eye, because the scarf was made by Kevin O'Brien, a local textile artist who works in Old City. As we walked together toward the coffee stall, I told him how to get in touch with Kevin and about his studio sales. The man told me he liked to give wonderful scarves to his wife, and wrote down the name of his favorite textile artist for me. He told me he'd be working at the addition to the Convention Center for a while. By this time I was ready to order, so I turned and offered to buy him a coffee. After we were served, I bid him good morning and went off to work with a wave. A few weeks later, leaving the Terminal with my iced coffee, I heard him hail me on the sidewalk, regretting that he'd missed his chance to return the treat. The Reading Terminal is a place where I feel at home, where I am more open to overtures from strangers, starting a conversation as if in midstream, then moving on.

Interestingly, those visitors to the Terminal did not meet at the stall where textile arts are displayed; however, the availability of handmade crafts makes discussions about them more normal here than they would be elsewhere.

As strangers pass by one another, they take in one another's pleasant looks, punctuated by only an occasional scowl or inexplicable frown. Individuals engage in an elegant, delicate social dance, as they exchange places and move about with a necessary awareness of the others. What begins as a consciousness of bodies moving in a shared space gives rise to courteous greetings, momentary encounters, and even mutual recognition. This interplay contributes to the wider synergy.

CLOSING TIME

At 5:00 p.m. the workers begin to pack things up and close down their operations for the day. The security guards start to move about, announcing in booming voices, "The Terminal is now closing." The din decreases gradually as the stores and aisles empty out. The cash registers grow quieter. As the denizens file out the doors and disappear into the passing traffic, they leave behind a setting quite different from what it was at midday.

Now, paradoxically, the workers grow busier—washing down grills, putting things away, and preparing to say good-bye to their friends and co-workers. They chatter among themselves, reviewing the day's events and joking as they work. The staff at one restaurant breaks down the kitchen equipment, washes the pots and pans, and wipes down the stainless-steel countertops. A small crew of Asian men cleans the fish cooler and hoses off all the surfaces. Across the way a young black man at a Chinese eatery cleans up, placing large black rubber floor mats alongside the showcase. The Amish farmers pack away the jelly jars and cover the produce. The workers at Ochs Meats transfer everything from the display case to the walk-in refrigerator. At the shoe shine stand Leroy puts away his polish, brushes, and rags. Everyone seems to get busy.

During this closing time, a subtle but significant transformation occurs. The members of the staff begin to mind the customers less and to mind their own business more, even turning to personal concerns as they look forward to the end of their workday. They talk more among themselves and focus on the customers only if they seem threatening.

Late-arriving shoppers scurry about to make their final purchases before 6:00 p.m., when the outside doors actually close. In the small restaurants a few patrons finish their coffee at the counter. The dimming of lights sends out the unmistakable message that it is closing time. The security guards grow more insistent, gradually raising their voices and becoming firmer in demeanor.

After enjoying a very late lunch at the Buffet, I've gotten the message and prepare to leave, but first I roam around a bit, taking advantage of the fact that others are still lingering and that the workers are engaged in closing down. At the Honey Store across the way, the staff has gotten a head start on the other stalls, for the store is closed on Sunday and its wares must be secured for the weekend. The workers carefully wrap the stall in protective netting. A middle-aged white woman, evidently the manager, expertly unfurls the spool. As I stop to watch, she eyes me with suspicion. So I move on through the Terminal, pausing here and there to take things in.

In front of the piano I encounter the young African American who has been playing at the Terminal for tips ever since he appeared there as a "boy wonder." His two jars full of dollar bills rest on top of the instrument as he talks with a young Asian man whom I overhear asking, "Where can I get a beer around here?" This is a truly odd question, especially at this time of the evening, when people are clearing out. As I approach, the musician begins to finger and gather up his tip jars. I feel his wariness. Remarkably, he answers that the Asian man can get a drink over at the Beer Garden, even though he knows that it will be closing in minutes.

The Asian man soon leaves, presumably to try to fetch his beer, but it is just about 6:00 p.m. I strike up a conversation with the musician. "I know you from way back," I open, "when you played over by the shoeshine stand." "Yeah," he says demurely, "I been playing here for a while." "How old are you?" I inquire. "I'm nineteen!" "Wow, I remember when you used to sit and play classical music and a little jazz over there. It was very impressive." "I'm still doing it," he responds, hitting a few bars of a jazz standard. "How did you ever begin doing this?" I ask. "I just walked up and asked if I could play, and then asked the manager to put me on the list, and he did, and I been playing ever since." A guard approaches us. "Time to go," he instructs. "Time to go." As we say goodbye, he gathers up his things and I move along.

The whole place grows darker, as the workers cut the lights, one there, another here, and then two or three over there, haphazardly, not all at once.

Earlier in the day the denizens and customers had the run of the place, but now the security guards usher the stragglers out of the main food court area and toward the Down Home Diner, which stays open until 7:00 p.m. and opens onto Filbert Street. "It's time to go, time to go. Don't care where you go, but you got to leave here!" the security guards shout as they walk up and down the aisles. "Everybody out!" No longer relaxed, the denizens scatter about like chickens before the place closes down. The guards are now responsible for securing the premises. They scrutinize the customers, treating each as a problem to reckon with, as if some might be dangerous and others might stray or otherwise cause them trouble. An African American security guard sizes up a customer. "You can finish your meal," he says, gruffly. "But you must now go out the Down Home Diner! All other doors are closing." "This is your way out," he shouts at another straggler. "You must go out!"

I stand talking with Tyrone, the black security guard, in an aisle separating the Down Home Diner from the open area. He tells me, "We close all entrances to the station and then send people out through the Down Home Diner." A middle-aged black man approaches and wants to take care of some last-minute business. "I need to pick up a package," he cries, looking over the sea of canvas-covered businesses in the semidarkened area. "We're closing up," says the guard, stopping the man. "But the package is waiting for me. She told me to come on back," he explains. The guard listens sympathetically and permits him to enter. As we continue to talk, he reveals that his biggest concern is with stragglers who might get locked inside after closing.

In Philadelphia the Reading Terminal Market is but one of many such locations that may be viewed, conceptually at least, as existing under a kind of cosmopolitan canopy. Other examples with a similar ambiance are Rittenhouse Square Park, Thirtieth Street Station, Whole Foods Market, the Italian Market, various local fitness centers, hospital waiting rooms, the multiplex theater, and sporting venues. Most typically, under the canopy, within the exterior walls or within the prescribed street boundaries (as in the case of Rittenhouse Square), the atmosphere is calm and relatively pleasant, as a mix of people go about their business, at times self-consciously on good or "downtown" behavior, working to "be nice" or civil to the next person. Here they sit, eat, and walk, sometimes meeting new acquaintances or bumping into people they know.

The denizens return from time to time to conduct their business, while becoming more familiar with one another as well as with the social ambiance of the place. Eventually they come to "know" the regulars without ever having met them. A major theme of this type of setting is civility, and people are continually encouraged to behave courteously to one another; at times denizens can be solicitous and extraordinarily helpful to complete strangers. Such neutral settings, which no one group expressly owns but all are encouraged to share, situated under this kind of protective umbrella, represent a special type of urban space, a peculiar zone that every visitor seems to recognize, appreciate, and enjoy. Many visit not only for instrumental reasons—to have a meal or just be "out and about"—but also for the experience of being among those they believe they are likely to find here. In navigating the public spaces, visitors have little sense of obligation to the next person other than common civility. They then leave with the memory of a good experience and are likely to return another day, perhaps to relive that otherwise uneventful experience. Personal accounts attest to this phenomenon.

On a cool Saturday afternoon in October, after spending the morning at the Reading Terminal, a young black man named Oscar returned to his West Philadelphia home tired, disgusted, and angry. His wallet was missing, and he was certain that someone, possibly two men he had encountered at the Terminal, had "run a game" on him to relieve him of his wallet. He thought he knew when this happened, and he had a definite description of the guys who had set him up. Upon returning home, he related his travails to his cousin Moses, who owned the house where he lived. He cursed the two strangers he was certain had taken his wallet. He simmered for the rest of the afternoon; later he felt utterly dejected.

By midweek Oscar was beginning to get over his loss. He didn't care about the money, which was only about twenty dollars, or even his credit cards, which by now Moses had helped him to cancel. The real loss was his leather wallet.

Having it stolen really hurt because this wallet was special. His baby sister had worked for years at an upscale leather-goods store in Center City and had given it to him as a token of her love. He had long cherished the wallet, imbuing it with pride and deep sentiment. He wondered what he would tell his sister. Maybe he wouldn't tell her but would try to find some sort of replacement. A week passed, and then two weeks.

On Friday afternoon at the end of the second week, he heard Moses call up to his third-floor apartment, "Hey Oscar! There's something for you down here. Mailman left a package for ya!" Oscar ignored Moses's calls. Later that evening he went down and opened the package. He was surprised to find his wallet intact. Everything was there, including his twenty dollars, his credit cards, his photos, his driver's license, everything. Whoever found it at the Reading Terminal—and Oscar strongly suspects it was a white person—simply mailed it back to him. The package had no return address, so he was unable to thank the finder.

The return of his wallet left Oscar with a great feeling about the Terminal and the quality of people who frequent it. Equally important, Oscar and Moses share this story repeatedly whenever the subject of the Reading Terminal comes up. Acts of goodwill are propagated through such stories and reverberate through the city.

A middle-aged white woman who lives in the suburbs of

Philadelphia tells a story—to others, as well as to me—that epitomizes the mutual enlightenment that may be gained in the casual cross-cultural exchanges that occur in and around the Reading Terminal Market. Marylyn is from southern Africa, so her awareness of the delicacy and mutability of interracial interactions is especially acute.

On one sunny spring day she exited the market with her arms full of bags and headed toward the corner. As she approached the traffic light, she decided to spit out the gum she had been chewing. When she spied an open trash can, she seized the opportunity. Unable to finger the gum because both her hands were holding her groceries, she simply leaned over the trash can and spit out the gum.

Just as she did this, a car full of young black men pulled up to the light and waited for it to change. With no apparent prompting, one of the black youths leaned out the window and shouted at her, "Hey, lady, don't spit in that trash can! Don't you know that people got to eat out of them cans? You shouldn't be doing that. Don't you spit in that trash can, lady."

Startled, but rapidly recovering her poise and smiling, Marylyn replied, "Oh, you're just teasing me. Can't you see that my hands are full?" She thought they were trying to scare her, so she turned the tables, teased them back, and engaged them in small talk. One of the youths said, "You talk funny, lady. Where you from?"

"I'm an African," she replied. "No, you're not, can't be African! You don't look African to me." "Well, I am," she asserted. "I was born and raised in Nairobi, Kenya." Astonished, the youth said, "Then speak some African." She then accommodated with "Jambo," which means hello, and other Swahili words. They were amazed. Cracking up, they made big fun of her, but not in a mean-spirited manner. They cajoled her, asking her to teach them to speak Swahili. "Speak for me," they begged. She continued to entertain them in Swahili until the light changed, and they were off.

When Marylyn returned to her predominantly white, middle-class neighborhood and shared this story with friends, they questioned her. "Weren't you scared?" "No," she said—but felt the need to explain that these boys meant no harm and that she had actually enjoyed the interaction with them.

Segregated neighborhoods and the cosmopolitan canopy exist simultaneously in Philadelphia. Under the canopy, people perform race. When they present themselves as civil and friendly, they may simply coexist. On occasion, however, they may interact, learning something surprising about others they had not known before. This practice can have an effect that extends far beyond the canopy. When people who have visited the Reading Terminal Market or other urban canopies retreat to South Philly, North Philly, or the suburbs, they share the story of their visit with friends, communicating to them the ambiance of cosmopolitanism as well as some of the discoveries about others that the canopy permits. When people have positive experiences again and again, this scenario becomes expected and, over time, is built upon. The most socially productive behaviors are encouraged and eventually become established, even institutionalized. Over many years of observation I have seldom seen an angry person at the Terminal Market. At the Gallery, where we make our next "virtual visit," altercations and fist fights sometimes break out. As the word spreads, places develop self-reinforcing reputations. At the market, where respectability reigns, visitors and denizens alike are strongly committed to civility.

3. | THE GALLERY MALL:
THE GHETTO DOWNTOWN

When compared with the broad diversity of classes and ethnicities found inside urban canopies such as the Reading Terminal and Rittenhouse Square, the Gallery Mall is considerably less heterogeneous. Initially designed to be a venue for upscale shops and department stores—a downtown equivalent to a suburban mall—its location above a subway interchange with lines running out into Philadelphia's black ghettos created a shopping and gathering place mainly for lower-middle-class and working-class blacks.

The earlier ambitions failed in part because of the mall's location on a stretch of Market Street where urban blight had already set in. When the Gallery opened, the Convention Center and the upscale Marriott hotel were not yet built, and the Reading Terminal Market was still awaiting its rejuvenation.[1] With the demise of the architecturally significant

Lit Brothers department store, the retail spaces at street level along that section of Market Street had gone steadily down market. The blocks of Thirteenth Street from Market to Walnut were still the city's center for vice, and some of the effects spilled over for several blocks toward the Delaware River.

Periodic economic downturns also made it difficult for the Gallery to compete with more established retail areas such as Walnut Street from Fifteenth to Rittenhouse Square. Lower-end stores began to replace more expensive shops, and the color of the clientele changed as well. The more moderate prices that became available started to attract more of the black working-class people who already patronized the street-level businesses nearby. Here, in the gap between the well-to-do areas of Center City west of Broad Street and the emerging chic of Old City on the edge of the Delaware, black people from the neighborhoods ringing Center City and readily accessible by public transport found a comfortable place to shop and congregate. At some point in the last decade, the transition became complete, and the Gallery acquired a clear and lasting reputation as a "black place," catering to black patrons from the lower economic classes.[2] Latinos and Asians with similarly low socioeconomic identities create what little diversity there is at the Gallery. The few white patrons are also predominantly working class.

That reputation is intimidating to the majority of potential white customers and discourages them from visiting the Gallery and mixing with its clientele. The predominance of black patrons at the mall evokes stereotypes of ghetto violence and criminality; in truth, middle-class blacks avoid the setting as well. Those whites whose own inner-city experience has made them streetwise are less likely to be inhibited by such stereotypical thinking. A few venture into the Gallery only when accompanied by black companions.

The food court in the Gallery's lower level has become especially important as a social hangout for middle-aged to elderly black men and the few women who gather here to "take in the day," to people watch and engage in their own variety of folk ethnography. The group that gathers here daily is made up of people roughly like the "decent" ghetto dwellers characterized in my earlier work *Code of the Street*. As reflected in their conversation and idle talk, their worldview is decidedly ethnocentric and suspicious of outsiders, especially whites.

In these respects, the Gallery Mall and its food court both challenge and extend my thinking about cosmopolitan canopies. Interaction between racial groups is observable here. Patrons do find a certain comity and goodwill, but their sociability seems cramped by the ever-present awareness that ghetto street violence—the violence commonly attributed to black ghetto streets—may intrude at any moment. Hence, there is an edge to the quality of public interaction here, an edge not so prominent in the other canopies I have described.

And yet this public space is a destination and hangout for ghetto residents who choose to leave their own neighborhoods each day and come downtown to interact with others, mostly like themselves with regard to race and class, but from other parts of Philadelphia.

What follows is a chapter devoted to a description of public life beneath what might be viewed as a special kind of canopy, more parochial in nature, perhaps not fully welcoming to one and all, but welcoming enough to be less than hostile to strangers venturing therein.

ENTERING THE GALLERY

You can enter the Gallery from various directions, including through some of the stores, notably Big Kmart on Tenth, but the grand main entrance is at Ninth and Market. A large sign announces "The Gallery," and underneath a wide set of steps leads to the lower level. On most days small groups of young black men hang out on the steps, leaning against the side of the building. Sometimes older, disheveled-looking women with bags and canes, or an occasional prostitute, join them. A few homeless people at times gather on these steps, occupy the benches, or simply mill about on the sidewalk, begging passersby for money, sometimes aggressively. Affronted or intimidated by this scene at the entrance of the Gallery, many middle-class people, black and white alike, pass on by, rather than descending the steps into the Gallery. Those for whom the loitering crowd is a more familiar street scene will not be put off by that presence.

As you descend the steps at Ninth and Market, you see the atrium, a large open space where from time to time various community groups put on shows. On the left is a window where lottery tickets can be bought. Usually three or four people, most often black, wait to buy a chance at a fortune. Just around the corner a young Korean man and his assistant operate a newsstand. In front of the newsstand, vendor's carts peddle cheap watches, videos, and framed photographs of black celebrities and heroes. The vendors themselves are somewhat diverse. I've noticed a young Korean man, a young white woman, and a Hispanic woman minding individual carts. Farther down the way a young African American man sells cell phones. The stores in the Gallery include f.y.e., an electronics store; Modell's for sporting goods; Radio Shack; and NET, a clothing store for young urban men. One business that shows how blacks have made this space their own is a bookstore that sells only books with a black perspective. Promulgating Afrocentric interpretations and ideology, few of these books can be found in mainstream bookstores.

In the Gallery the outside comes inside, but within limits. The mall is an interior, yet much of what occurs on the surrounding streets happens inside as well. The hustlers who sell cheap jewelry, incense, and pirated movies and front stolen goods occasionally come in to sell their wares surreptitiously. Sometimes incidents do occur, especially in the food court. There is a certain defensiveness as you enter. In this way the Gallery is different from the Reading Terminal. The security guards are challenged more often. They know that this is not as easy a job as being a guard at Reading Terminal;

their physical safety is more at risk. Yet those who come from the streets can feel at home here. The themes, ideas, and associations derive from the ghetto, although civility prevails. The Gallery is a humming, buzzing, fun place, where black people come not just to shop and to eat but also to see and be seen by others like themselves. Though not cosmopolitan, life here is very public.

THE FOOD COURT

Along this corridor a steady stream of people passes, mostly black, with an occasional Asian, Puerto Rican, or white person. In the middle of this long corridor a set of tables extends for about thirty yards before you come to the food court itself. The court is a large, hangar-like area full of tables ringed by fast-food places, including a Taco Bell, a KFC, a Caribbean stand, and other franchises. Tables for four provide a place for people to eat and congregate with their friends and associates. Typically the patrons are taking a brief break, enjoying lunch or coffee and a snack, or refreshing themselves for continued shopping.

But that is not always the case. A substantial number of people buy their refreshments and then linger for much of the morning and afternoon, meeting their friends and hanging out in the area. On weekday mornings a mix of people is always there, though most are black, middle aged to elderly, from the local neighborhood. Many have become regulars, and their presence has created a virtual senior center—a kind of haven to which retired folks from the local ghettos come regularly to keep up with their friends.

The food court differs from the street market in that it is cool in summer and warm in winter, and is kept clean by the Gallery's management. It is a very accessible space, since many of the denizens are able to get there from their neighborhoods by public transportation. Because this setting is indoors and downtown, it has a certain air of security as guards frequently wander about the premises. Some of the men comment, "Well, this is better than the 'hood. I ain't got to worry about being shot at."

The regulars come here not only to see their friends but also to be entertained and amused by the social energy of the setting. The corridor of the food court serves as a runway offering a virtual show for many patrons. The choice seats are along the corridor or "pass through," where the men sit and "watch the action." They watch the ladies, young and old, parade by, commenting on their dress, their bodies, and even their supposed personal lives, as if they "know their business." Small groups proliferate, providing the participants with a form of social capital, or social sustenance, allowing them to laugh easily, to complain out loud, or simply to enjoy themselves with others who are there for some of the same reasons.

These men are generally retired and appear in decent health. For them—and the occasional woman among them—being here may be compared to hanging out on the street corner in the 'hood of an earlier and less turbulent time.

Many come to "see what's happening," which seems to be something quite satisfying in and of itself. Their trek to this setting each day provides a purpose to life, so they try not to miss a minute of it. If they haven't been around, they are filled in by friends when they reappear. The regulars enjoy being in the thick of things and talking about strangers with their friends.

As passing mothers publicly chastise their small children, trying to make them mind their manners, the men comment on the women's child-rearing skills. If they curse out little children loudly, men roll their eyes and make critical remarks the women might overhear, trying to sanction them. The men try to guess who's who as people pass. "See her in the yellow with the big titties? The guy there, he's a pimp, that's her pimp." After a black man sharply dressed in white passes by with a dumpy black woman pushing a baby in a stroller, the older men laugh at how ridiculous he looked. Masculinity is not about pretense and strutting self-display, they seem to be saying. The "corner boys" are here too, as are black men who may be in their forties but still dress like corner boys, with their baseball caps and ornaments. There are some younger adults in their twenties who may be unemployed but somehow get by. Grandmothers bring their grandchildren. The occasional white businessman walks by or stops for a bite to eat. A lady passes by with a bunch of balloons. Muslim men and women are identifiable by their distinctive dress. A few vagabonds meander about and beg but manage to avoid the notice of the police. A group of Ethiopian or Somali girls wanders through, followed by a group of white girls with sodas and shakes. A cohort of elderly Chinese men has laid claim to a table. Interestingly, comparatively few Chinese people are here despite the proximity of Chinatown, which occupies roughly the same east–west blocks as the Gallery, but three blocks above Market Street. This fact underscores the basic homogeneity of those who come to the Gallery: the high school girls, the young men, the older men, the couples—almost all of them are with others of the same race and age group. The self-segregation is striking, although not total.

WILLY AND HIS FRIENDS

An extended primary group, like the denizens of the food court at the Gallery, is a loose collection of people who gather and hang out together in the same public setting on a regular basis.[3] Their interactions exhibit some features of primary groups and some features of secondary groups. These people typically know one another well, or at least claim to, even when they don't know one another outside this setting. They are familiar enough to be able to tease one another good-naturedly and have running jokes about one another. So there is a certain safety and comfort in an extended primary group.

It was through hanging out at the Gallery that I first met Willy, a seventy-seven-year-old black man who was a regular member of the group that congregates in the food court. Willy was from the huge North Philadelphia ghetto. In the old neighborhood he lived with his sister, but he visited the Gallery almost daily.

Over the course of a year, as I came to know Willy and his friends, we shared numerous stories about our lives in Philadelphia, about others whom we knew, and about life at the Gallery. In sitting there with Willy, I could see that he was well liked by the others who frequented this space, for as they arrived, they warmly greeted him, and as they departed, they respectfully said their goodbyes.

There was one person with whom Willy had a very special relationship: his "wife," Sarah Jane. Often, at a certain point in the day, Sarah Jane arrived and asked whether Willy was ready for his coffee yet, and when he answered in the affirmative, she would disappear for a few minutes and return with a coffee and donut for him, which she had bought from the Dunkin' Donuts down the way. She also occasionally brought a coffee roll for me, which I appreciated. Willy felt taken care of and even attended to by his "wife." Significantly, they conducted their relationship only here, where it was effectively consummated by these little exchanges, which they conducted every day.

After a couple of hours, Sarah Jane might break out a chicken sandwich with pickles for "her man" and hand it over to Willy. Willy would accept the sandwich as though he were owed it. It was all he needed and all he wanted, as well as what he'd come to expect. For the next fifteen or twenty minutes, Willy would sit on the bench eating the sandwich. Then he would signal that he wanted a soda. All he had to do was to display "that look," and Sarah was off to the KFC across the way to fetch him a Pepsi to wash down the chicken. Sarah fussed over "her man." They knew each other only in this place; they needed and wanted no more.

Sarah Jane's devotion and his Gallery friends' affection were signs not of deference but of deep respect. Here Willy could get something that he could not get in his old neighborhood, and his sense of that recognition made him feel good inside. On occasion he shared this feeling of appreciation with me: "I'm glad I got Sarah, Eli. I'm a lucky man. I mean that. She's always ready to do for me, and don't ask me for nothin' back. Just wanta take care of me—man, I'm sho' blessed."

On a warm Monday morning in May, I arrived at around 10:30 and went directly to the area where Willy and his friends hang out. At this time of day the seats are mostly empty. We agree that it is good to have our backs to the wall—actually more of a partition—and sit and watch the men and women parading by, knowing that others are watching us watching them. Those sitting at tables directly on the corridor that runs through the mall all face the walkway. Mainly they are men socializing among themselves or eying girls as they go past. A young Puerto Rican man calls out to a very pregnant black girl: "When are you due?" "August," she answers. "August!" he echoes as she continues on her way. This is really just a way of engaging her in a moment's conversation. Willy and his three or four friends watch over this part of the Gallery like hawks, and they seem to have the best seats in the house. Young women walk by, putting on a show and know-ingly catching the eye of Willy and his buddies. The passing parade also includes young white and black students playing hooky from school, middle-aged shoppers, and other retir-ees, as well as a number of homeless people.

Willy and his friends say that anything can happen here, and to hear them talk, it does. He tells me that two months ago two eighteen- to twenty-year-old "white lesbians engaged in a vicious fight over a young black girl," hurling all kinds of expletives at each other. It erupted "out of nowhere." Shop-pers and diners stopped what they were doing and moved closer to view the action. Eventually, Willy said, "it took about twenty cops to stop the fight. Hair was pulled out, rings from noses were snatched, and blood was everywhere. Finally, the fight was broken up, and the girls were arrested." While the regulars do expect to see a fight from time to time, this is not the main reason they come to the food court, nor are such fights so likely to escalate into wider violence as equivalent confrontations back in the 'hood.

On Saturday evening around 5:30 in early January, the area is filled with a majority of black people and a few Asians, Latinos, and whites. Today's outside temperature is about twenty-eight degrees, and the Gallery patrons are dressed warmly: the women bundled up in long blue or gray down coats, the men in caps, overcoats or "puffies," and scarves. In the common areas, people mill about; a constant parade of shoppers and diners moves up and down the runway. Most of the four-top tables and seats are occupied by black middle-aged to elderly men and women—a few women here, a few men there—and the younger black people are up and about. Whole families are in evidence, here for an evening's entertainment or dinner out, though the fare on offer is all fast food. The scene resembles an extended gathering of people who might be strangers, but could well become friends. I meet some of my old friends who hang out here, and we find our spot on the runway and catch up. After about an hour of spontaneous group talk that jumps from subject to subject as it shifts from speaker to speaker, my turn comes. I share with them an incident that I witnessed in the Radio Shack earlier in the evening.

As I entered the store, there was a commotion just inside the front door, where a crowd of about twenty people had gathered. A black male customer and the Filipino store manager stood face to face arguing, with a large black security guard standing between them. The black customer looked about fifty years old and the manager about forty. The black man was upset about the way he had been treated by the store personnel. I gathered that he had wanted to exchange one item for another, but the item he wanted was out of stock. Disappointed, the man complained that he had come all the way from North Philly, and since he was returning home empty-handed the store should pay for his carfare to compensate him for his trouble. The manager said the man's request was ridiculous and there was no way that he would comply. When refused, the black man became loud, and the manager summoned the mall's security. The guard's presence emboldened the manager, who began to instruct the black man about store policy in a most officious way. The customer became even more agitated. Through all of this the guard was ostensibly a silent bystander, but he represented the authority of the civil law. Finally, the guard had had enough and calmly took out his radio and called for "backup," signaling to all that this incident was over, or the police would arrive to arrest the man.

The black man seemed to understand this threat, but he took a parting verbal shot at the manager, saying, "I'm not afraid of you, you can't threaten me." The manager then mumbled something under his breath. To this implicit threat the black man countered, "You need to get out of my face before I punch you in the mouth, in front of this guard." As he made this comment, his voice trailed off, as he shook his head and walked out of the store.

Soon the backup arrived, but the customer had left, the incident was over, and the store began to return to normal. Business was again conducted as usual. Seemingly oblivious that he was speaking to a black man, the manager explained to me, "Yeah, he wanted carfare home, and when I refused, he wanted to get loud, thinking that I would give in. No, no, can't do that. That's how they are, that's how it goes."

My friends enjoyed the story. Ignoring the store manager's offensive remark about blacks, they laughed at how "crazy" the black customer was to think that the store should give him his carfare. Then someone else shared another story *on a similar topic, so the conversation went on over coffee and donuts. We were having a good time.*

Sometimes Willy or his friends walk around as though they are "at home," perhaps with a piece of chicken from KFC or a pastry from Dunkin' Donuts in hand. Friends fetch coffee for others who cannot move so well. Fellowship and sociability is the order of the day. They sit and read the paper, talk with one another, or enjoy periods of silent observation. The *Daily News* is the newspaper of choice, as it is among so many ordinary Philadelphians. Local events often become a topic of conversation, along with random items in no special order: "You hear last night that the power went out?" "Anybody hit the Lottery?" They talk about what they watched on TV, and what deals they can get from their cable providers. They also talk about what happens to them and their friends and families back in the neighborhood. Violent acts there are a common topic. A lady got punched in the face; shots were fired in another brawl. One man chimes in with his reaction: "Time for me to go, know what I mean? Just one more year and then I'm gone." Who is making what money is another perennial subject; that someone is making "plenty money" is big news among a group where even temporary affluence is rare.

At times arguments break out as the men debate historical incidents, especially those involving black people. The one thing the men will all agree on is that the black man is almost always a historical victim, and that what the white man did to the black man was "low down and dirty." They conclude that "the white man is against us" and that "his day will come." It will be "payback time," and "he'll get his." This perspective operates as a background understanding born of a history of ethnic competition in the city. In the safe black place that has been created at the Gallery, the men feel very free to be themselves. They can be loud and boisterous and frank in their comments, released from the inhibitions they might feel when among whites. Their orientation has been shaped by their place, and sense of place, in history.

Willy was a fixture of the Gallery, as regular as an employee in his attendance at the food court. When he stopped coming around, his Gallery friends grew concerned. I began to worry that something had happened to him. A while later I encountered A.J., a middle-aged man whom I met there when Willy was present. When I asked about Willy, A.J. told me that Willy had not been around "in six months." He commented that a number of others "just stop coming around" or had died during the past year. It is clear that some of these men don't really know one another by anything other than their first names, and their interactions and friendships tend to be confined only to the space of the Gallery.

The sociologist Erving Goffman, who analyzed interaction in groups, noticed that a person displays his "front" for others to observe, for he is aware that he is "on" and that much is at stake in any interaction. His or her performance can be highly consequential, so it must be managed as on a "front stage." In these circumstances the "backstage" is more guarded and kept strategically hidden from the audience for whom the performance is expressly given.[4] Things that go on at the Gallery are on the front stage, where people can represent themselves in whatever way they want. The denizens are acquainted in the here and now, but don't know one another's backstage. Eventually word spread around that Willy had been seen wandering aimlessly around his North Philly neighborhood, peering into trash cans and seeming generally disconnected.

The concern of Willy's Gallery friends did not extend beyond their relationship in that setting. They did not go and seek him out in his neighborhood, learn the reasons for his sudden behavioral change, or try to encourage him to return. Their relationship had been confined to that space and was nontransferable. Many relationships formed under the canopy are one-dimensional: they exist in a specific space and do not develop further, or progress deeper, outside that setting.

Conversation among the denizens of the food court is stimulated, rather than interrupted, by the passing scene. People's personal histories might come up, but as a rule anecdotally. The men didn't know one another before they met here, and they still don't know one another well. They define themselves as much by what they say about the passing scene along the Gallery walkway as by the stories they tell about their past.

Members of these groups are most often self-consciously, ethnocentrically black. Within the race, African Americans congregate separately from African immigrants. Mixed groups appear among the more transient visitors to the Gallery. Three construction workers, two black and one white, share a table for lunch. A white woman, a black woman, and a black man walk by together; perhaps they are co-workers. Some of the high school groups are also mixed. And there is the occasional biracial couple. These visitors are reminiscent of the diverse clientele of the Reading Terminal Market, but the defining presence in the Gallery remains the predominant black population, and few of the white visitors are there on their own.

Big customer flows at certain times impart a distinct rhythm to the day. Older people slowly file in during the morning. Some while away the whole morning here. As noon approaches, the food court gets busier. The crescendo in the noise level all but drowns out the background music. From about 11:30 to 1:30 students from nearby schools and workers from area businesses crowd into the food court for lunch. Some students are there earlier, playing hooky. The mall offers everything they might want. The girls are in their purple-and-gold uniforms. The boys wear the required attire, chino pants and blue-striped, man-tailored shirts, but they put their own stamp on it, wearing their pants below the butt and leaving the shirts hanging out; in defiance of the school dress code, it gives them a special look. Small groups of them visit the shops, generating a low-grade anxiety about shoplifting among the clerks. When two or more black youths enter a store, the managers go on alert, watching them carefully. Occasionally someone will grab something from a store and run out, and the black clerk (many of the clerks are black here) will run after him instead of calling the authorities. More than in the suburban mall, the "code of the street" is operative here. Now and then birthday party lunches are held in the food court. Twenty or so people, mainly women, will build a common table, buy food from various vendors, and party heartily. There is laughter, loud talk, and camaraderie. The crowding does not disrupt the comity. A black girl there with her family goes up to a white man sitting alone to ask whether she can take the empty chair at his table, as her group of five squeezes around a four-top.

After about 1:30 the place becomes noticeably quieter. For the rest of the afternoon and evening, crowds come and go. Activity ebbs and flows, although it is never completely silent. During the quiet times some of the Asian food vendors hand out free samples in an attempt to attract customers. Some young couples are lost in their own world, absorbed in each other. Groups of older people, men with men and women with women, as well as a few lonely individuals, are there all day. Kids come back and hang out after school, or they cut classes in order to socialize at the Gallery. They connect with other young people and check out the stores.

On the weekends, the students are joined by older youths who have left high school, with or without a diploma, and now have children, whom they bring with them. A carnival atmosphere is evident at times, never more so than at Easter, when people are buying new outfits for themselves and for their children.

In Philadelphia, working-class blacks get dressed up to give Easter speeches or attend Easter functions at church or school. For this they need bright spring clothing and new sneakers. Since the Gallery has all of it, the Saturday just before Easter is especially lively. Large crowds stroll about evincing a certain excitement. They may queue up for a hamburger at Mickey D's or simply sit in the food court and pass the time of day. A hustler appears and tries quietly to sell his wares. He might have fresh copies of *American Gangster* or *Big Momma's House 2* for five dollars per movie. He walks about and whispers, "I got something here! I got something here! Can I tighten you up?" After a number of people ignore him, he makes a sale, which seems to surprise him. The customer slips the young hustler a five-dollar bill, and he quickly plucks it up, wary of the mall security. The sale is made, and the two part company as quickly as they met. The hustler is now gone. And the customer is left to wonder whether the DVD is good, or whether this whole thing was a scam and he has lost his money. He may conclude the risk wasn't that great, given the stake to get a movie that was released just days ago.

Down the way and upstairs is a set of young men throwing big money around. One of them picks up four or five pairs of his favorite brand of sneakers from the Foot Locker store and pays for them with cash. It looks strange, since the boy is otherwise so shabbily dressed. He has drug dealer written all over him, and the local folk ethnographers know this. He displays everything about himself to anyone caring to pay attention, though not everyone is in the know.

At the entrance to the Gallery, a small group of young black men hangs out. Though the group's behavior is not threatening, it reminds the regulars of their dislikes and fears regarding the 'hood and creates an atmosphere that discourages middle-class shoppers, whether black or white, from patronizing the mall. One young man takes out a roll of cash, taunting the others. He brags about his money, "threatening" to buy one of his friends a new pair of sneakers, since the ones the friend is wearing are so "old and dirty." The others laugh. And soon they disperse.

In order to understand the signals given off by this young man, we need to know something of the background from which he hails. The average whites who visit this setting know very little about black inner-city culture, and what knowledge they have tends to be superficial. A few are quite "hip," or pride themselves on "knowing what time it is," and can read the cultural signs, or try hard to do so. Others not only fail to know what time it is but are basically incurious and oblivious to what is happening all around them. Their lack of curiosity may entrap them in a generalized conception of all black people as dangerous potential criminals.

Two things seem most striking about the denizens of the Gallery, old and young. The first is the comfort level that permits the uninhibited expressive behavior in public. At the Gallery the situation that usually prevails outside of black neighborhoods is reversed. Whereas in predominantly white settings blacks are inhibited by an uncomfortable awareness of "being on," here it is the occasional white visitor who is more likely to feel inhibited in expression.

The second notable thing is that Willy's cohort of "decent" folk from the 'hood amicably shares the space with young people and others who are often thoroughly "street," deeply immersed in the styles and attitudes so prevalent in the ghetto. In a manner quite like the effects of place and function that enable a degree of positive interracial folk ethnography in the leafy confines of Rittenhouse Square or among the shops and eating places of the Reading Terminal Market, the confined and security-patrolled setting of the Gallery enables a variety of intraracial folk ethnography to take place.

The Gallery is essentially a black community under a canopy, not cosmopolitan in the same way as the other canopies I've observed, but nonetheless a place where diverse elements of one racial community may mingle peacefully and express themselves more fully.

PUBLIC PERFORMANCES

Virtually everyone who visits the western end of the mall passes by the food court. As they do, they are assessed by the small gallery of observers. Sometimes the onlookers comment on the performances of passersby with open acknowledgment that behavior in public—even so simple an act as walking in a mall—constitutes a performance. The walkway is a kind of stage upon which performances are ongoing. However, performers are not always self-conscious. Most often they are alone but involved with themselves, taken with their own show. Less often two or more people perform together, urged on by an audience of one or more.

The performer becomes the audience and vice versa. Denizens walk about, taking it all in, scrutinizing other people and the setting, exhibiting a readiness for anything that comes their way. They are here at least in part to see the show. They are aware that here they can see most anyone in the world and that, by implication, anything can happen here. An older black gentleman, about sixty, sits observing the runway. Dressed in a white jersey with a white "gangster cap" cocked to the side, he slowly nurses a bottle of Pepsi. Displaying a style that mimics the ghetto "cool cat" he may once have been, he takes in the scene, apparently ready for anything, but seeming to mind his own business.

He glances furtively at the people around him and then focuses back on the runway. He looks down at the floor, then up to study the passersby, stares vacantly into space, and pans the runway again. He flicks a piece of lint from his shirt, then takes out a bottle of lotion and carefully applies it to his hands, arms, and face. He rubs his hair, touching up his appearance. Though taken with himself, he is very much aware of his surroundings. On the runway his eyes have found and now follow an object to reward his long fixation on the traffic: a twenty-year-old white male with his pants below his butt, resembling the white rapper Eminem, with a young woman with dirty blond hair who appears to be his girlfriend or wife pushing a baby in a stroller. Next comes a fortysomething heavyset black woman with two elderly black women, followed by a thirtysomething Asian couple. Then comes a shapely young black woman wearing shorts and a halter. She's listening to her iPod, the white cord dangling down. The man is transfixed. He studies her every move. Finally, their eyes meet and lock. She's even with him now, about to pass by. He looks her up and down, struck by her display. As she passes, he demonstratively turns his head. Both know what has just happened. Some onlookers know, too. All are attracted to this instant. Then, as suddenly as this show began, it is over, as she proceeds toward the Radio Shack.

Traversing the public spaces of Center City, whether the Reading Terminal, the Gallery Mall, or elsewhere, you cannot avoid overhearing one side of numerous cell phone conversations. Most people pay civil inattention, sustaining the pretense that no one else is listening in. Cell phone callers in the Gallery proceed with abandon.

Aline, a flamboyantly dressed young woman who was talking on her cell phone, had a lot to say to her friend and seemed oblivious of those nearby. "Ronny cared about me. He texts me all the time. He always wanting to know what I'm doing, who am I fucking. You know, I'm looking good today. I'm so irked. Tellin' my business. When you hear 'something' right away, bitch—why can't you call me an' tell me?! You ought to be a better friend to me. I'd tell you. I'm buyin' her [her daughter] some clothes, least I'm lookin' for some. Prom clothes. Got to go to the bar to show my face to let these motherfuckers know that I'm still here. You studyin' them? I don't give a fuck about 'em—they know what they can do for me. I'm wearing hot pink today, lookin' good, too. I been throughout the Gallery and didn't find nothin'." After her call ends, I compliment her on her nice pink outfit, ask her where she's from, and inquire about her day. She tells me that she's from Camden but comes to shop in Philly because "the Old Navy in Camden is much higher than the one here." People come from New Jersey and from Delaware: "Delaware is all right—don't too much bad happen in Delaware, not like it do about Philly. My grandmom is eighty-two, and I'm tryin' to get her somethin' every year. But things are just too expensive over there; that's why I come over here. And Cherry Hill, that's for 'white people' [she lowers her voice to a whisper], and they got all them high-priced things over there. This place is more for the black people. Camden is bad, badder than here."

Those who speak on their cell phones in public have a certain awareness of being overheard. Indeed, some of what they say may be intended for the benefit of eavesdroppers, not just their interlocutor. They imagine, see, and hear themselves in the mind's eyes and ears of those nearby, as well as in the other person's responses to what they say. At the heart of this phenomenon is the need for self-expression and recognition. In the process people communicate to others not only their sense of self but also the parameters of what Georg Simmel called the "aura of the self," which extends beyond the body to become an expansive sense of personal space in public.[5] People's public talk may be a bid for turf and territory, a claim on public space that is up for grabs. Their phone talk serves as an indirect assertion of the self, an effectively staked claim affirmed by others' passive acceptance of their vocal presence.

THE CHALLENGE OF THE GALLERY

The streets that surround and provide access to the Gallery are populated by a mix of African Americans, Latinos, and Asians but relatively few whites. That reflects what lies within the mall itself. For many Philadelphians, but particularly the white middle class, this exhibition of colored people—black preachers exhorting passersby through a megaphone, homeboys hanging out on the stairs, black women pushing baby strollers, Latinas with small children carrying bags, homeless elderly white men sitting alone smoking cigarettes, groups of black girls joking loudly—is a signal that this place is not for them, and many go no farther. Personal safety is an important consideration, for in the public mind any concentration of black young people is associated with danger.

But recently on the streets of downtown Philadelphia, the "flash mob" has appeared, a roving group of mostly black high school students initially organized through social-networking websites such as Facebook and Twitter. But this is not publicly defined as the irreverent, fun-loving absurdist kind of flash mob described by the journalist Bill Wasik.[6] At the appointed time, often around three or four in the afternoon, after being released from school, young people gravitate to a designated location. Once there, the crowd becomes a mob, forming a throng that gradually gathers force as it roams the downtown streets, wreaking havoc on businesses and terrifying pedestrians.

The mob rolls through randomly selected downtown department stores like a wave, sweeping over everything in its path. In this uninhibited atmosphere the youths yell and scream, or throw snowballs at pedestrians, but on occasion they punch people. Then smaller bands, offshoots of the larger mob, break off as they pass through department stores, confronting the clerks and helping themselves to whatever merchandise they can. Eventually the city police or the store security confront them, and in short order they are carted off to jail and charged as juvenile offenders.

As quickly as this storm appears out of the blue, it is over, but the effects are lasting, powerfully redefining the public spaces of the canopy zone. Afterwards the canopy must recover its reputation as an oasis of comity and goodwill in the city. The media coverage of those events, in newspapers, television, and on the internet, is unrelenting. As a result, young black males— and, increasingly, females—become ever more defined as people to fear, even though, in truth, the wild mob was sprinkled with white youths. Denizens worry as they travel about, expecting the worst and looking out for the kind of people who might engage in this sort of activity. The figures that most rapidly come to mind are young and black, and particularly male.

Those deeply disturbing incidents, and the reactions they

cause, reinforce the profoundly negative reputation of the iconic ghetto. In the minds of many Philadelphians, black or white, the black ghetto is the symbol of what Everett Hughes called a "master status," which defines a person's place or position in society regardless of his or her individual characteristics.[7]

For many outsiders, especially whites, the central cultural manifestations of the ghetto are anonymous black males and, to a lesser degree, black females and their children. When these figures are encountered in public, their master status—race—supersedes whatever other characteristics the person might display. The young black male is approached with a deficit model: he must prove himself to be law-abiding and trustworthy, which he is seldom able to do to the satisfaction of his white counterparts in the short time allowed. Unable to make sense of him, to distinguish his status and, by implication, what may be his nonrelationship to them, the strangers opt to distance themselves or avoid any contact. The young black woman with children in tow triggers another set of stereotypes. This figure is simultaneously pitied and despised, rather than simply feared; she is imagined simultaneously as downtrodden and overly assertive, burdened by motherhood yet hypersexualized. Respectable she is not.

The black person may in fact be middle class, law-abiding, and decent, perhaps even better educated than the whites whom he or she encounters briefly in public places. But ascertaining the particulars about individuals requires time and work, burdening the encounter with a tax that neither party may be willing to pay. The black person must prove himself or herself worthy of being treated politely. The white person must work hard even to recognize this individual as an exception to prevailing racial stereotypes. Most offers of interaction are cut off or declined. The Gallery, whose denizens look as if they hail from the black inner city, represents a huge challenge that many whites and middle-class black people are not really willing to face. So they just don't go there.

From time to time young black people, especially males, make the news by committing dramatic crimes that shock both blacks and whites. Usually, as with the flash mobs, such events occur unexpectedly. Apart from the mayhem within the black ghetto that is reported in the newspaper and on public airwaves, the crime that is most upsetting to the city's collective conscience is that which might be termed a "racial crossover" crime: when a white person is the victim of rape or murder. Most Philadelphians take notice, and the stereotype of the dangerous young black man becomes most salient. The suggestion is that it could happen to anyone, white, black, or brown, but it has just happened to a white person minding his or her own business who did not deserve this fate.

When violence occurs at the Gallery, the story may travel throughout the city. If someone is robbed at gunpoint or seriously injured, it makes the papers and the nightly TV news. Recently, after lying in wait for the right victim, three homeboys robbed an older black man in a Gallery men's room. One boy served as a lookout, and when the coast cleared the other two carried out the deed, robbing the

man when he was most vulnerable. The boys were apprehended almost immediately. Incidents like these happen
occasionally in downtown Philadelphia, in the trolley concourse, or on deserted streets, and the perpetrators who are
taken into custody are almost always young black men from
the ghetto.

These incidents feed stereotypes, giving all Philadelphians, both black and white, a particular perspective on
the ghetto. Among blacks in the Gallery, however, familiarity
reigns. Black folks who come to shop and to hang out here
realize that this place is safer than many ghetto streets. With
security guards and foot traffic steadily coming and going,
with neon and bright white lights bathing long corridors and
corners, ordinary black people feel safe among their own.
Compared with whites and others who are not familiar with
black people, blacks more easily make subtle distinctions
that can enhance their sense of safety among other blacks.

Many people see this "ghetto" style as an oppositional
culture, but it is also their expression of themselves as hip,
cool, "down"—in other words, distinctively black. Profoundly disconnected from mainstream society, they pay
it little mind, focusing on their own unique expression of
themselves and their culture. Much of what even the decent
people in the neighborhood call "street" is here conflated
with black identity. There are variations on this presentation of self, but they all are a play for street credibility. Too
idiosyncratic a style calls "street cred" into question. So this
sets a standard for the young black male, who is the most

authentic person in terms of this mode of expression. The Gallery gives respect to the street way of being, or at least acknowledges its importance. The place has an intense edge at times, which distinguishes it from a setting such as the Reading Terminal, where anyone—even someone utterly lacking in street smarts, visitors from out of town to the Convention Center, or suburbanites with very little experience of the code of the street—can go and feel capable of handling the scene as well as the next person, whoever that person might be. Feeling that way about the Gallery requires insider knowledge of the particular ethnic world that is black Philadelphia.

Walking the length of the Gallery complex reveals how extensive it is. Past the food court an increasing number of stores stand vacant, and the place becomes less populated. People use this corridor as a pass-through to the trains. The layout brings to mind New York's Grand Central Station in miniature, but this area is not busy; pedestrians are conspicuously absent. Development plans for this area have been made for more than a decade, including the recent grand scheme to bring a casino to this part of the Gallery Mall. But they have remained largely unrealized. So the shops and stores now sit empty, "in waiting" for development. The infrastructure was built in anticipation of a high-volume business that simply did not materialize. The Gallery never became the grand mall that the developers imagined. The elaborate infrastructure remains, but the largely black, working-class, and poor clientele cannot fully support it. Since gambling seems like one of the most common of human activities, cutting across social and racial lines in its popularity, perhaps a casino will transform the Gallery into the most cosmopolitan in all of Philadelphia. For now, though, the Gallery symbolizes the 'hood.

4. RITTENHOUSE SQUARE: THE PRACTICE OF CIVILITY

Under the canopy, within the exterior walls of the Reading Terminal Market or within the prescribed street boundaries of Rittenhouse Square, Philadelphia's premier public park, the atmosphere is usually calm and relatively pleasant, as a mix of people go about their business, at times self-consciously on good or "downtown" behavior, working to "be nice" or at least civil to the next person they encounter. Here they sit, eat, and walk through the square, sometimes making new acquaintances or bumping into people they know.

The definition of the square as a positive place dates back through generations of urban history. This park has an enduring identity as a setting for the rich and upper class, and though that is no longer as true as it once was, it is a social conception that resists change. The occasional act of incivility or crime poses little challenge to this accepted definition of the setting. Indeed, when visitors arrive, engaging in something bordering on urban pilgrimage, they effectively borrow status from this place. They become marginally more sophisticated for having visited, bettering themselves through this implicit social bargain. Hence, the setting gives rise to an infectious cosmopolitan attitude of civility, encouraging complete strangers to model this public style for one another. In so doing, denizens become preoccupied with expressing civility toward others that enhances social control in this unique public space.

A square block in Center City, covered by a canopy of old-growth trees and enhanced with well-kept flowers and shrubs, it is an oasis of green space in a sea of residential and office buildings, concrete, and asphalt. Under this canopy a diverse, if transient, community of all persuasions meets and gets along in an informal and friendly atmosphere. In many respects this setting, including the numerous twenty-story apartment buildings, the large elegant hotel, the church, the bookstore, the shops and cafés that surround the park, is the quintessential cosmopolitan canopy, under which diverse people constantly exposed to one another occasionally interact, people watch, and become familiar with one another.

The bustle is striking. Nothing is more wonderful than a warm spring day in the square, when the place comes alive with activity. Denizens interact, smiling, laughing, and engaging in general camaraderie. The benches situated along the paths that crisscross the square fill slowly, and an infectious levity is created by seemingly carefree visitors. During inclement weather people may not be so relaxed, but by noon, even in winter, the square is almost full of people, engaging in various activities, from dog walking to taking their daily constitutional.

The square is a place where people of all ethnic and class backgrounds adopt "downtown," civil behavior, contributing to a "code of civility" that is powerfully present here. In the popular imagination it is a prestigious and generally wonderful place, and everyone from rich to poor knows it to be special. This local knowledge[1] travels beyond the boundaries of the setting, ever enhancing and institutionalizing its reputation as a safe and relaxing place for interesting people watching. Moreover, there is "always something going on."

A typical day in the life of the park reveals a good deal about these dynamics. By 7:00 a.m. the square is already full of activity. It awakens to the sounds of honking horns and the rumblings of vehicular traffic, the footsteps of pedestrians, the murmur of their conversations and their occasional loud voices, as well as the twitter of birdsong. The dog walkers are out by now, drawn by their charges, which are sometimes distracted by squirrels scampering about.

Soon they are joined by younger and older people. Children loaded with backpacks and lunch pails, sometimes with a dad, a mom, or a nanny, and sometimes with classmates, cut through the square on their way to school. Older white women clad in brightly colored athletic suits gather in small informal walking groups and circle the square, their white hair wrapped in neat buns. Business people, college students, and working people crisscross the square on their way to work or an early morning meeting, at times catching a taxi from the queue outside the Rittenhouse Hotel. Occasionally, they must step over a homeless person or endure aggressive begging, which momentarily throws them off, but they are inclined to ignore this interruption and to move along.

As midday approaches, the nannies with their charges are out in force. They mosey through the park, pushing baby carriages or strollers, or lead small children. Very much aware of one another, they sometimes form social bonds as they stop, converse, and get to know one another. Middle-class mothers of small children who regularly visit this space do the same, at times planning excursions with the friends they have made. On occasion they sit on the benches and allow their children to play together, while they socialize among themselves. The common sight of a black woman with white children or a black woman with an elderly white woman or man is becoming less provocative, and caretakers are increasingly likely to be Asian or Russian.

UNDER A GREEN CANOPY

My family and I moved into one of the apartment buildings fronting the park a number of years ago. I had never lived in a high-rise before and thought it would be a good vantage point from which to study a more privileged population than I usually work with. Move-in day was, well, interesting, to put it noncommittally. We used the back stairs and elevators and so got a sense of the backstage. I saw that people were not used to black males in their midst. I received many odd looks, though I encountered no serious problems. I began by meeting the doormen and maintenance men, who were all African American, as well as the desk clerks, two young Irishmen from working-class Kensington and an older Scottish woman. It took time for other residents of the building to get used to me. I often went up the elevator by myself until the unaccompanied women who might have stepped into it with me, but didn't, realized that I was not up to no good and was, like them, just going up to my apartment.

As I jogged around the square in the morning, I got to know many of the doormen of the buildings on the park. Several were Irish and had grown up in Southwest Philly, a place where they still might exhibit ethnocentric attitudes. But here on the square they were on their best professional behavior; after all, it was their job. The black doormen were all polite, considerate toward everyone, and quite friendly with whites, though none exhibited an overly deferential or obsequious "Uncle Tom" attitude. Nor did they show any trace of a stereotypical "ghetto style," since anyone acting "ignorant" would not last long as a doorman on the square. They functioned as security guards, requiring every visitor to indicate the apartment to which they were going and then contacting the resident for approval before granting entry into the building. They also ran errands and provided myriad services for the elderly and other residents of their buildings. Equally intriguing were the Ethiopian attendants at our parking garage. I tipped them regularly so that they would take good care of our car. But I also engaged them in conversation, which was not their usual experience with middle-class black men. Relatively recent immigrants, they worked hard at their jobs and were unusually deferential toward the persons they served, who were often, like my family and me, residents of the upscale apartments on the square. And although they understood that customers are not always right, they often felt the need to defer to and effectively excuse the public for passing offenses.

I also frequently visited the Free Library on the square. On any given day it was populated with a diversity of local people, from college students to the homeless. Those at loose ends would leaf through books and magazines, and were left undisturbed for what seemed like hours, especially on rainy days. In addition, I got to know the regulars at a number of other establishments in the area that I frequented, including Houlihan's, an Irish bar and restaurant then located on the square, and Tuscany, a coffee shop.

Sometimes I would sit on a bench and watch people come and go for hours. I was struck by the ways different sorts of people seemed to dance around one another in the park, avoiding potential conflicts and collisions. On the sidewalks, in cold weather, the homeless would occasionally spread themselves out on steam grates in an effort to keep warm, or go across the street to one of the benches to bundle up with a friend; they might sit there until a policeman came along and urged them to move on. These actions were arbitrary at times, because the homeless people would be minding their own business, only to be confronted by a policeman for no apparent reason. Homeless women were more rare on the square. Over time I learned that some fastidious women who lived in the nearby apartments would refrain from sitting on the benches because they worried that the homeless had sullied them.

Rittenhouse Square Park hosts many special events: the annual art show, summer concerts, occasional political demonstrations, even a formal dinner dance to raise money for park maintenance. It was eye-opening to see the swirling array of residents, workers, and visitors, from rich white folks to poor blacks from North Philly, the white working class from South Philly, and students who live in the cheaper apartments in the area. Young white musicians from the nearby Curtis Institute, whose lovely, ornate building fronts the square, sometimes perform classical music on the pathways for donations from passersby. Artists set up easels. Would-be actors mix with businesspeople and retirees. People using walkers navigate the curb cuts alongside others pushing baby carriages. Foreigners who are not easily racially classifiable complicate the imposed American dichotomy of black and white. What a fascinating place Rittenhouse Square is! Being there at all times of the day and night allowed me to see its combinations and permutations, its many moods and faces. In nice weather the square was like a carnival; I found it hard to tear myself away.

The folks who stroll the pathways are distinguishable from those using the square in a utilitarian way. Pedestrians on a mission, who are trying to get to a meeting, work, or the store, treat the park as a cut-through and are obviously in a hurry. For those just out for air and the sights and sounds, Rittenhouse Square is a destination. People come out to see and be seen. Some walk about arm in arm, engaging in public displays of affection and expressing polite indifference toward others. Some are here to see the show, although they know on some level that they are likewise onstage. Occasionally, now, men kiss in public. A few people stare, defining the scene as a spectacle, but most are preoccupied with their own activities.

Black women who care for children or the elderly form a conspicuous group. Some push baby carriages or supervise the play of white toddlers. Others stroll alongside elderly white people or push their wheelchairs. As I listen to their speech, many sound West Indian. A good number of elderly people are unaccompanied by caregivers and walk unassisted or with the help of a walker.

Young people, ranging from college students to professionals, make up an amorphous group. On their days off they dress informally and use the park as a playground. After lunch on Sunday afternoons they congregate in the bookstore cafés to study, see their friends, and meet members of the opposite sex—or same sex, for that matter. For the most part these young people are white. Their black counterparts tend to be present here in very small numbers; they are sprinkled in with the sea of white faces, one here or one there, only occasionally three or more together, but never in groups that others might perceive as threatening. This upscale crowd displays the latest fashions and electronic appurtenances, but most often conspicuously without dogs or children in tow.

The park is also a staging area for spiritual proselytizers warning that doomsday is near at hand. But in this park doomsday seems very far off.

Significantly, there is no firm definition of the place; the scene changes with the time of the day, and with who is present, who drifts by, and who leaves when. People tell social time this way and take their cues from what is observed. In many ways this is an attractive setting for leisure, a place to be at ease. It advertises itself as a respite from the busy life of the downtown, offering all a chance to slow down. It may be visited on a whim, approached for a shot of pleasure. Each group seems to find its own niche. What emerges is a kind of peaceful coexistence, as various groups appear to agree on the specific times each uses the square. With a sense of what has transpired before and what happens around them, they know when to come and when not to, who will likely be around and who not, and most important, when enough people like themselves will be out and about. They informally negotiate this peculiar form of turn taking and then hold one another to the deal—not by force of any sort, but by their own bold presence. Others respect the resulting order and express it by using the space when they are most comfortable with those who are present at the time, and they get what they bargain for.

EYE WORK[2]

When blacks and whites encounter one another under the canopy, they typically hold each other's eyes only for a few seconds. The duration of this look reflects an instantaneous assessment of the likely future for this nascent relationship; those of the same color typically make longer eye contact. Blacks engage one another longer simply because a black person might actually know the other black person, or know someone he knows, or might have a future connection. This possibility encourages mutual interest, but it exists less for blacks in relation to strange whites, and vice versa. Many African Americans who have never been formally introduced feel compelled to acknowledge or even greet each other in public. With the huge influx of immigrants of color from around the world, this simple formulation becomes ever more complex. Recent immigrants of color are not familiar with this traditional practice and feel no need to engage in it. When eyes meet across a boundary, the gaze is very often averted or cut off. Too much attention simply floods the situation out.

Under the canopy, where an ethos of civility reigns, the parameters of these types of interaction are stretched, but may also be confused. Interracial eye interaction may grow more complicated. People may well be quite curious about strangers, and even find them irresistible. Rather than gawk or stare, however, people surreptitiously steal looks, only to look away rapidly when they are discovered. Most evade being caught in this little game. A significant amount of people watching occurs in this setting.

A wealthy, retired white woman related a story that illuminates why some people enjoy people watching:

> Our friends who live in Philadelphia go to Rittenhouse Square all the time. Every day, after they have their coffee, they walk over to the park just across from Rouge. One day we went with them. Since we're from the suburbs, we thought it was cool. We sat on a bench and began checking out the people, all different kinds of people, like what they were wearing, how they looked, and we critiqued them. Then we started telling stories about them, like a game of "Whispering Down the Lane." One person would start: "See that couple, holding hands? Well, they're really not married. . . ." The next person would go on: "But they want to be married." And the story would progress and grow, with each person making up juicy details. Here we are, adults, getting so silly and a little off-color in what we were saying about the people we were watching. "These two guys, they are not really business partners, they are lovers, ha-ha." We were just having a lot of fun watching all the people.

On a spring day Rittenhouse Square is filled not only with attractive young women and men but with older people and a fascinating mélange of others. Observed carefully rather than categorically, park denizens come in all colors—

black, white, olive, brown, and shades of red, all equally attractive to one another, homosexual or heterosexual. In order not to make a spectacle of themselves, some voyeurs don dark eyeglasses. Those whom I have surveyed indicate that they are aware that they are being watched. Some relish playing the game of cat and mouse, watching people watching them.

On more than one occasion I have spotted young women eyeing young men. They do so under cover, looking closely while being careful not to ogle. They cover themselves by staring off into space and then slowly focusing in on the object of desire. Thieves I've spoken with employ a similar strategy. These men eye women's pocketbooks, while taking the measure of the owner and evaluating the feasibility of the deed they are contemplating. At times young women approach strange men, while looking at them more directly. Men tend to look directly at women, upping the ante and underscoring the stake in the encounter.

Here black people look white people directly in the eye, though sometimes self-consciously. In other circumstances such looks might well be forbidden, but under the canopy they are more often taken with impunity. Older black men from the South have vivid memories of having to answer for "reckless eyeballing," for ogling white women who were protected by southern racial etiquette and, ultimately, by white violence.

When the risks seem high, these looks may be stolen, often when the other's back is turned. When it is not, a friend might well cover for the person, alerting her, "That man is looking at you!" The target might rise to the occasion, looking the man directly in the eye, causing him to avert his gaze, and effectively putting him back in his place. What might have become "a move" is interrupted. This category of stolen looks is most intriguing, drawing attention to those who cross a brightly etched cultural line and, for the most part, commit such acts surreptitiously.

"IT'S ALL ABOUT THE GOAT"

Some of the visitors to the square form identifiable social groups and use particular zones within this space for their own purposes. Mothers from their midtwenties to midthirties make a daily pilgrimage to a statue in the southwest corner of the park. They are mainly white, although some are South Asian, West Indian, or African American. Their destination is a small bronze goat set in the middle of a large semicircular area with low-rising steps. "Billy" is life-size, almost spindly, unintimidating in scale. Children are encouraged to climb on the goat and play with one another in the vicinity, while the mothers stand nearby or sit on the steps to engage in adult conversation. Many of these women start out as strangers, but before long they get to know one another. This place and time offers them a respite from the exclusive company of children. A steady parade of women with buggies and strollers comes and goes; when one woman leaves, another takes her place. Sometimes the mothers bring their own mothers. Later in the afternoon their husbands or teenage children might join them, and the family might go out to dinner in a nearby restaurant or walk home together.

This women's friendship group becomes a visible element of the park community. Babies may be breast-fed here; toddlers are catered to. Adults seem to gain a sense of connectedness that compensates for the isolation of full-time child rearing. These women live within walking, stroller-pushing distance of the goat. They come alone or in twos or threes and stay for one to two hours. Gathering at the goat is an important part of their day. Although one woman told me, "It's all about the goat," the real reason she comes is sociability. I've been told that a generation ago, mothers and children gathered in the center of the square by the lion statue at the reflecting pool. The focal point has shifted, but the social dynamic has remained the same. Here women form bonds, finding something for themselves as well as their kids. Black women who are employed by affluent white couples to care for their children also belong to this group. The park is one of the few places where black working-class and white upper-middle- or upper-class women can interact on common ground.

From the point of view of social control, the presence of mothers and small children may deter public aggression and encourage civility in the square. A sense of safety and protection—the essence of the canopy idea—is inspired by the ongoing social activity of public mothering.

THE ETIQUETTE OF BENCH SEATING

As the park fills, especially on a beautiful day, people gravitate to the benches, staking their claims as seating space becomes scarce. The act of choosing a park bench can be done without much thought, but more often it is done in accordance with an etiquette that defines the situation for everyone involved. Typically, visitors refrain from sitting on a bench already occupied by a stranger when alternative seating is available. This rule may not apply when the person has an ulterior motive. Most often, if there is a nearby empty bench, the stranger will sit there rather than impose himself and violate the other person's space. As a rule it is not until seating is visibly scarce that habitués will crowd others on a bench. In these circumstances violations may be viewed as excusable or appropriate by those being joined.

Evident here is a strong concern about sending an ambiguous, unwelcome, hostile, or wrong message. If someone violates this rule, the person being joined can get the impression that the person taking the seat is trying to move in on him or her, for, if this were not the case, why wouldn't the person take one of the available seats on another bench? When the seat is taken in spite of the availability of other seats, the person being joined has reason for concern. If the violator is considered an unacceptable seatmate, the person may try to discourage him or her, or simply leave. The action serves as evidence that something is amiss. If the person is deemed attractive, he or she may well be excused and even encouraged, with the un-offended party showing approval by responding with small talk. An account by a young black man illustrates the delicacy of these negotiations.

One evening on my way home from work, dressed nicely in a suit and tie, I stopped to have a seat on one of the benches in Rittenhouse Square. I was twenty-nine at the time, and I sat down next to this older Caucasian woman, who was maybe about forty-five. When I first sat down, we didn't talk, but then something amusing happened, and she made a comment and then I made a comment. This was followed by a long stretch of silence until something else happened, and we both commented on it. Finally, she opened up a conversation by asking me whether I was on my way home from work. I told her that, yes, I was coming from work, but I was looking for a new job. She shared that she had played hooky from work that day to take her mother out to lunch for her birthday. She said she lived in Rittenhouse Square. I was working in real estate at the time, and we chatted about that for a while. We had a really good conversation, and had it not been for that atmosphere, maybe the conversation would not have taken off.

I'm a six-foot-one-inch black guy, dark-skinned, about two hundred pounds. I always joke that I fit the description of about every young black male criminal you see on TV. So

I understand that people aren't always comfortable talking to me. I've learned to smile a lot. If I'm thinking hard, I might have a look on my face that appears angry, but if you talk with me, you'll see that it's the opposite. It's just that most people don't get that far.

Under the canopy, strangers can feel secure and comfortable enough with one another to extend themselves and interact across racial lines.

Some denizens of the park are almost never acceptable seating partners: those who through their demeanor signal that they are homeless, criminal, or incapable of civility. This list of undesirables includes those whom the general public is prepared to label as deviant. It is important to acknowledge the arbitrariness of such designations. These rejections often say as much about those applying the labels as about the people who are treated as deviant.

Strangers may spontaneously engage one another socially in the park. On a hot August afternoon, I saw a young white woman walking her English bulldog puppy. They had obviously been out for a while, and the dog appeared tired. The dog stopped and sat down in the middle of the path, so she stopped and waited. She stood there for a bit. The dog was panting because of the heat and humidity, and she was accommodating. Suddenly, a Middle Eastern–looking man sitting on a bench with his girlfriend summed up the situation and spoke, "Too hot for him, huh?" She responded with a slightly exasperated smile, "Yeah, he's young and tires easily." The man good-naturedly smiled his sympathy. She waited for a while longer. The dog started to move but after a few steps plopped down again. The young woman placed her hand on her hip and waited. After another minute she gathered the dog up and carted him off—but not before again acknowledging the stranger.

The rules of civility that are demonstrated and observed here are taken for granted by regulars, but they may pleasantly surprise newcomers. On a warm summer afternoon, I was sitting on a bench next to an elderly white woman reading a book. When she decided to leave, she had trouble rising. A man sitting alone on the next bench over came to assist her. She graciously accepted his hand without so much as a word, rose up, stood for a moment, nodded her thanks, and walked away. He returned to his seat and continued reading his newspaper, as though he had simply done what was expected of him. Those of us who observed this act realized that we ourselves might expect such help or be called upon to render it.

EBB AND FLOW

The energy level of the park picks up again with the lunch-time crowd, as offices empty and people pass through on their way to a restaurant or settle down on a bench with their lunch, be it takeout or brown-bag. An interesting mix ensues, as some people are moving to and fro while others are eating lunch and having conversations. The noise levels rise, and more people arrive. People playing chess, Frisbee, or other games seem to appear out of nowhere around lunchtime.

Dogs are everywhere, at all times of day, and their owners smile and converse as they admire one another's pets. Most dog walkers accompany one or two pets of their own, but sometimes a professional appears with as many as seven or eight canines. An upper-middle-class person intently focused on the task of walking a dog may stand out in the more casual milieu. A young black man with a white-and-brown English springer spaniel talks on his cell phone while the dog does its business. He has no pooper scooper or doggie bag, and he leaves without cleaning up behind him. Other dog walkers frown, but say nothing. As dogs sniff one another, play together, and occasionally get into a fight, their owners exchange information, praise particular virtues of their dogs, and even pet others' dogs if possible. The dogs' interaction stimulates their walkers to interact, but they seldom form a group like that around the bronze goat.

Musicians are especially common in the midafternoon and on weekends. On a bench along a main walk, a middle-aged white man strums a guitar, his sheet music at his side. As people pass, he provokes interest and even looks of admiration. Across from him on the grass about fifty feet away, a small group of young people enjoys listening to heavy metal from an iPod. The musical styles never conflict, for they are too far apart. Farther away five disheveled-looking white men sit in a circle on the grass, their backpacks nearby. As one shouts out a song, the others listen attentively. These men, who range from youthful to middle-aged, laugh and play together. In time they get a little loud, for they are enjoying themselves in this company. Others walk stiffly by, trying not to be bothered, to ignore them, but their actions belie this performance. The benches around these men are curiously empty.

Afternoons, like midmornings, are quiet. But in the late afternoon the pace picks up again. The hustle and bustle of rush hour invades the park as people cut across to their apartments or parking garages. Then things calm down, and people move more casually through the square on their way to late dinners at home or in restaurants. The activity on the pathways continues well into the evening.

WHAT A DIFFERENCE THE NIGHT MAKES

At night, the character of life in and around the square changes dramatically, from a setting that is somewhat benign to one that is potentially more sinister. As the old proverb puts it, "At night *all* cats are gray." A certain wariness comes over the pedestrians using the streets and pathways, replacing the daytime lightness, levity, and trust. The change is betrayed by the set looks on their faces. During the day people could discern the next person, but now they can make out only a bare outline. Skin color becomes a more important marker. In many open spaces, a black male whom both whites and blacks might have taken as a friendly stranger is now regarded as a potential threat and may require greater scrutiny. What by day would have been neutral or friendly gestures from a stranger may become highly suspect. Now people using the square must become instrumental folk ethnographers, taking in information about strangers, trying to categorize and handle whatever comes their way. The paths are brightly lit by streetlamps, but the mood of the park changes.

At this time the pass-through function of the place takes precedence. People passing through the square tend to stay on the perimeter, leaving the center of the park to those who may be homeless or otherwise desperate. A shared understanding is that you must be adventuresome to traverse the square at this time of the evening, and even more so as the night wears on.

On the streets bordering the square, the sidewalk cafés host constant parties. All this activity, as well as the lights, encourages people to feel safe in the square. At 7:30, the foot traffic is still going strong, allowing everyone to believe that others might come to their aid if needed. That assumption remains to be tested, but it emboldens visitors at this time of night. As the activity tapers off, only the roughest people remain. This fact places the law-abiding elements at some disadvantage, which they sense and which motivates them to leave the park. Finally, by about ten, the square has quieted down considerably. At this point the park is gradually given over to the homeless, some of whom have already begun to curl up on a bench for the night, and in time more of them follow.

The denizens of the square, law-abiding and crime-prone alike, follow certain rules of engagement. The law-abiding assume that those out to take advantage of others become successful by picking their people. The implication is that those who fall prey to criminals are themselves to blame. It is important to act in ways that communicate to potential stickup men that you are not that person, that you do not qualify as a victim.

Stickup men may concoct some ruse to catch the person off guard, requesting the time or directions, or simply taking a seat next to an unsuspecting target. Most urban dwellers pride themselves on being wise to such ploys, a stance that often results in standoffishness toward anyone who seems at all suspect. Primed to watch for "suspicious" behavior and, by implication, "suspicious people," regulars have reason to practice defensiveness when approached by strangers in the park at night.

People who use the park often have already become good folk ethnographers: most likely they have engaged in people watching for hours, sometimes sitting on benches only half reading the books open in their laps. Simultaneously, they learn to read the signs and symbols their counterparts display, familiars and strangers alike. Even more important, they learn to place what they see in perspective. Through this process concepts and symbols emerge and a vocabulary develops, allowing them to make greater sense of the world of the square. The ragged shirt, worn-out shoes, and white skin color of a middle-aged male, the black skin color of an elderly female, the three nondescript homeless men sitting on a bench with their belongings and conversing with one another—all these elements figure in the task of reading people and situations.

Black skin seems so powerful a symbol of possible danger that it supersedes all other observable qualities. If Philadelphians expressed their opinions honestly, they would tell you that black males particularly bear watching. Blacks who come to the square at night learn to handle the particular way suspicion plays itself out in the nightlife there. The square's cafés and restaurants seem more glamorous than sinister.

Workers, young business executives, and students mix as the restaurants, cafés, and bookstores become places to meet others or simply to go for a good time. Expensive and fast cars are on display in front of the trendier spots. A limo pulls up, its passengers get out, and early drinkers and diners wonder, "Who was that?" They surmise that the car must belong to the restaurant's owner or some other big shot. On rare occasions, a celebrity is sighted, as a star athlete or other well-known face graces the street. When media stars come to town, they might visit one of the nightspots or restaurants to sample Philadelphia's nightlife. Allen Iverson, Dr. J (Julius Erving), and Jamie Foxx, among others, have been spotted on the square. Night or day the feeling among Philadelphians is that Rittenhouse Square belongs to everyone—or almost everyone. It is an intensely cosmopolitan space in the generally cosmopolitan context of Center City.

The homeless and those who resemble them, who may be housed but are otherwise aimless, are especially conscious of the routines and rules that define this urban milieu. Some sleep in the park during the day and roam about the city at night, when they must be more alert; others sleep here because they feel secure enough. They have a clear conceptual map of the whole territory, marking the relative safety of its public areas. This perspective escapes most others, who use public space less intensively.

It takes careful observation at odd hours to meet the homeless, since they try to remain unobtrusive. Early Monday morning is a good time to find those who have slept in the park, since it is otherwise pretty empty. A black man sitting on a park bench wipes sleep from his eyes. For a few moments he just sits there, ignoring the passing traffic and seeming to feel at home. Then he digs into his backpack, takes out a roll, and munches his breakfast. He props his feet up on the armrest and reads the local paper. He is comfortable here, treating the park bench as his living space—which, for all practical purposes, it is. Fifteen minutes pass as he catches up on the news. An elderly white man shuffles by, hands deep in his pockets. He systematically searches the trash cans, looking down at the ground as he makes his way around the park. Nearby a middle-aged black man is just waking up. He changes his rumpled shirt for a fresh one and goes for water. A strong smell of cologne follows as he passes by. Back at his spot, he tidies up, placing papers and bags in a nearby trash can. A white man hanging out close by spots a woman letting her dog crap on the ground and starting to walk away. He calls to her, "Whoa! Pick that up." She just gives him a look and keeps walking. "Nothin' I could do," he says, shaking his head.

RUSTY'S STORY

My interest in Rusty was piqued when I spotted him speaking with a policeman. After the officer left on a scooter, I walked over and sat down beside him. "Good morning," I said. "Good morning," he returned. "A lot of people are out in the park this time of the morning," I observed. "Yeah," he said. "People are waking up," I remarked, trying to make nonthreatening small talk. "Yeah, they're all around," he agreed. Then I introduced myself: "I'm Eli." "I'm Rusty," he responded. Though he was noticeably less well groomed than I, both Rusty and I are black, and this was perhaps enough to allow Rusty to feel he might be able to trust me, to speak at length to me about his life. After a few minutes of small talk, I asked whether I could interview him, and he said, "Sure." I set the tape recorder on the bench; we both ignored it.

"How long you been out here in the park?" I open. "I got a room. I was in the park four years. Four years back. I just got my room two weeks ago. Four years to last week. I was in rehab. Got myself together. Free of alcohol. Things are better now. If I didn't do that, I'd be out here killin' myself. A lot of people do live out here. City Hall, you got a lot of homeless down there. See, there are places they can go,

but they don't wanta go get help. They come beggin' me. I don't have nothin'. I just got off the street. I used to walk around, around, terrible. I got a place to live now, down on Taylor Street, now. See, like I say, I'm cleaned up. Used to be plasterer. See, I had some surgery done." He lifts his shirt to show me his scar. "Like I say, I'm cleaner now. I'm cleaned up.

"I was runnin' around like that, you know. Socks stickin' to my feet, in need of a shower, a shave. That's no way to live, you know what I mean? Pickin' cigarette butts up off the ground. That's no way to live. Just started realizing, somethin' ain't right here. I shoulda had a house, you know. I got a daughter, got a wife. I just took myself down. I cared more for the bottle than I cared for them." I ask whether drinking is common among those who live in the park. Gesturing vaguely toward the homeless people in Rittenhouse Square, he responded, "Aw, they all drink. Most of them drink. They're just drinkin' their troubles away, but they don't realize how much trouble they're makin'. You see 'em with a 'water bottle.' Ain't no water in that bottle. Straight-up vodka in that bottle.

"So the cops got hip to that, you know. See, with a 'water bottle,' they catch you once drinkin', see you with a 'water bottle,' they walk right over to you, 'Lemme see, lemme smell that water.' If it ain't water, they'll take you in. Officer Mangione does that. And all he does is hang out in that booth over there." "Mangione?" I ask. "Yeah, he does. Now he's workin' nights and mornings, and he's not here in the daytime. A lot of people are mad 'cause he stays on top of things, you know what I mean? He catch you drinkin', you're gone." "Does he take you to jail, or does he just kick you out of the park?" "Oh, he gives you a citation, and if you don't go to court, then that's on you. You don't go to court, you get a warnin'." "Then they look for you?" "Yeah, they look for you. He'll look you up again, and if he sees you, he'll look to see if you got a warrant, see if you been to court. [If] you ain't been to court, then he'll lock you up. He'll give you a chance, you know what I mean? [It's] not like you did a murder or anything. You only got caught for drinkin'. I can see if it was somethin' bad, you'd be scared to go to court. I don't like the court myself. I got locked up once. Last year, on my birthday. Yeah, got locked up for drinkin'. Went away for two months for that. I had no bail, nothin'." "What was that like?" "Oh, it was terrible. Never again. It's not worth it. When I buy vodka, I'm buyin' a bottle of jail, really. I go through a change of personality, a Jekyll/Hyde thing.

"Now I like how I am. My wife, she sees it too, sees a change in me. I don't curse, hardly any more. What are you gonna curse for? I hear that cursing, I say, dumb person. No need for that. There was a lady down here—I don't know if she's down here any more—she's been down here a couple weeks now. Homeless. That's somebody's mother, or somebody's grandmother. Why would you wanta see her out in the street? Maybe she don't have no money, ain't got nobody. Maybe that's just the way she wants to live.

"See, a lot of 'em guys who go to shelters, they don't wanta go to 'em shelters. Up at Haven House, a guy got strangled in there. That's why people don't wanta go in there. They steal your stuff. I was in there. You got to sleep light when you go there. No cops there, but they got guards. Just the same as the cops. Treat you bad, though. You got a lot of homeless. They're all startin' to come up here, now. They used to hang out in Love Park. Love Park is too dangerous. This is nicer. More nice people and stuff."

Rusty explains that he sees Rittenhouse as a "good" park mainly because there is not as much crime there as elsewhere. He is still horrified by the murder he witnessed in Love Park. "A woman stabbed another woman in the chest with a machete. I heard her gurgle, and then she died. That was bad, so I stopped going there." Still, Rittenhouse Square has its own dangers. "I was robbed here at the Barnes and Noble about a week ago," Rusty explains, pointing toward the bookstore across the street. "A guy came up to [me] 'bout ten at night and showed me what [he] claimed was a gun. I said, 'That ain't no gun.' He claimed that it was, and then I just gave in because I didn't want to get beat up or nothin'. He said, 'Gimme your money,' so I did, and said, 'Just don't take my ID.' He let me keep my wallet. He got my last twenty dollars."

A park maintenance man appears and empties the trash can and changes its plastic liner. He picks up trash off the benches, keeping the park neat and free of litter. "Every day he does it," Rusty comments. "It's his job, but I'll pick up stuff. People like me, the homeless, they'll make a mess. If you sleep on the bench, take your paper, put it in the trash. But these guys just leave it lay there. I used to lay on the bench, with the paper. Out in the cold.

"I traveled a lot too, around the city, and to other cities. I went to Boston, I went to Florida. It's nice to travel and get away. But you bring you with you. It didn't change my drinkin' style. I still drank. I said maybe in a different place, I won't drink. Sure, that was a joke. I'm bringin' me; I'm bringin' me. I go to meetings over here at seven in the morning. Went to the church over here. Then at eight or nine they have AA meetings. Without that, I'd be drinkin' again. Keeps you sober, hangin' around with some sober guys. Used to be, all I knew was to drink a bottle, come and sit on a bench and drink. But now I'll get me a soda, or coffee, or a snack, you know. I do that now and enjoy life."

Rusty looks over at the children playing nearby under the watchful eye of adults. "Little kids, they're great. I ain't seen my grandkids yet. One's a year and a half, and one's six months. I ain't seen 'em yet. My daughter's mad at me. I'll let her feel her way. When she's ready to talk to me, she'll talk to me. I'll always ask, 'How's the babies doin',' you know? Long as they're OK, I'm OK. I can go down there, but I don't wanta start a ruckus, get the kids upset. When she's ready to talk to me, she'll talk to me. I call my wife, you know what I mean. When I see little kids out here, they're great, ain't they? I just wonder how people can hurt kids, you know, molest them and stuff. And all these beautiful *women out here. God's got a place for people who do that stuff. I love women, but I'm a married man, you know."*

We watch the squirrels and pigeons scouring the ground for food. *"You know you got the mice around here all night. And the rats, they run all around. Around the trash cans, they're all over here. They get up in these cans. Yeah, the mice jump. I seen 'em, I watch them jump on that bench. You'd think they had wings, ha-ha. They don't like you feedin' the pigeons here either. The mice and the pigeons and the squirrels and the rats, that's the wildlife here. There's some hawks here, too. Two of them sleep up top of that building. Haven't seen 'em in a week or two. You know, they keep the pigeon population down. When they swoop down, all you see is feathers. They're like missiles, them hawks. Ever see it? You should have been here that day when . . . 'member them little dogs? Like a Toto dog, a Scottie maybe. I was sittin' over there, right where that man's sittin'. Then the hawk came down, picked the dog up, then he dropped it. Must have been kinda heavy. Lady said, 'Did you see that?' I said, 'That's nature, lady.' Then he went and got a squirrel."*

Rusty explains that the homeless have to know their way around. Mangione is a *"good cop"* and allows the men to sleep in the park as long as they don't *"act up."* But the sprinkler system will get you all wet if you don't know which bench to sit on, or where to sit on the grass. *"See, the sprinklers go on from eleven-thirty to one. They come on at night. I'll sit here and I'll watch. They don't do it out of spite. They water the grass at night because if they water in* the daytime, people can't sit and enjoy the park. I was here one time, and I got wringing wet. I woke up and the sprinklers were . . . shssss. I got so wet. I was freezing, too. And I know this kid Chucky. I say, 'What'sa matter, kid?' 'Did you get wet?' he asked. 'You need pants and a shirt?' He blessed me, gave me pants, a dry shirt.

"Really nice of him to do that. There's a lot of good people in the world. Remember that big dinner they had here a couple of months ago? They had tents up. Yeah, I was sittin' over there. I was in this mess. Rich people go in there. They come out, and they give me all their chocolate and stuff. 'You hungry?' they say. Hand me twenty dollars, and I say I ain't takin'. . . . But then I take it. Handin' me money. Two ladies came over, sat beside me, 'You look kinda down, now.' Looks at her friend and then at me, 'You doin' all right, now?' Says, 'I'm gonna go now,' looks down in her pocketbook, hands me a twenty. I say I don't want this. And she says, 'I know you're broke, and I know what it's like to be broke, and maybe that's why you're disgusted. Maybe this will cheer you up.' And that was very nice of them. Twenty-dollar bill. Very nice of them to do that, yes it was." A cute dog and its young female owner pass us. "He's a Boston terrier named Max," Rusty explains to me. He greets the woman, "Hey, how you doin' this morning? I seen you yesterday." "Yeah," she says; "his name is Max." She passes on. "Lot of nice kids out here," he comments. "And they go to school. Mannerly, too.

"But you got these thugs comin' here, too. And they wanta bother people. They smoke the dope, smokin' that crack. They get their own little clique going on, sittin' 'round in a circle. I see that, I take a walk. I don't need that. They got me Tuesday; they robbed me. You got to watch out. See, when you sleep out here, you got to watch out. You got to sleep like a cat. A cat never sleeps, you know what I mean? Take catnaps. Call it a catnap. I always sleep with one eye open, and the slightest little sound, my eyes would open up real quick. It's dangerous out here."

Rusty has been the recipient of spontaneous generosity from the poor as well as the well-to-do. He shared a story with me. "Yesterday, guy wanted to use my lighter, and a lady asked me, 'You wouldn't happen to have a cigarette, would you?' I said no, I didn't. She said, 'Is there a store around here?' I said, 'Yes, there's a CVS up the street.' She says thanks. Goes up there, comes back, brings me a pack of cigarettes. I got blessed that day."

Around the square there are clear disparities in the levels of wealth and well-being on display, yet neither the rich nor the poor seem ready to cede the park to those on the other side of the class divide. People don't always expect to be panhandled, but those who are often give what they can. Perhaps the panhandlers cannily know just whom to ask.

Friendships between men of different races are openly exhibited here. Those relationships are not often obviously homosexual, but simple friendships or even casual acquaintanceships. On a park bench a black man will be with a white man; on the path a white man will be walking with a black man, talking and laughing in a reciprocal and utterly equal way.

The ever-changing scene makes Rittenhouse Square Park especially entertaining. Unlike the Reading Terminal Market and the Gallery Mall, the park has nothing for sale or formally on display. What it has to offer is the active life that fills the park and surrounding square, a kaleidoscope of urban dwellers in all their variety pursuing their personal pleasures in full sight of others.

Mixing goes on at all levels. Five young boys sit together in the park smoking weed, passing the joint around in broad daylight. Dressed in jeans and T-shirts, with backpacks nearby, they smoke and talk, talk and smoke. The black boys both have long bushy hair; the three whites have long hair as well. Two men, one black and one white, sit on a bench for a while. They laugh and talk. Then the white guy, out of the blue, asks the two white women across from them, "Excuse me, but do you have the time? I don't mean to bother you, but what time you got?" One of the white women says, "Four-twenty." Then the white man returns to his conversation with the black man. Evidently they are friends making plans to meet on Monday. The black man asks the other man to wait for him if he is not there at the agreed-upon time. They talk about what to eat, how to get the money for food, and what one owes the other from the last time they were together. On closer inspection these men appear to be homeless, but their situation is not entirely clear. What is clear is that they take their friendship for granted and are bonded here in—or perhaps *by*—this urban space.

The variety of black folks on display is as striking as the interracial character of other groups. In the center of the park two black chess players are deeply involved in their game and have drawn a few spectators. Each takes his time, pondering every move. A well-dressed black woman who apparently lives in the neighborhood strolls by with her gray-and-white schnauzer on a leash. In just a few minutes a white woman appears, similar to the black woman with respect to grooming and self-presentation. Old American conceptions of race give way under this particular cosmopolitan canopy.

Effects of this cosmopolitan concentration spill out of the park to nearby businesses. Rachael's Nosheri, a popular lunchtime restaurant and take-out place, is owned by a Jewish man and his daughter, after whom it is named. A young woman who seems to be a member of the extended family takes telephone orders, handles the cash register, and manages the restaurant. All the employees are black. They make all the sandwiches and platters behind the counter, where customers order and pick up their food. The employees also deliver food to offices, stores, and apartments in the neighborhood. They form a strong group in and of themselves, with collegial bonds to the owners and personal relations with their regular customers, whom they call by name. The clientele of this Jewish delicatessen is ethnically mixed. Black customers seem less likely to eat in the restaurant and more likely to take out what they order; perhaps they have offices in the area and are here because of their work, not leisure.

Similarly, DiBruno's, a cheese-and-Italian-specialty store nearby, having originated in the heart of the Italian neighborhood in South Philadelphia, has its Rittenhouse Square branch staffed by Latinos and serves a cosmopolitan crowd. The staff at the local Cosi, which sells coffee, pastries, soup, salads, sandwiches, and desserts for modest prices, today happens to be entirely African American, which is unusual; the ethnic makeup of the staff changes frequently. Professionals and their support staff, blacks and whites alike, come from the nearby offices at lunchtime and during their breaks, taking their purchases out to a bench on the Square or sitting down to eat.

BLACK AND MALE ON THE SQUARE

Over the course of my ethnographic research, I have discovered at least one interesting exception to the cosmopolitanism of the Rittenhouse Square area, and that is in the spaces around the square occupied by upscale eateries. These restaurants—Rouge, Devon, La Colombe, Blue, and the Parc Brasserie and Bistro—attract a well-heeled, mostly white clientele. At Rouge, a Parisian-style bistro, the Sunday brunch crowd comprises people who have come from church as well as those who have slept late. Tables are occupied by young couples who do not yet have children as well as older folks in twos and fours. Seldom are there solo diners. Known for featuring locally grown ingredients in its complex dishes, the place is busy with patrons. The music, a mix of late-1970s soul and white rock, is played at a subdued volume that does not interfere with the conversation.

Ethnically, the clientele appears pretty WASP, but generic "whites" may well include Latinos, Italians, Jews, and others of European descent. The one who does not fit in here so easily is the black male. Not that he is excluded. I eat at Rouge often when I come to the square, because I like the food. But when I enter and leave the restaurant I must prove myself as a bona fide paying customer, not just some black guy who wandered in off the street to use the bathroom or beg for money. Rouge, like the other restaurants fronting the square, is somewhat permeable to the street life because of the sidewalk tables it services and the huge glass windows that swing open in nice weather and turn the whole interior into a space with an open-air atmosphere. I sometimes eat at the sidewalk tables and sometimes indoors, depending on what is available and on the season.

One warm August day I came to the square to meet an African American physician friend for lunch at Rouge. A little before our meeting time he phoned me on my cell to say that he would be delayed by about thirty minutes. I sat and observed the goings-on in the square, moving from bench to bench and traversing this walk and that. It was a beautiful day, and I was in a very good mood. At about 12:45, while I was sitting and writing in my journal, my friend Michael approached. We greeted each other, and he apologized again for being late, which I shrugged off. We then headed toward Rouge for our lunch.

The noontime crowd was sitting outside enjoying the sidewalk-café ambiance. As we approached, an African American hostess greeted us, which was quite striking because it is so rare to see a black person working for any of the high-end restaurants fronting the square; usually the waitstaff is young and white. The hostess was quite gracious, even friendly toward us, as she offered to take my knapsack for safekeeping. Then she gave us the option of a choice sidewalk table or inside. Michael and I decided to sit outside, where we could enjoy the pleasant day. We sat and perused the menu. After placing our order, I remembered that my cell phone needed charging. I decided to ask the nice young hostess to recharge it for me inside.

As I entered the restaurant, I was confronted by a sea of white people, some dressed casually, others not so—this was the business lunch and casual upper-middle-class crowd—and I was pretty blasé about what I was going to do. But no sooner had I stepped inside the restaurant than a heavyset white man rose from the bar and confronted me, asking, "Can I help you, sir!?" A few of the other diners turned their gaze toward us. I was surprised by the show of aggressiveness and the sharp tone of voice. But I kept my cool and gazed about for the hostess, explaining to the white bouncer that I wanted to see the hostess. "Can I help you?" he asked again, his voice rising. I then said, "I'm looking for the . . ."

By now, the hostess had spotted me and approached with what seemed a rather forced smile. As she did, she greeted me, acknowledging that I was a bona fide customer. With this recognition, the heavyset white man retreated from his defensive mode and returned to his seat at the bar. The hostess was very pleasant, even solicitous, as she took my cell phone and charged it. After returning to my seat, I could not help discussing with Michael what had just happened. Having faced this sort of treatment on numerous occasions himself because he is black, he agreed that something was amiss here.

Still, it wasn't so very amiss that we couldn't take up where we'd left off before the slight rent in the canopy that I had just experienced. We ate a fine lunch, the only black patrons of the establishment. Why is it that the black male seems to stress the fabric of the canopy at this particular point? The restaurants that cater to upscale customers around Rittenhouse Square generally don't hire African Americans to work in visible positions. Whether this discrimination is by design or not is an open question. It may well be that the black persons with a certain stylish appearance and cool but deferential demeanor who might fit in with the waitstaff are already employed elsewhere. African Americans are quite visible as bank tellers and clerks in retail stores, as well as doormen in the apartment buildings around the square. Given that all those are service positions, it seems clear that these restaurants actively exclude local black people from their workforce, or at least keep them from showing their face to the public. It is highly unusual to see or encounter a black waitstaff member, male or female. This discrimination means that few blacks benefit financially from these successful upscale businesses downtown. It also takes its toll on the comity of the city by reinforcing alienation and cynicism among certain wealthy black Philadelphians. Although many in the black middle class tend to blame poor blacks for their inability to find jobs, this argument wears thin in the face of such visible discrimination.

THE DOORMEN

Where black males seem to fit comfortably into the scheme of things at Rittenhouse Square is in the role of parking valet and doorman. Rarely, black males are distinguished as doctors, lawyers, professors, and other professionals. When such men do appear on the square, unless attired in a suit and tie and accompanied by other professionals, it is hard for others they encounter to recognize them as professionals. In public it is easier for most blacks as well as whites to assume that the black male is an ordinary person of the working class who resides in the ghetto. Black skin is taken as biographical information that says most of what people want to know.

The black men who meet and greet residents and visitors at numerous apartment buildings and the Rittenhouse Hotel serve as eyes and ears on the square, and as they wait and watch they learn much more than most people assume they know. They take good care of "their people," meaning the numerous residents in the vicinity who have come to depend on them. Those who are least able to fend for themselves, especially the sizable elderly population residing in the high-rises, rely implicitly on the doormen, who in turn form a community devoted to their well-to-do residents. Responding to their needs becomes second nature.[3]

When my family lived in Rittenhouse Square, my wife and I especially enjoyed our evening constitutional. After we completed our walk, my wife would sometimes return to our apartment while I spent some time with George, the black doorman one building over. His building was more elegant than ours. We had a simple front desk with one or two attendants, but his building had a small, private entry space off the main lobby where the doorman would sit and keep a close eye on the sidewalk and curb in front. During his shift, George anticipated his chance to greet the building's tenants as they left or returned to their apartments. He had a small TV set that was always tuned to his favorite channel, but he watched it only sporadically. Whenever he spotted one of his tenants coming or going, he would rise to greet them: "Hello, sir," or "How are you, ma'am?" "Can I give you a hand?" "Good evening, sir." This was his constant refrain. From my time with him, I could see that George's attention to his tenants went well beyond the service that residents in our building expected to receive.

One evening George and I were deeply involved in a discussion of his grown daughter's troubles with her boyfriend when a middle-aged female tenant pulled up in her Volvo station wagon filled with groceries. Stopping in midsentence,

George jumped up and rushed out to the curb to render whatever assistance he could. From his action I thought the woman might be in some sort of distress; I was surprised to find out that she simply needed help with her purchases. George was there to provide it. He quickly lowered the tail-gate and went to work almost mechanically, gathering up her bags and neatly placing them on the floor inside the building's vestibule. Within a couple of minutes, the Volvo was unloaded, and she left to park it in the adjacent garage. Now he returned to me, and we resumed our conversation, picking up where we had left off, talking about his life with his daughter in Southwest Philadelphia, one of the rough-est neighborhoods in the city, notorious for drugs, crime, and violence. Living there requires a significant amount of street smarts. While George's demeanor and conversation with me indicated his understanding of the ghetto streets, he was equally able to be polite and unassuming toward his ten-ants in this fancy building on Rittenhouse Square. And his readiness to be at their service was clearly appreciated. When the woman returned in about ten minutes after parking her wagon, he placed her packages in the elevator for her, and she presented him with a five-dollar tip.

On another evening I was in front of the very fancy Ritten-house Hotel, which fronts the square, waiting for the parking attendants to retrieve my car, when I struck up a conversation with Terry, a twenty-five-year-old African American doorman, about the quality of life in Philadelphia. "I love Philadelphia," he enthused as he held the door for entering and departing guests. "Yes, it *is* a great place," I agreed. "And it's even more so now that we gon' win the Series," he boasted. (He was wrong, alas.) With that, he tried singing a few bars of the Phillies' cheering song. "La-di-dah," he warbled, but he wasn't sure he had the tune right. I offered a different version of the song, and we took turns trying to figure it out. Then we began to discuss the particular ballplayers—Jimmy Rollins and Shane Victorino—who had contributed to the recent playoff victory that had earned the Phillies their berth in the World Series. At this point, Sean, another doorman, who had been observing our conversation, chimed in to praise Victorino, remarking that he thought Victorino was Latino and that he himself was half Italian and half Irish. "I don't know what he is, but I do know he's a hell of a ballplayer," he commented. Then he began singing what he thought was the cheer.

Soon Terry and I joined in. Suddenly, an elderly Jewish hotel guest who had been watching this whole exchange joined as well. We all took this opportunity to join together in singing the praises of the home team. In the vicinity of the square, this seemed a very natural thing to do. Though racial and ethnic identities are never "forgotten," there seem to be places where such particularities can be put on the back burner. And this amounts to a high level of civility and even a kind of caring.

An elderly white woman, an astute sociologist and a friend of mine who has lived in Rittenhouse Square for decades, now uses a walker to get around and regards these men respect-fully as her protectors. Their assistance enables her to live downtown and to immerse herself in the activities around the square. The black doormen not only fulfill their duties to her conscientiously but are unfailingly courteous and consider-ate of the residents, whether white or black, young or old, in their own or in adjacent buildings. She notes, "They know and interact with one another, and I believe that they talk with one another about the tenants of their respective apart-ment houses. Not only does the staff in my building watch over me with respect and protectiveness, but they have made me known to the staff of the apartment house just across the street, who greet me warmly when they see me pass by. I have been told by friends who come to visit me that when they have bumped into persons who work at the door or at the desk of my apartment house in another part of Center City, they have been recognized and greeted as well."

She tells a story that, to her, epitomizes the overall civility that characterizes racial interactions in Rittenhouse Square.

Once when I entered the bank around the corner to obtain some cash from the ATM machine inside, I had an interesting encounter with a middle-aged African American man with some gray in his hair, wearing glasses, and infor-mally but neatly dressed in slacks, a T-shirt, and cap. I had just obtained my cash from the machine, and he was waiting patiently to be the next to use it. He kindly and gently told me to take my time. When I thanked him and assured him that I was just pausing to put the cash in my wallet, he said I need not hurry. He went on to tell me, quite spontaneously, that he often made the same remark to his mother, whom he helped every day to do her grocery shopping. I commended him for that, and once again for his kindness to me. That was the way he was raised, he replied. It was the way that I was raised, too, I responded.

By this time, he had gotten the cash he wanted from the machine, and then kindly opened the door for me so that I could easily exit. This incident illustrates the sort of kindness that I experience as I move about in my neighborhood with my walker. The consideration is extended most often, though not exclusively, by African Americans. I surmise that these black men and women may associate me with their elderly mothers and that their concern for others has been inculcated and reinforced by their relationship to the black church, as well as by experiences they may have had in paramedical jobs in hospitals and nursing homes, or as home health aides.

In my friend's experience African Americans take special care of those whose limited mobility may give rise to difficulties as they navigate public spaces around the square. Perhaps they identify with them as members of a marginalized group. Most important, they care for and respect their elders, and others benefit from their kindness.

In the wider American culture race relations can be tested and feel fraught and even frayed by interactions in public, in the same way they can at times feel soothed, as in the interaction at the bank described by my informant. But no forward movement in this long process is possible unless the races share space at close enough range to interact with one another.

LA COLOMBE

La Colombe is a coffeehouse located off Rittenhouse Square on Nineteenth Street that some connoisseurs think serves the "best cup of coffee in town." Its daytime regulars are mostly young professionals who sit by themselves to study or do work-related reading. Some come with friends or meet others they know, creating a social-club atmosphere in the late afternoons and evenings. The customers here are more homogeneous than the people found nearby in Rittenhouse Square Park. Those who congregate at La Colombe are predominantly white and exhibit the signs of middle-class status and aspirations for upward mobility. As they greet one another, they display an awareness of professional credentials. Overheard snatches of conversation relate to ongoing projects and job-related contacts. This setting facilitates social mixing within a limited range; professional status functions as a peculiar kind of social coin. Regulars seem to find comfort through publicly communing with others like themselves, either socializing with them or simply sharing space as they concentrate on their work. National origin and even race or color seem to take a backseat to social-class homogeneity. At times the place feels like a study hall for grown-ups.

On first impression this setting appears entirely white. After repeated visits, close inspection, and reports from regular customers, I discover that a few blacks do venture in, sit down, and stay awhile; and when they do, they visibly fit in. Occasionally a lone black woman or man enters, gets coffee, and is out the door and gone as suddenly as she or he arrived, perhaps back to the apartment to hit the books. At other times a small group of black men, ranging from artists to educators, hang out here, enjoying the coffee and socializing, savoring the atmosphere that accommodates people like themselves, though in limited number. Often the black people who frequent this place are well educated; they "talk white" with little or no audible effort and engage in articulate-sounding conversations. Overhearing them without seeing their faces, they might well be mistaken for middle-class whites.

The habitués at La Colombe play down the importance of race, seeming to privilege a certain professionalism instead. But when a black stranger comes in the door alone and without the obvious emblems of middle-class status, others take note of him and may make assumptions regarding his social place. An extraordinary amount of eye work must be performed. At first, with no actual knowledge of the person, but with the evidence of ordinary casual dress, most of the clientele might infer that they are observing someone from the ghetto. Limitations on racial acceptance emerge—the subject "bears watching." Gradually, as more information becomes available, including the fact that nothing eventful has yet transpired, the others in the coffeehouse begin to relax and to carry on.

No black people work at La Colombe. Given Philadelphia's large and varied population, that seems to most blacks a deliberate exclusion rather than a mere accident. A young white man and a young white woman work the counter. They prepare coffee, serve European pastries such as brioches and croissants, and attend to the cash register. A thirty-year-old Hispanic man keeps the place spiffy. He is quite attentive to the shop's appearance, wiping down the front window, sweeping up, and emptying the trash. Blacks who linger over coffee may feel their minority status, even if they fail to acknowledge it out loud. Acknowledging this to themselves might raise hard but fundamental questions about their own social place.

All the issues that confront the black community thrive in the microcosm of Rittenhouse Square. Wirth and Simmel suggested the size, density, and heterogeneity of the population help to define this area as a "scene" or a "happening place."[4] The square and its environs possess all those qualities, yet the black upper-middle class continues to be conspicuously underrepresented in the mix. Blacks who have had considerable social and economic success in mainstream society are not always comfortable in the public space frequented solely by their white counterparts, a state of affairs reminiscent of the situation described by the African American sociologist W. E. B. Du Bois over a century ago.[5] Much has changed for the black community since Du Bois's day, yet this aspect of the relationship of the black middle class with the predominantly white society appears to be as challenging as ever. How do cosmopolitan blacks and other minorities navigate such confusing environments, which are tolerant enough to admit them, and even at times to welcome them, but which also remind black people of the extent of their own marginality? Feeling that discomfort, I turn to this question in the next chapter.

5. THE COLOR LINE AND THE CANOPY

In 1903, W. E. B. Du Bois presciently remarked, "The problem of the twentieth century is the problem of the color line."[1] At that time, the color line was clearly demarcated and its rules were universally understood and generally deferred to in northern cities like Philadelphia as well as in the Jim Crow South. The significant changes that have occurred in race relations since then have generated ambiguity and bewildering complexity in interracial interactions. The promise and real achievements of the civil rights movement have not remedied structural inequalities, and black skin color remains a powerful marker of second-class status. Norms of "color blindness" coexist with persistent patterns of discrimination, and interpersonal relations across the color line are highly charged.

Since the 1960s, affirmative action and other public policies promoting racial incorporation have reduced racial conflict and led to the growth of the black middle class, whose members enjoy an enhanced, although still tentative, sense of social inclusion. These efforts, however, provoked in an increasing number of whites feelings of unfairness and a generalized sense of threat.[2] In addition, a social and economic split developed between the black working class and the new middle class as deindustrialization, globalization, and other forces eliminated the manufacturing jobs that once provided blue-collar employment in the city.[3]

White people and, later, upper- and middle-class black people followed the jobs out of the city, leaving inner-city working-class and poor neighborhoods that became generally perceived as dangerous, poor, and black and, therefore, undesirable. Ghettos expanded, public services declined, and police, schools, and other institutions often abdicated their responsibilities to serve and to protect black citizens.[4]

By 2007, before the latest recession began, Philadelphia's manufacturing industries had declined so sharply that they employed less than 4 percent of the labor force, whereas in 1970 they had employed 20 percent. According to a 2010 Pew report, "In 2009, the city remains a place where the poor and working class form the majority. One out of every four residents lives below the poverty line—a greater share than in most big cities—and the median household income is half the suburban average. The old economy has left a lot of Philadelphia behind."[5] Black workers encounter great difficulty finding family-sustaining employment in health care and education, the only sectors that are expanding. Consequently, many black neighborhoods are marked by concentrated poverty.[6] In such distressed neighborhoods, the drug trade and other elements of the underground economy have moved in and proliferated, providing economic opportunity for the most desperate elements, where the wider economy provides little hope.

Today interracial interactions are much less predictable. Many heavy racial burdens have been lifted, but blacks can still find the color line sharply drawn at any moment. When this happens, it strikes almost any black person like a bolt out of the blue, leaving him stunned, but particularly when it happens in spaces dominated by whites whom he formerly trusted. In the "nigger moment"[7] the black person is effectively "put back in his place"—a situation that many in the middle class thought they would never have to navigate. Blacks are prepared to think that the offending white person has simply had enough of the "uppity" black person and reverted to form, treating him or her disrespectfully.

The most problematic aspect of social relations under the cosmopolitan canopy appears when the color line is suddenly drawn, and an issue that people had assumed mattered little comes to dominate the whole situation. Tensions may arise over turf and territory, particularly when a member of one group considers a member of another to be out of place, or even threatening. In these circumstances, the "gloss" that people put on to smooth their interactions can wear thin. The celebration of diversity, the practice of civility, and even the pretense of tolerance itself can all break down, exposing the racial fault lines that still exist in contemporary American society.[8]

The everyday experiences of black people who move through urban public spaces and mix with whites in the workplace reveal these fault lines with special clarity. Although members of other visible minorities, especially Hispanics and immigrants of color, can experience marginalization or stigmatization, black people encounter the contemporary color line in a relatively pure form, uncomplicated by matters of language and immigration status. Their perspective on the limits of the cosmopolitan canopies that are emerging in Philadelphia and other major cities sheds light on the disparities, revealing that America in the post–civil rights era is not quite the "postracial" society that some proclaim.

The social gulf between black and white Americans that is linked to lingering racial segregation is only in part a matter of persistent—indeed, intensifying—economic inequality between the black poor and everyone else. The social isolation of impoverished blacks in ghettos where they seldom interact with mainstream institutions and have a limited hold on the labor market, the dysfunctional educational and law enforcement systems they do encounter, and the myriad social ills that accompany concentrated poverty—all limit the lives and aspirations of too many black urbanites. It is clear that as the social ills of the iconic black ghetto grow ever more dramatic and acute, those residing in the wider society, including many blacks themselves, come to conflate black skin color with ghetto residence and, in self-defense, often prejudge black people to be problematic or even dangerous. When dark-skinned visitors approach the canopy and begin to partake of its wondrous social benefits, they are tolerated, even sometimes embraced, providing they exhibit "good behavior," but they may have to endure an extra measure of scrutiny by their hosts.

Beyond the ghetto racial inequalities persist in less visible but nonetheless potent forms. The post–civil rights era has been formed by a highly successful racial incorporation process that vastly increased the size of the black middle class and allowed many of its members to approach parity with their white counterparts. Yet many middle-class black people still find themselves occasionally treated as if they were indistinguishable from the most stigmatized figures that represent their race in the imagination of fearful whites. Racial profiling is a routine occurrence for black males, and black females are often insulted in racially degrading terms. The stigma of blackness, compounded by the contagion of ghetto stereotypes, continues to afflict African American professionals and executives, even in their own homes in predominantly white neighborhoods.

Today places like the local Four Seasons hotel are patronized by well-to-do black professionals and public officials. As the number of upper-class blacks grows, it is also more and more likely that a random black person encountered in public is the son, nephew, daughter, or cousin of such accomplished individuals. In the past the caste-like system of racial segregation made it very unlikely that blacks would hold such positions. Now, after some black people have achieved upward mobil-

ity through the incorporation process, the American occupational structure has changed, and the consequences have
reverberated throughout the wider system of social stratification. Those changes make for certain dilemmas and contradictions of status.[9] The success of a few blacks has had collateral
implications for the collective status of the race, raising its class
profile. Because a random black person could theoretically be
anybody, the position of the black person encountered in public becomes increasingly complicated. Upper-class blacks serve
as significant role models for the younger members of their
race, inspiring and encouraging them to follow the lead of
their elders. The social consequences of this phenomenon are
crucial; as a critical mass of such leaders emerges, the status of
the black community rises, militating against the lower caste-
like status of black Americans as a group.

At best, however, the black middle and upper classes
enjoy their status only provisionally. This chapter explores the
ways in which the promise of the cosmopolitan canopy is challenged by recurring situational racial discrimination or by the
occasional racial incident. In examining the places, times,
and circumstances in which the color line is drawn, we learn
not only about the social dynamics of racial inequality but
also about the possibilities and limits of cosmopolitanism as
an organizing theme of public life. A study of the problematic
aspects of public interracial interactions allows us to probe
different strategies by which both blacks and whites cope with
racial dynamics at work and in other more public venues.

LIBERTY PLACE

In Center City, not far from Rittenhouse Square, rises Liberty Place. A pair of elegant office towers, this marvel of architectural design in metallic blue glass serves as testimony to the city's renaissance and supports Philadelphia's claim to be a world-class destination. The buildings are state-of-the-art in their physical as well as social environment. Compared with the Reading Terminal Market or the Gallery Mall, this setting is decidedly upscale and rather antiseptic. Almost everything is clean, orderly, and safe, effectively monitored by security—young black people, male and female, clad in crisp white shirts and dark blue pants. That the trash cans are seldom allowed to overflow is the kind of minor detail that makes a significant difference. Things are a bit more uptight here, spiffy and formal, than in the street outside.

The food court, located on a mezzanine that looks out onto the atrium, features an array of stalls and an open floor plan for casual dining. Its ambiance expresses a contemporary spirit of possibility. Most of the customers come from offices of the national and regional corporations located here; others work in retail businesses nearby. Residing in the city's rich variety of local ethnic and suburban neighborhoods, people of all colors meld, but the polished young black individuals stand out, displaying a look of cultivation and poise. They interact amid a multiracial group of middle managers, secretaries, accountants, administrative assistants, and salesclerks who all share tables. Customers occasionally wander in from the upscale boutiques and stores of the mall area or from the hotel that is a part of this complex.

The blue-and-gray glass interior has a corporate feel. Built in 1987 and in 1990, the huge modern structures showcase space that is airy, the marble unmarred. Dining tables are regularly bussed, and trash is picked up frequently. The message is clear that every well-behaved person is welcome here, regardless of his or her background. Clerks and servers are Latino, Asian, black, and white, and the clientele to some degree mirror this mixture. A cosmopolitan aura prevails. Decorum is subtly yet effectively enforced. The homeless or mentally ill who come here seeking to escape the summer heat or winter cold are discouraged by the security guards, who are savvy enough to understand the cues such undesirables display.

As they carefully read the crowd, the guards generally know whom to discourage, seldom misinterpreting the signals people give off. The guards' behavior is something of a performance for those who partake of this public space. Their actions communicate that the norms observed here set certain limits on allowable behavior. Panhandling is strictly forbidden, and on occasion the guards demonstratively escort a person to the door or put him out, discouraging return trips and informing onlookers about the rules of this place. Only a few homeless persons seem not to get the message; those repeat violators are well known to the guards, who eye sketchy-looking visitors suspiciously.

The food court is unusually active today, its small shops

offering a variety of cuisines. Its denizens include well-dressed workers from the adjacent downtown area. Service-oriented workers take lunch and coffee breaks away from their workplaces while socializing with friends and colleagues. A young black man with chiseled features, in business attire, lunches with a young black woman at a table over by the window. The noontime light hits them just right. The exquisitely polished image he projects is very much at odds with that of the stereotypical ghetto male. The well-dressed, soft-spoken young man and woman with dark-brown skin let all who witness them know they are exceptions to reigning racial stereotypes. And they are not alone.

In this upscale setting, the foreboding image of the ghetto is balanced, though not entirely offset, by the critical mass of young black people having lunch and going about their everyday business. They represent powerful racial advertisements. Here well-dressed, middle-class black people have a chance to be taken as normal, even as ordinary. Equally important, those present representing the wider society are subtly but powerfully challenged in their previous stereotypical thinking as they are exposed to the emerging class and multicultural complexity of the cosmopolitan canopy. In truth, they all represent a cross section of middle-class Philadelphians: white, Latino, Asian, and black people who have gravitated here from the city's ethnic working-class enclaves as they have achieved upward social mobility. In this new space, subtle but far-reaching cultural exchanges are being quietly but effectively negotiated. The otherwise off-putting master status of black skin color in the young male is negated by counterrepresentations of civility and professionalism. And the image of the intolerant Caucasian person is being tested and may be situationally cast aside. All this is for the common good, as more and more Philadelphians regard this scene as normal.

An important social education is being obtained here, as people from the far reaches of the metropolitan area have an opportunity to develop new understandings of people of color. Significantly, similar observations and social lessons are increasingly available to black people themselves. No longer must each black person who is the first to be employed by his or her firm be painfully visible among whites or eat alone; now he or she can sit unobtrusively in a multicolored crowd.

THE WORKPLACE AS CANOPY

We now move from the tranquil and more public cosmopolitan canopies, where little other than polite greetings and other expressions of goodwill are felt to be at stake, to the more private and somewhat more bounded spaces of the workplace. This situation presents us with a different order of challenge. While characterized by some of the more ordinary features of the canopy, the workplace and what goes on there is unique in a number of respects.

Most important, in this setting people develop a more clearly defined stake or interest in the behavior of their counterparts. Here issues become more freighted with politics,

which can become conflated with daily tasks; workers negotiate for place and position while trying to get along in the
organization. Specifically, actors are more inclined to make,
and to retain, mental notes on one another, keeping track
of others' relative status in the organization. In these settings people are more carefully guided by one another, and
by their background understandings of the world, which are
based largely on "local knowledge" acquired from the public streets of their urban communities and on their "sense
of group position."[10] The local neighborhood, long associated with racial and ethnic particularism, is reflected in the
modern Philadelphia workplace, and tensions occasionally
become pronounced.

In the workplace, encounters with members of other ethnic groups occur in the context of a more self-conscious strug-
gle for existence than that which is present in the more public
canopies. Yet workplaces are canopies nonetheless, albeit institutionalized ones. Here people hailing from the diverse ethnic neighborhoods of the city gather under one roof to work
together, thereby acknowledging that some degree of mutual
trust is essential for the good of the organization. By law and
policy, as well as a matter of self-interest, most Philadelphia
workplaces are no longer the nearly all-white settings they
were in the mid-twentieth century. With the incorporation
of more visible minorities, comity and goodwill are encouraged and offensive behavior in interactions among members
of different racial and ethnic groups is negatively sanctioned.
Beyond this, employees are encouraged to check their eth-

nic, racial, and other particularities at the door and to exhibit professionalism and tolerance toward those who are different from themselves. In exchange, employees receive the chance to rise in the organization, or at least to hold a place in good standing if their work merits it.

Still, ethnic affiliation is a persistent fact of organizational life, and workers form affinity groups on the basis of ethnicity, identifying themselves by what they share. These affinity groups may draw invidious distinctions between themselves and others, forging their identities to some degree by whom they oppose. Virtually every issue becomes political as groups vie for position and power. Not only do these affinity groups petition the organization for specific programs or support, but, more important, they define and underscore differences in the workplace. In these circumstances employees with a particular background in common are encouraged to look out for one another.

The division between an authentically cosmopolitan canopy and a mere pretense is difficult to discern. In order to succeed or to survive, group members often take strong defensive action. In negotiating the terrain, they adopt a smooth façade that deflects close scrutiny and allows them to float from situation to situation, negotiating their way around the organization.[11] They get along with their co-workers, engaging in small talk around the water cooler or in the lunch room, smiling, laughing, and getting by among the people and situations they must deal with throughout the day. The main thing is to do the job effectively.

At five o'clock a different picture emerges. The comity and goodwill of the workplace abruptly shuts off. Black professionals agree that it is at this time that they feel the greatest distance from their white professional counterparts. Revealed for what it was all along, their work-related communication seems strangely superficial, even empty. The diverse group works together but seldom bonds across the color line. When such bonding does occur, it is surprising, perhaps worthy of comment. Ordinarily the more cosmopolitan-oriented people cross their respective ethnic and color lines, at times forming especially intimate friendships. They even become cultural brokers of a sort, modeling this behavior for others who remain "work friends" throughout the day. A few people straddle the color line, which underscores it. But they tend to be the exception rather than the rule. Work is left at work. When it's over, almost everyone heads out to the parking garage or the street to what seems another world, to meet real friends and buddies, or simply to head for homes in segregated neighborhoods.

As they go their separate ways, black professionals I've gotten to know complain that in chance encounters on the streets, in local cafés, and on public transportation their white co-workers, eyes glazing over, sometimes act as though they didn't know their black colleagues, as though they had never met them before. Conditioned by a long history of dealing with white prejudice that has made them sensitive to racial slights, many blacks discern a pattern. Some blacks find such blank stares deeply offensive and perhaps indicative of how their white colleagues really feel about them. If the unexpected encounter is to be consummated, they lament, they must take the initiative themselves. In their defense, the white co-workers might say that they are just melding into the crowd, putting on the blasé, impersonal mask that Louis Wirth described as necessary in order to navigate the dizzying urban environment.[12]

RACE AND PROVISIONAL STATUS

Particularities, whether of ethnicity, race, gender, or sexual preference, are not expected to count in the workplace today. But this ideology of universalism is belied by the social acceptance of the master status–determining characteristic, in which a single trait trumps a person's other qualities.[13] People with such a characteristic are seen first and foremost as representatives of the group that is defined by that characteristic rather than as individuals. Race is a prime example; gender, sexual orientation, and physical or mental capacity are others. This dynamic has strong implications for anyone with a "negative difference"—blacks, women, gays, and the disabled, among others—because it saddles them with provisional status. Blacks who first broke into white settings, such as Jackie Robinson and Paul Robeson, felt this burden keenly. As the incorporation process has progressed, expectations of full acceptance have grown, yet many blacks who have gained positions in majority-white organizations still experience their status as provisional. Blacks see carrying that provisional status as part of their identity.

At first provisional status was based on the fact that people without the experience of working in mainstream institutions were being deliberately placed there, often through affirmative action programs, without having previously demonstrated their merit. Blacks themselves could see a certain logic in this provisional status. As they proved capable, however, and as greater numbers of blacks joined them, their expectations of unqualified inclusion grew, yet that desired situation has not developed. Provisional status is now a function of collaborative action on the part of both whites and blacks. Paradoxically, affirmative action, which was meant to remedy the problem of black exclusion, has underscored provisional status by blurring the distinction between meritocratic hiring and promotion and tokenism. This ambiguity has created doubts among both whites and blacks regarding the true capabilities of black professionals: were they hired because they can really do the job, or because the company needed to have a visible black presence? As a result, despite the ideology of equality and meritocracy, blacks remain second-class citizens in the organization. Moreover, there is a lack of trust on both sides. Whites are uncertain of blacks' credentials, while blacks, aware that they lack power and credibility, can remain uncertain as to their real position.

A veneer of racial civility usually characterizes the predominantly white workplace. Nonetheless, when a black individual is treated day in and day out as an outsider, he can become aware of his provisional status. But he feels his status most acutely when he is tested by a false accusation, an unfair evaluation, or denial of a promotion. Such actions can be ambiguous, but they are always complicated by his outsider status, which has deep implications for his credibility. For the ordinary people he encounters every day, his presence may be tolerated, but he typically symbolizes a person with "much yet to prove." Thus, his real integration with existing workplace "in-groups" or cliques is usually limited, and yet these elements wield significant power over him; his co-workers, particularly the ethnocentric whites among them, can be revealed as being most resistant to his presence. When politics emerge these interests often coalesce, leaving him with little actual leverage or reliable support.

After experiencing these patterns of arbitrary treatment in a context of racial civility, he can feel by turns both appreciated and resented. As issues of power and respect become intertwined, he may become confused and disillusioned. These challenges are then processed on a human and emotional level, a situation that can crystallize his vulnerability— reminding him that he occupies a persistently provisional status. Ultimately, his situation may devolve to a point of crisis, attracting attention and becoming closely watched, with the resolution providing important lessons about the nature of the workplace for all, but particularly his younger co-workers.

In the early nineteenth century Tocqueville observed

that the existence of a hierarchy with a privileged class gave France a more stable system than that in the United States, where the lack of a hereditary aristocracy leads to a competition for status.[14] Everyone in this country is vying for place and position. In the contemporary United States the black person is still at a disadvantage. The weakest competitor is the person with a stigma attached to his or her identity.[15] No stigma has been more persistent than black skin color.

In the course of the workday, people with provisional status may gain greater insight into their situation as they encounter acts of both omission and commission. They may be subtly ignored at the office or even treated as invisible. Their projects may not be taken seriously. Little indignities may be visited upon them, reminding them that they are not full people in the eyes of their colleagues. These processes leave members of this group more conscious of their place in the firm.

Once people are sensitized to this situation, they begin to look for such instances. They scrutinize their experience in the company. They note the new employees, watch how they are treated, and measure them against themselves at a comparable stage. They single out others who have been in the firm for a while, reflexively checking into their histories, their trials and tribulations. Again and again, the provisional status of the person is confirmed, as the reality dawns—that he or she has always been a token member of the team. He notes that he was not asked to do this or to do that. She realizes that she is not invited to the gatherings, such as lunches, drinks, or golf outings, that her white counterparts can take for granted. Everything hits home when a younger white colleague—a person for whom he should be able to play the role of mentor—begins to counsel him! The younger colleague tells him about the ins and outs of the firm's politics, information that only an insider would know, such as the specific plans of the organization with respect to prospective hires and directions it might be considering. As this occurs, the provisional status can no longer be denied; it must be faced up to. In those circumstances the person may become either temporarily demoralized, or energized with her new understanding of herself and her position in the firm.

Many accept their provisional status as a matter of course. They have a ready racial context for anything that happens in the workplace. People in the majority group interpret this behavior and pass judgment on the minority person depending on how secure they are in their own entitlements, their sense of position in the general scheme of things. They entangle themselves in questions of whose place it is to do what in which circumstances. The calculation affects the context in which meaning is made of behavior and symbols displayed in that context, including clothes, speech, and actions. This dynamic has implications for both sides. To have provisional status means to be circumscribed in your actions to the extent that they might challenge or be seen to threaten the hegemony of the dominant group.

MARCEL AND HIS CO-WORKERS

The dynamics of interracial interactions at work are shaped by blacks' and whites' differing experiences outside of the workplace. I found Marcel's perspective enlightening.

One Sunday afternoon after returning from New York by train, I drove my 1998 Ford Explorer out of the Thirtieth Street Station parking garage and soon realized that it had a flat tire. I walked to the Firestone shop across the street from the station to get some help. But they could not send anyone over, so I called AAA for roadside assistance.

About half an hour later, Marcel, a young black man, arrived. After checking out the problem, he inflated the front right tire to see whether it would hold air. It did—at least enough to allow me to drive to the Firestone shop. By then, though, Marcel and I had become engaged in a conversation, first about the Phillies and then about city neighborhoods, people, and places, and the work experiences of young men like himself. My curiosity got the better of me, and he agreed to be interviewed. So I turned on the tape recorder and asked him a few questions about himself, his friends and co-workers, and his perspective on life. Over the course of our hour-long conversation, I listened to Marcel talk about his family, his work history, and his attitudes about race and ethnicity in the city.

Marcel is a tall, well-built, dark brown-skinned black man of twenty-four. After growing up in a two-parent working-class family in the black community of West Philadelphia and attending racially segregated schools there, he is employed by an automotive parts and service company in West Philadelphia. His co-workers and supervisors are for the most part young white men who hail from various white working-class neighborhoods in Philadelphia, Delaware, and Maryland. All, including Marcel, participate in the metropolitan area's car culture.

These young white men generally have had little direct, positive contact with black people. Marcel is aware that, in his co-workers' and supervisors' eyes, he has something to prove. His is a provisional status. But he is very curious about them, and they are curious about him as well. At work, his co-workers are civil, and even friendly at times. Yet they associate Marcel with the ghetto; it's all they have to go on when making sense of him. Marcel treats the 'hood as an icon either to embrace or to distance himself from. In his dealings with whites, it is never a nonissue.

Outside his workplace, Marcel sees himself as an average young black man. He has a girlfriend and his "homies." He avidly follows all types of sports, particularly the local professional teams. Like many of his black friends and acquaintances, he makes occasional visits downtown, which he regards as a nice place to visit with his girlfriend, to shop, or, when he was younger, just to hang out. Marcel takes a deep and abiding interest in his car, which he maintains with great care.

In this respect, Marcel is quite similar to his white co-workers. He feels accepted by these young men, even though they come from divergent backgrounds. Like other work-places, including parking garages and delivery services, that draw workers from the local neighborhoods of Philadelphia, the auto parts and service shop is a site of social convergence, and in many respects it shares aspects of the canopy. Marcel is one of the very few blacks employed there, and over the years he has come to understand that blacks rise more slowly to positions of authority than do their white co-workers. When looking at these men, Marcel does not distinguish Irish and Italians; in his eyes, they are simply white, which he considers both an identifier and a status.

The workplace has given Marcel an opportunity to observe white people up close on a sustained basis for the first time. When he was younger, whites were socially distant. His exposure to them was limited to school teachers, clerks in downtown stores, fans at sporting events, and the popular media. At the shop, he interacts positively with white men his own age. Typically, problems are resolved with relatively little friction. Together these men, including Marcel, constitute a primary group. They form "work friendships," relationships that center at work and are generally left there after quitting time. However, Marcel feels that if something were to hap-pen to him, his work friends could be counted on to offer their support, and he knows he would do the same for them. His workplace serves as a window onto white society. Over lunch and during breaks, Marcel has a chance to share his own life with these young men.

Once, as they discussed their everyday experiences, the

subject of encounters with the police arose, prompting Marcel to tell his co-workers how often he had been stopped. When he asserted that he was stopped at least ten times a year, they thought he was exaggerating.

What Marcel observes as he drives around the city leaves him not angry but resigned to the status quo.

I see black people always being stopped by the police. And I'm a prime example of that. I don't know anybody at work that gets pulled over as much as I do. I get pulled over, and I'm not even joking, say ten or twenty times a year. I drive a white Dodge Charger, 2003. I do have rims on it, and I do have tinted windows. A lot of times, they [the police] say, "Well, your tints be too dark. But if you show me your license and registration . . ." They just tell me to make sure I take care of it. It can be the same cop that did it two months ago, but he do the same thing. I'm never given a ticket; I'm not fined for it. The violation wasn't serious enough for a citation; the frequent stops are a form of harassment.

I know people who never got pulled over, guys I work with. Or maybe they get pulled over 'bout two or three times. They never receive tickets either. But I get pulled over fifteen or twenty times and never get a ticket. These are white cops, definitely. Take the guys I work with. These guys work in the garage. Truck drivers, mechanics. White boys. They pass.

I'm kind of used to it. When I was a little younger, it would make me mad, 'cause I knew that they wasn't pulling me over because I ran a red light or because I ran a stop sign or because I was speeding. I know why they were doing it. It use to make me mad, and I used to talk back to 'em, get an attitude with 'em.

But now I'm getting older, it's just, "Yes, sir. I don't know why you stopping me, sir, but you must have a good reason. Here's my registration; here's my license." They take it, come back. "Thanks, have a nice day." It makes my life a lot easier. Before, I might get pulled over, talk back, get an attitude with 'em, and they might have me sittin' there for thirty minutes, forty minutes, just sittin' there. Now, what I do is just tell 'em, "Yes, sir" and "No, sir." Now when it's all said and done, they done in about fifteen minutes compared to forty-five. They already getting paid; they on the clock anyway. They can have you sittin' there all day. My time is more precious. "Alright, you have a nice day, too."

At the shop, we all friends. We get along, have lunch together, chitchat, whatever. We compare notes on our police experiences. They say, "I never got pulled over," or, "I got pulled over once or twice in my life." And I be like, "No way." So I might even call them on the phone, "Yo, I was on such and such street, and I just got pulled over by the cops." Or I take a picture of the stop with my cell phone and send it to 'em. They say, "That's crazy." Now they know that guys that are like me, my homies, get pulled over quite a lot.

In Philly you have "Operation Live Stop." If you don't have registration or insurance, they can take your vehicle.

They probably think that because you are from a certain descent, you probably don't have a license, you just driving. Once you do verify that you do have a license, you all right. But the white boys don't get stopped.

Marcel knows his place and expresses resignation: "That's what it is." He does not resent his co-workers who are white. "It is just the hand they were dealt, not their fault. It's not like they set up the system."

This viewpoint, which reflects Marcel's direct interactions with white co-workers, is uncommon among those who remain isolated in the black community.

WHEN PEOPLE MEET

When blacks and whites encounter one another for the first time, either inside or outside the workplace, a complicated set of attitudes is set in motion. First and foremost, an informal power differential is almost always at work. Lurking deep in the background is the legacy of slavery and racial segregation, along with the putative lowly caste position of the black person, and what this special social history has come to mean for both participants. That such issues can arise and become consequential implies that all black Americans can be considered members of an underclass, regardless of their putative status.

Blacks and whites acknowledge these truths differently. Black people, after all these years operating under the yoke of slavery and second-class citizenship, are far more able and willing to accept this reality than the average white person. It is not a truth many are inclined to discuss openly with their white counterparts. Many white people are simply ignorant of that fundamental but inconvenient truth, and would likely become disturbed if their black counterparts were to bring it up. While they may understand, and even assume, the reality of their structural position, their bosses and superiors at work, including some of those who are black, are encouraged to entertain the notion of a postracial America. Out of respect or deference for the occasion, black people generally keep these feelings to themselves, especially in the office, yet they can easily surface when blacks socialize among their own. In fact, such issues casually serve as bonds or even as organizing principles of their more particularistic social relationships.

Given these considerations, when a black person meets a white person for the first time, he occupies a structural position that may prevent him from fully trusting his white counterpart. Typically the black person has at least a superficial history of the black experience—that whites enslaved his ancestors, that his people continue to live in a racially segregated society, and, above all, that while there are many "good" white people today, many other white people are still consumed by race prejudice, and he cannot tell beforehand which are which. He also knows that many prejudiced white people remain in good standing with those whom he might consider "good."

On the job the black person is bombarded with new white people every day, people with whom he must interact in a professional manner. While those white people may well be able to relate to him in a nonprejudiced way, he knows that their attitude toward him will depend on what is at stake in any transaction they conduct. Moreover, he knows that to maintain his gloss and protect his own sanity, he must try to give the next white person the benefit of the doubt while being aware that even this degree of trust may be seriously misplaced.

When the black person enters a new workplace, she scans the setting for a friendly face. Before her is a sea of ambiguous white faces. Some may appear hostile and others polite, but she cannot tell which whites are genuinely pleased to have her in their presence. Those whites are indistinguishable from others who may feel threatened by her arrival. The black faces, in contrast, seem unambiguously welcoming. They speak and smile at the same time, in contrast to the whites, whose nonverbal meanings must be second-guessed and whose smiles may hide hostility.

The black employee knows that on any given day he will encounter numerous white people, many of whom he is sure are racist to some degree—but to what degree, and how must this reality figure into his relationship with them? Those people may well have misgivings about, or even a visceral dislike of, black people. The gloss of the canopy provides cover, allowing some people to mask their truer feelings. Some good comes from this, for prejudiced people are practicing tolerance, which may eventually take root. But because, in these circumstances, people have not yet been called out as racists, have not shown this side of themselves to blacks or to anyone else, they are an unknown quantity; the gloss protects their image. Nonracist white people give them the benefit of the doubt and excuse their racial orientation. Those people are able to then pass themselves off to their liberal white counterparts as postracial. But the black person, whose well-being hangs in the balance, cannot be so cavalier.

As best he can, he tries to manage others, keeping his distance from those he does not know. He may come to understand that he must also better manage his white friends, who he had not assumed could be so friendly with racists. He witnesses their fraternizing with astonishment and realizes that he needs to rethink these relationships. The black worker's only solution then is to give up on whites, or to relate to them personally with extreme caution. The reasonable way to proceed is to keep the whites he meets in their own provisional status, acknowledging that they have much yet to prove.

THE SOCIAL SITUATION OF BLACK PROFESSIONALS

I was excited as I entered the Center City office building, clad in a pin-striped suit, on a warm, sunny day in early autumn. I was meeting with the vice president for human resources of a major corporation, who had agreed to talk to me about the situation of black professionals in his firm.

First, though, I had to pass security. Everyone must display an ID card, attesting that he or she has a legitimate reason for being on the premises. While employees with white skin can often take their right of entry for granted, black employees, particularly black males, cannot. They know that at any moment, the full weight of security can come down, collapsing the distinction between themselves and more ordinary black males on the outside.

The black security guards inhabit a special limbo. They protect the employees and the building's premises from people who physically resemble themselves. The guards both identify with and feel a certain distance from the local disfranchised black community. At the same time many of them feel some dissonance regarding their connection with the organization, whose employees are predominantly white or relatively well-assimilated blacks who often display little appreciation or sympathy for people like them, particularly as they negotiate the social dynamics of their peculiar status. Indeed, the guards, along with other minority employees, may be positioned as buffers between the insiders and the blacks on the outside. Moreover, depending on the proximity of the workplace to the inner-city ghetto, policing this line may be especially fraught with confusing and dangerous scenarios, practically as well as psychologically.

Many people who work in the company that I visited identify themselves as white Anglo-Saxon Protestants. Even if this is not true of many individuals, the wider white-dominated culture privileges WASPs to such a degree that most others, regardless of their differences, tend to view the distinctive symbols of this group as legitimate and even, in many circumstances, as normal. Typically, these individuals form a working conception of the organization that further privileges their own group. When considering black people, they display little sympathy for their plight or for their position in the company. They often feel that the organization is egalitarian enough and that nothing needs to be done to encourage the presence of minorities, least of all black people. They may think, and even say, that blacks should be "on their own" by now and blame them for creating their own problems.

In this context, many black employees take for granted that they are on continual probation within the organization and that the workplace can turn hostile at a moment's notice, no matter how long they have worked there. In dealing with their situation, they understand that certain white colleagues, subordinates as well as supervisors, are always on the lookout for minor missteps and that any suggestion of vulnerability on their part can be politically devastating. Entirely aside from matters involving competence, the black employee, even when viewed as a team player, is also seen as—and feels himself to be—marginal.

Having survived the discomfiting security scrutiny, I took the elevator to the twentieth floor, where I entered a glass-enclosed suite. There I encountered the receptionist and asked for Robert Hopkins. She informed him of my presence and announced that he would come to greet me. A tall, square-jawed, brown-skinned man soon appeared dressed in a gray glen plaid suit, blue paisley tie, and wingtip shoes. Introducing himself in the presence of the receptionist as Bob Hopkins, he showed me into his office. As we spoke, I gathered that we both were somewhat taken aback. From our carefully cultivated telephone voices, we had each expected the other to be white. It took us a little while to recover from the shock.

After taking our seats, we made small talk and inquired about each other's background. Hearing that I was a professor at the University of Pennsylvania, he asked what courses I taught, and I answered, "Deviant Behavior, among others." This revelation was followed by silence, but then we both began to crack up and, after acknowledging the irony of our respective situations, laughed out loud, since we both might be considered deviant as successful black professionals in white-dominated institutions. With this realization we hit it off, becoming instant friends. In the conversation that followed, Bob agreed to make room for me in the organization and promised to provide me with information, office space, and contacts. He introduced me to a number of executives and over time this group grew as I met their friends and associates on and off the job.

While I was doing fieldwork in the firm, Bob and I would meet occasionally for breakfast or lunch at restaurants in Center City, comparing notes and discussing my tentative findings. Bob was a very helpful analytical guide and informant, mainly because he saw my project as an opportunity to learn more about his own organization. For six months I interviewed employees in my borrowed office and met them for lunch and drinks after work in various downtown venues. During those informal conversations I was able to gain a sense of what corporate life is like for black and white workers.

The first person Bob had me meet was a middle-aged black middle manager and sales representative, Jerry Thomas. As I entered the suite where Jerry worked, a well-dressed black female receptionist greeted me. When Jerry appeared, he approached me with a firm handshake that quickly evolved into a "black power" shake. Jerry was a tall, handsome, brown-skinned black man with a noticeable gap between his two large front teeth. He wore yellow trousers and a yellow striped shirt, hardly a "dress for success" out-fit. His self-presentation contrasted sharply with that of Bob Hopkins. And it was clear that Jerry was comfortable with the visible difference between himself and the vice president, as well as the white executives. Relaxed, spontaneous, and quite open, Jerry soon volunteered his sense of pride in not putting on what he considered to be a conformist appear-ance. He was self-consciously "Black" in a white firm, ran his own department, and in the minds of many was a fine black executive. Yet he was not long for the company, and this situ-ation eventually afforded us a more candid exchange.

Jerry's office, located in a back corner of the building, was elegant, with personal photographs and track trophies displayed on his desk and on the walls. Automobile models were mounted on a stand against the wall, and two of his most prized cars were prominently displayed on his large mahog-any desk. As we became acquainted, Jerry inquired about my background, including where I was raised and what schools I had attended. We discussed jazz and sports, and other cur-rent events, getting a read on each other.

I noticed that Jerry was surrounded and protected by a group of black secretaries and assistants. His department had a concentration of black people who seemed to work exclusively for him. Later he commented that he liked having his "own people" around, for when they greeted him each morning he could "be sure that they mean it." In his tone I noticed a distinct skepticism toward the white management group. In contrast, Bob had not displayed this attitude; he seemed comfortable with his white counterparts in the firm and trusted the motives of his white bosses. For his part, Jerry expressed concern about the management and the plans it had in store for him. His questions to me eventually turned on whom I was "working for" and what I was going to do with the information I gathered.

Although these are understandable questions, it was clear to me that Jerry had special concerns. He was highly distrustful of whites. Later I learned that he felt that most whites were unrepentant racists who had been conditioned to have very little respect for blacks, even those they knew and seemingly befriended. These attitudes marked him as a racially particularistic person. Over time I gathered that he had little respect for white people and "their" institutions. Yet, ironically, here he was working for a corporation in which whites were firmly in control and for whom he was required to perform well professionally.

Initially, Jerry was not entirely comfortable speaking with me, either, someone who was successful and teaching at a fine institution. Since Jerry had no respect for the white man's system, he had even less respect for those blacks who sought to become a part of it. At the same time he understood that blacks need to get along in that system, and for this he excused them. Jerry knew that he too had to "play the white man's game." In doing so, he admittedly displayed a certain amount of "gloss," including smiles, handshakes, and silences, when the situation required it. But in his case it was a relatively thin veneer. Jerry was not happy about these adjustments, but he understood their necessity. As I got to know him better, I found that he considered himself "a master of the game," and in time he tried to show me how he played it.

Upon arriving at work each day, this proud, racially particularistic black man would cloak himself in protective coloration. As he often told me, he trusted his white co-workers "about as far as [he] could throw them." This attitude of carefully concealed hostility was his way of managing himself among white people, most of whom, he was convinced, had contempt for him.

Making these adjustments, Jerry acknowledged, made him ever more frustrated at blacks like Bob Hopkins. The vice president was just the type of black person he did not want to become, and at work he did all he could to stay out of Bob's way. Bob dressed meticulously in the uniform of the executive suite. He was exceptionally articulate in standard English. Not only did Bob come across as well-spoken, but he also knew how to act to win the confidence of his white counterparts. His self-presentation was polished, and he seemed to know just what to say and do to "make them like him," to put white colleagues and superiors at ease. He was also highly competent at his job. These skills, and the willingness to employ them, had somehow escaped Jerry, and he was aware of the difference.

As I came to know Jerry better, he began to relax in my presence. I even bumped into him in my own West Philadelphia neighborhood, and he came to see that I was not a threat to him. Over time our many frank and free-flowing conversations taught me much about the organization in which he worked. All was not well at the firm. Jerry painted a complex picture of his organizational life, in which he was harassed daily and eventually marginalized. In one critical story after another, he related his beefs with his white colleagues and the "bad faith" he had discovered between them. His complaints centered on his feeling of being treated as a token with the complicity of his colleagues. In addition to Jerry's views I also sought out opposing ones, hoping to see the firm from a comprehensive perspective. In the end I became as interested in these differing viewpoints and orientations as in the dynamics of the organization as a whole.

After successive substantive interviews on and off the job and coming to know Bob, Jerry, and other employees with whom they worked, I began to realize that the experiences of these black men represented two distinct poles of cultural orientation not just in the organization for which they worked but within the black middle class more broadly.

COSMOPOLITAN AND ETHNOCENTRIC
ORIENTATIONS

These poles, which are alternative but sometimes coexisting orientations toward the social world, may be broadly conceived as ethnocentric and cosmopolitan. For short, I call them "ethnos" or "cosmos." In what follows, Bob stands for the cosmo and Jerry for the ethno orientation.

Born into a middle-class black family, Bob attended segregated public schools in the Deep South, but when he was twelve his family moved to the North. His father worked as a fifth-grade social studies teacher, while his mother was employed off and on as an office clerk for a downtown department store in Cleveland, Ohio. Bob attended a university just outside of Dayton, majoring in history and graduating in 1976. Along the way he gained an abiding interest in finance and enrolled in the MBA program at a private Catholic university in 1977.

Bob began working for his present firm in 1980. Because of his talent, his winning personality, and the good fortune of attracting the attention of a prominent Jewish mentor, he was placed on the corporate fast track. As he rose through the executive ranks, he was directed away from his field of expertise toward his current position as vice president for human resources. Bob said somewhat regretfully that although he "really wanted to be in finance," the company needed him in the department that handles employee relations, training, salaries, and benefits. The brass anointed him with a special status vis-à-vis lower-ranking black people in the workplace.[16]

Because Bob was trusted by the white establishment and considered a team player, he often became the go-to person for influential members of the firm. Whenever the CEO or any other top officer wanted advice about a black potential hire, they ran him or her by Bob, even though the job opening was out of his original area of expertise. At the time the black applicant's training appeared not to matter as much as whether or not he or she was likely to fit in with the culture of the firm. Bob's opinion carried special weight with the top management: if his assessment was positive, the person was likely to get the job.

While whites were generally comfortable with Bob and regarded him as a wunderkind, many blacks who worked for the corporation were not. Their assessments of Bob ran the gamut from "another brother" to "sellout" or "Uncle Tom." These negative attitudes were not expressed openly, but rather displayed behind his back, and he learned second-hand how he was regarded at the firm. The label that stuck was "head Negro in charge." As the most esteemed black employee in the firm, Bob was supposed to know which black employees were trustworthy. This role put him in an awkward position in between the top management and the other black employees. Those above him held him responsible for managing his colleagues, whereas those below him thought he should represent the concerns of all black workers. Bob had not sought out the role of "race man" or cultural broker; the managers enlisted him into this role because it was useful to them.

In contrast, Jerry grew up in segregated North Philadelphia, a sprawling ghetto where black people seldom encounter white people; indeed, if they do, they may presume that the white person is lost. Jerry developed a deep suspicion of white people that was to some extent a function of his relative isolation. After performing well in secondary school, he attended a local college and promptly landed a job at the firm. Although Bob was hired approximately five years after Jerry, Bob outdistanced him in terms of promotions and compensation.

At work Jerry did his job and tended to keep pretty much to himself. When his white colleagues invited him to lunch or to their homes, he accepted politely but usually made up an excuse not to go; mixing with his white colleagues was a low priority for him. His constant refusal to have much to do with his white colleagues outside of work appears to have given his colleagues reason not to invite him to their homes, in turn giving him ever more reason to decline when they did. His life around the firm, with the exception of his black assistants, was spent in a peculiar isolation not entirely of his own making, but for which he admittedly shared some responsibility.

The contrasts and continuities between ethnocentric and cosmopolitan attitudes of blacks like Jerry and Bob are explored in the next chapter.

6. | ETHNOS AND COSMOS

Among blacks of all classes, owing in large part to the peculiar institutions that have historically circumscribed African American life, racial particularism like Jerry's is widely shared. I use the terms "ethnocentrism" and "cosmopolitanism" to refer to attitudes or orientations of black persons and the cultural assumptions and behavior resulting from them.[1] Generally, ethnocentric[2] people emphasize loyalty to their own group, which is defined by ascribed characteristics, such as skin color, while cosmopolitans emphasize individuality and achievement, including education and experience. These views appear to govern racial conduct in the black community and how individuals define themselves and others. These perspectives, in practice, are not mutually exclusive, and can be thought of as a continuum. Individual black persons live by one orientation or the other or by both simultaneously. Most people code switch from time to time, depending on how they read a particular situation.[3]

Both types[4] may be observed up and down the class structure of the black community, but there are often class correlations between them. Generally, ethnocentric attitudes are strongly associated with the working and lower classes, and to some extent they are produced by feelings of social isolation. The individuals who hold these attitudes often emerge from highly segregated or racially particularistic backgrounds, and many continue to reside in such communities even when they have options to live elsewhere, for this is where they feel comfortable. Historically, within the iconic racially isolated black ghetto, the "white man"—whether represented by the slumlord, the storekeeper, the police, the courts, or some abstract symbol of social and political power—was often stereotyped, particularly by the most alienated residents, as "a cheat," "a devil," the epitome of evil. These observations have fueled the ideology of black separatism in inner-city black communities.

One of the reasons that black people so often assume the ethno position is the intense and complicated need to shield themselves and their family members against prospective or actual racial injury. It is not an unrealistic adaptation; the legacy of African Americans' long experience of social exclusion is a persistent, deep-seated wariness of how they might fare in white company. Will they meet with outright rejection, true goodwill—or a smiling mask that thinly conceals a racist mindset?

Most ethnocentric blacks are highly distrustful of whites. Some deeply alienated black people hold an extreme version of this perspective and have come to believe that dominant whites have a "plan" to debase, to dehumanize, and ultimately to destroy African Americans (including the folk belief that HIV/AIDS is a government plot against black people). This plot is not only manifested in a history of enslavement, sexual violation, lynching, and racial exclusion but also visible today in troubling racial disparities in major societal institutions, from health care to education, criminal justice, and employ-ment. The persistence of the ghetto underclass is viewed as a manifestation of racial discrimination, as is the evident politi-cal indifference to high death rates from preventable causes, including drugs and violence.

While many blacks strive for positive relations with their individual white counterparts, most hold whites and the insti-tutions they dominate in some reserve and can understand the frustration and anger of the more alienated. Such ethno-centric views take root and fester in hyper-segregated, socially isolated, and disfranchised ghetto communities.

Generally, in order to be successful professionally, blacks, like members of other groups, have been encouraged to fit in with the workplaces, divesting themselves of their ethnic particularities as a matter of form. At the same time, as blacks become upwardly mobile, they often encounter whites who hold more cosmopolitan views, or who at least present them-selves in this manner. In today's workplace they also observe whites who are highly ethnocentric, but for whom the open display of such an attitude has not been a clear disadvantage. Many blacks view white ethnocentrism as prejudice. This fact, along with the occasional hostility blacks encounter from whites on the job, encourages them to value expressions of ethnocentrism among their own. But this form of ethnocentrism is often justified as a precaution as well as a defense against racial injury. Hence, blacks who hold this view become highly sensitive to slights and what they readily perceive as racial slight.

Because the black ethnocentric perspective on the social world expresses itself mainly in terms of color and culture, individuals of this persuasion are strongly concerned with retaining and emphasizing their racial identity, or Blackness, in a predominantly white class context. In these circumstances all whites are considered suspect on the race question, and selective experiences of many ethnocentric blacks bear this out. Martin, a self-described ethno, articulated this orientation.

A middle-aged black professional and family man, Martin was hanging out one Saturday afternoon around the piano inside the Reading Terminal, eating his lunch with a lively and racially mixed crowd. The piano player, who was black, was taking requests and was able to satisfy a wide range of music lovers. At one point, Martin's friend Regina requested a gospel standard, which was something between an old slave song and a modern gospel song. The piano player obliged, and all were getting into the beat and enjoying the virtuoso performance. After a few such numbers, however, one of the white patrons rose and spoke to one of the managers, who was white. A few minutes later the manager approached and politely reprimanded the black piano player, who abruptly stopped playing the "offensive" music. Martin was appalled that such a thing could be happening inside the Reading Terminal. Wasn't this a place for all kinds of people, where tolerance and comity prevailed? After a while he departed, disturbed by the racial insensitivity he had just witnessed.

People like Martin have resigned themselves to the notion that whites are unalterably prejudiced against blacks, and many have come to believe that almost any relationship with a white person that is not clearly instrumental is likely to be a waste of time. Ethnocentric blacks characteristically observe a racial etiquette based on these assumptions. Their primary-group relations—that is, their personal relationships—tend to be almost exclusively with other blacks. In their daily affairs they either decline social invitations from whites or accept them mainly out of politeness or curiosity, or to serve a particular political purpose. Their own social gatherings are almost always exclusively black. In support of their orientation and their actions, they recall the history of the black experience, point to white racism and persistent social inequality, and feel uncomfortable in the presence of whites in social situations. They perceive racial prejudice as a continuing factor in interpersonal interactions, though it is rarely expressed overtly in polite company. And they pay particular attention to the treatment of black males in public places, especially their own relatives.

Because they lead relatively racially circumscribed lives, even middle-class black people in Philadelphia may well be ethnocentric. Yet, in order to excel, to achieve upward mobility, or even to thrive in the everyday work world, black people must engage whites. Indeed, they encounter whites more often than most whites encounter blacks; they must get along with white people. To do so, they tend to assume a professional attitude of civility and feigned trust. They might "make nice" to whites, and even make work friends with those whites who extend themselves, but these relationships typically go no farther than the workplace.

Beyond this group, however, some black people embrace the cosmo orientation. They not only tend to be middle to upper-middle class but have been positively exposed to the wider society and have had some positive relationships with white people. Sometimes their Christian upbringing is enough to persuade them to espouse this more humanistic perspective, but many of these individuals are interracially married and serve as cultural brokers between blacks and whites. They effectively bridge the racial divide.

Those living by the cosmo orientation appear to be much more accepting of people who are different from themselves, while holding on to important aspects of the ethno position. Exposed to the realities of their caste-like position every day, at work, on public transportation, or on the street, they know that racial inequality continues to be a fact of life in Philadelphia and that America is still far from being a postracial society. Yet they are willing to give white individuals the benefit of the doubt, and in their relations with them hope to be treated fairly. But since they typically don't really know the whites they encounter, they have to take them at their word and at their self-presentation. Yet they always remain unsure. When the cosmo meets a new white person, a nagging question arises: is this a "good" white person, or am I dealing with a stealth racist?

In contrast, the core ethno does not even entertain this question: he assumes that whites are unrepentant racists. Every white person he encounters starts with a deficit or has something to prove. It is likely that the white person will ultimately fail the various unspoken tests designed to determine whether he or she is "good."

The ethno knows that on the job he must deal with people who have little respect for him and may see him as a physical or economic threat. He understands that it is utterly impossible for them to treat him as an equal. He believes that they will tolerate him, or at least put up with him, but that is as far as their relationship can go. He is acutely aware that there is a limit to their tolerance of him and that, when he reaches that limit, all hell may break loose. He lives with this truth every day.

Significantly, the cosmo is not ignorant of this perspective, and because of the profound racial barriers it assumes, most of her close friends are black. As she moves comfortably in middle-class black and white circles, she tries to approach each new white person she meets as an individual. She tends to give whites the benefit of the doubt. Consistent with her education, sophistication, and class position, the cosmo is prepared to play down the importance of color and to see it as an insignificant issue. At social gatherings she values the opportunity to mingle and socialize with middle-class Jews, Italians, Irish, Iranians, and others—people who might view the world not strictly in terms of color or ethnicity and might be somewhat distant from their own ethnic backgrounds. In settings that include a diversity of people, the cosmopolitan black person is reasonably at home. Moreover, she is inclined to see herself as an individual, playing down the importance of racial affinity with black people and trying to choose friends based less on their color than on common interests and other affinities such as hobbies, school, church, or work. These people are often on the make and usually want to avoid limiting their social lives to just one group. They pride themselves on being cosmopolitan.

COSMO AND ETHNO SOCIAL GATHERINGS

The ethno party is usually a homogeneous affair. During the workday ethno people engage in a good deal of code switching between the cosmopolitan and the ethnocentric poles. The ethno gathering presents a respite from all that. The party is a place for black people to let their hair down and be themselves without having to perform race. The subtle implication is that the ethno orientation places your group above all others and is intolerant of those who are not your kind. This sort of gathering serves as a refuge from having to guess all the time whether the whites with whom you are dealing are either "for" or "against" you. The relaxation is badly needed, and many blacks, even the most cosmo, can savor such times.

The ethnocentric middle-class black person is simply not that interested in white people. Within the black community, competition for status does not include whites. Socializing and keeping up with one another happens in racially circumscribed contexts. As a rule, socially blacks matter most to other blacks, and what whites think about them is not relevant. The ethno party supports this attitude.

A few cosmos might be in attendance at an ethno party, but in settings like this they themselves might code switch and behave in more ethnically particularistic ways. The conversation takes off naturally, with stories, nods, and interactions that define the situation, reflecting one kind of person or another. If the ethnos win out, then that's the kind of party it becomes; if too many cosmos are present for things to go that way, then the ethnos become constrained.

When the situation is defined as cosmo, many people who may otherwise be ethno try to pass themselves off as cosmo, even when they experience dissonance with this performance. Those who experience dissonance are usually educated, middle-class people who come from relatively isolated working-class backgrounds and who typically have had less exposure to persons who are different from themselves. Often, their fathers and uncles were Philadelphia tradesmen or laborers and their mothers domestic workers, and they grew up and lived for a long time within ghetto or ethnic enclaves of the city. Such an upbringing can condition people to be suspicious of those who by their look or presence challenge deeply cherished values of ethnocentrism.

As we move toward a day when these particularities matter less and less, the ethno perspective may lose its force and cosmopolitan tolerance may take its place. Compared with those of the previous generation, more and more of today's young black people attend predominantly white private schools and grow up with white friends. A few even have married whites. As they grow and become educated, they see that no part of the city is off limits to them strictly because of their race or color. With their white counterparts they attend the symphony, or they eat out in fine restaurants. They begin to move easily in the white world and to feel comfortable in it. Unlike the ethno party, which reinforces the ethno perspective, the cosmo party—with all kinds of people in attendance, performing tolerance and civility—is a proving ground for this behavior, a practice session that prepares people to accept egalitarian cosmopolitanism in the wider social world.

There exists a tipping point at which people from more ethno backgrounds—whether white or black—may be overwhelmed in cosmo social situations. They may not appreciate the degree of cosmopolitanism they witness, and may feel uncomfortable, disturbed, even provoked. But here they are forced to stretch their minds to encompass and acknowledge the diversity of black as well as white people present. The situation becomes a learning experience; the next time they are in such a situation, it might be less offensive to them or, at least, less difficult to navigate.

CODE SWITCHING BETWEEN COSMO AND ETHNO

Charles, a black professional who works in a predominantly white organization, exemplifies the ethnocentric orientation with a cosmo gloss. This tall, good-looking, dark brown-skinned man in his early fifties works as an accountant for a large financial services firm in Center City. His wife, Carmen, a brown-skinned Puerto Rican, holds a prestigious position with a local communications firm. Together they have two lovely young children, who attend private academies on Philadelphia's Main Line, where they are among the rare black students. Charles's neighborhood and workplace associations afford him numerous opportunities to interact with a wide range of white people, from the working class to the upper class. These interactions never fail to amaze and provoke him, and he loves to share his accounts with me. In many respects he is more comfortable with his own people than with the members of other groups whom he knows from the corporation. The legacy of racial segregation continues to be an important theme in his life. This worldview shapes the framework by which he lives, setting his agenda and ordering his priorities.

Many of his white colleagues believe color caste is a thing of the past. His carefully composed behavior toward these whites confirms this for them. But what he reflects back to them is mainly gloss. He humors them, gaining their trust and then using them instrumentally. To get by them, he engages them in superficial small talk. This banter is empty, and both he and they know it, but his white co-workers are reluctant to call him on it. He must play this game with them. And it has to remain a game; for he cannot take them seriously without losing his self-respect.

His comfort level is strongly related to his color-caste status. Charles was raised in Chicago during the 1950s and 1960s. He attended black schools, worshipped at a black church, and lived in a black neighborhood. All his close friends were black. In sum, his primary-group relations—the interactions through which he came to define himself—were racially particularistic. He harbored no hostile feelings toward his white counterparts; he did not even dislike them. Growing up in an essentially black world, he simply didn't know them. While associating mainly with black people, he competed socially with his black peers, forming his own standards and values in the process.

Today Charles must make his way in a white-dominated world, particularly his workplace. His formal college and professional education socialized him into "white ways" and prepared him for life in the wider society and the middle class. White people more easily dominate this culture in a number of ways, ranging from how they speak to how they treat one another and what they appear to value. In order to get ahead, Charles has had to learn these ways and even to make them his own. In so doing, however, he sometimes overcompensates. His clothes are always a bit more stylish than those of his white counterparts and his presentation always somewhat more polished. Whether it is accurate or not, he has the feeling that he must perform in their presence. His adaptation to this situation can be seen in the nearly new high-performance car he drives. He takes care to be correct in his behavior, speech, and appearance, for he is constantly scrutinized in a way his white counterparts are not. He understands that he is held to a different, and more exacting, standard, even if this is not always the case. He responds with a degree of care that may become ritualistic. He sticks to his own rules even when they may be incompatible with the larger goals of his organization. He'd rather "go by the book" and be mediocre than risk being wrong or opening himself to criticism. This sense of insecurity is inherent in his situation, and his presentation of self reflects it.

Many successful blacks feel that they must hold back when reaching out to other black people. The system works in such a way that a successful black professional may feel constrained by his own precarious position. While he himself may be trusted, often he is unsure just how much change the system can tolerate. He has been able to get around the white people at work, but, uncertain that other blacks will be as successful, he must be wary in vouching for them. So he "plays his white folks" in order to secure his own continued success.

At home Charles and his family keep largely to themselves. He lives in a predominantly white, upper-income neighborhood, where white strangers are constantly trying to make sense of him. They even whisper that he might be a drug kingpin, according to one of his white neighbors who befriended him. Charles and his family attend a large fashionable Baptist church in North Philadelphia. He wants his children to have a black identity, but not so much that it holds them back. No one in his family associates with anyone in the ghetto, though he tries to remain close to his extended family. Politically, he and his wife support candidates who advocate initiatives that promise to better the condition of black people. Yet this support is always offered from a distance.

On a warm and sunny Saturday afternoon in the spring, Charles and I sit at the Chestnut Hill Starbucks, drinking lattes and looking casually out the large window, watching the passing crowd in this upscale area, largely white but dotted with a few black faces. When Charles and I meet, we always compare notes about what has been happening, sometimes simply marveling at how far we've come in life, how different life is for black men like us than for our fathers and grandfathers. We share stories about the state of the world and about the white people we've encountered along our way. Sometimes we joke that sharing these stories is a way of maintaining our sanity. Today he has a big one. After we settle into our perch in the window, he begins.

Yesterday Charles's Lexus was being serviced, and Brad, one of his white colleagues, offered him a ride home, which Charles accepted. Soon he realized he'd made a mistake: "I forgot myself." He didn't know this man very well; they were only casual acquaintances at work. Charles grew nervous as the small talk about the Sixers gave way to talk about local politics—where Charles is careful not to go—and then turned to their families. Brad was very curious about Charles. But his comments seemed to center on the question, "How does a black man like you get to a place like this?" When they arrived at Charles's driveway, Brad blurted out, "You live here?" "Yeah, this is it," Charles replied. "This is where I live." As Brad's late-model Toyota came to a stop, he got out and walked around, asking, "Where does your property line run?" and heading around the side of Charles's house. Charles explained how they found their house and how much they liked the area, but he could tell that Brad was not fully satisfied and wanted more. "He wanted to come inside and check out my house, but I just put him off, and finally I got rid of him," Charles said. "Man, I thought the dude would never leave."

We both chuckled, underscoring what middle-class blacks understand about race relations. Black people in Charles's position hesitate to allow strangers into their homes, especially whites. "You never let just any white person in your house," he told me. Charles felt that he had allowed his white colleague to obtain a glimpse of his backstage. With the right white people, such familiarity might not necessarily be a problem. But a man like Charles must deal with all types of white people. Some may appreciate him as a person or even as a potential friend, but others in the workplace are resentful, tacitly but firmly believing that black people are taking jobs that rightfully belong to people like themselves. With such an attitude, they do all they can to put Charles back in his place. Charles's concern was that when Brad returned to the firm with "all this information" on him and his digs, word would then spread that he lives in a "mansion in a rich neighborhood," inspiring jealousy and envy among peers at work.

Charles is anxious to distinguish the "good" white people, who mean him well, from the "bad" white people, who mean him ill. In this effort, he becomes a close student of white people, noting their ways, proclivities, and hang-ups. He is acutely aware of the strange attitudes harbored by the kinds of whites with whom we both work. A primary goal of people who inhabit this slice of the black middle class is self-protection. But the problem is interpretive. Bombarded with so many different white people every day, he places each new contact on probation. He traverses the shoals of the workplace, managing his identity while also trying to manage those he encounters.

As a defensive strategy, Charles "floats" at work. To those who scrutinize his personal performances, he appears rather superficial. His gloss deflects attention and enables him to get through his day. He flits from one person to the next, a one-liner here, a two-liner there. By remaining a "moving target," he passes as a cosmopolitan person.

Charles is savvy enough to know that to present his ethno side would be inappropriate and would likely get him into trouble on the job, impeding his progress and undermining the comfort that he has worked so hard to establish with his white co-workers, many of whom themselves are also recent and perhaps socially insecure arrivals to the middle class. Emerging from the ethnic neighborhoods of Philadelphia or from those of other cities, those white people often have relatively little experience with black people, and many are not likely to be positively disposed toward them, much less to befriend them. Yet, to be professional, they too must present an acceptable front, both to their white co-workers and to people like Charles.

Charles has made his own study of the workplace. He knows from experience that a person who is comfortably upper-middle class is likely to be less prejudiced toward people like himself than an insecure white person from the working class. In fact, a white of the upper-middle class might feel affirmed by his presence and even work to assist his upward mobility. Yet he can never be sure quite how interracial interactions will play out. Charles must juggle life in two worlds, and his guardedness causes significant discomfort.

RACIAL ADVERTISEMENTS

For cosmos life is more complex and variable. When they face such ordinary trials, race is not the foremost issue they consider; instead, cosmos bend over backwards to look for nonracial reasons for unfortunate outcomes. When confronted with a crisis or setback, others see the racial angle as a sufficient explanation of events, but cosmos are not convinced. This view emerges from their educational foundation and the premium they place on rational thought. Cosmos can't quite get their head around the arbitrariness of racially related behavior and resist this analysis at every turn.

Those who have espoused elite values are often careful to manage their public image so as to uphold such standards in every detail. They are perhaps fearful that their behavior might inadvertently betray their origins.

I encountered one cosmo family at eleven on a Friday morning a few days before New Year's in the foyer of the Four Seasons hotel. He was a light-complexioned man of about fifty, sharply though conservatively dressed in a dark suit with a white shirt and necktie, a black cashmere overcoat, a black bowler hat, and shiny black dress shoes. She was a brown-skinned woman of about forty-five. She wore a stylish brown dress, dark-brown shoes, and an overcoat with reddish dyed mink. Their three children—a girl of fourteen, a boy of ten, and a girl of seven—were dressed fashionably in designer clothes. It was clear that great attention had been given to the children's appearance, and in public they beamed.

The family approached the foyer with no luggage, which suggested they were on their way to visit friends or relatives rather than leaving for the airport. It seemed that they had arrived late for Christmas, because the children carried presents: the older girl had a large box wrapped in green paper with gold string and a bow; the boy a smaller, equally tastefully wrapped box.

As they waited in the foyer for their car, the woman traversed the lobby and disappeared, while the husband monitored the children. As he stood by the front door out of the passageway, he motioned to his young son to do the same, gesturing as though he were directing traffic. The boy responded quickly to his father's nonverbal instructions, while the girls sat on a platform and leaned against a pillar. Soon the mother returned from the gift shop, a third package in hand, and rejoined her husband, who continued to stand up straight, military style, tending his flock. In a few minutes, the uniformed bellman informed him that his car had arrived. The man gathered up his family and corralled them into the black Cadillac Escalade. After making sure that everyone was safely situated, he walked around the car, slipped into the driver's seat, and drove away.

What are the societal implications of this scene? This man might not be recognized as African American if his darker-complexioned wife and children did not accompany him. If they saw him by himself or in an otherwise all-white group, many white Americans—though not so many African Americans—might take him for white. In truth, he probably has some Irish or German ancestry, but he does not play up that part of his background. Indeed, he is careful not even to seem to be trying to pass for white. Like most black people in this country, he can trace his ancestry back to both Europeans and Native Americans, but because of the history of the caste-like system of race relations he emphasizes his African ancestry.

At the same time it is likely that for generations his extended family has belonged to the small black middle class. This is less obvious for his wife, though it could be just as true; members of the old black elite varied widely in skin color. Previous generations may well have served the black community, but the black middle class is no longer enclosed by racial segregation. It is likely that this man is a lawyer, a doctor, or a business executive for a large corporation. He came to Philadelphia during the holidays to visit relatives and chose to stay at the Four Seasons. Perhaps they will be off the next day, returning to Atlanta, D.C., Chicago, or Columbus. White passersby might make less informed inferences, but they would probably be impressed by the family's appearance of wealth and privilege.

The whites in the lobby and the black bellmen learn something about race in contemporary America by observing this man and his family. If they discuss him, they may remark on his dignity and poise, or his evident care for his well-behaved children. If they do not discuss him, that too is significant, for it implies that they take the existence of a wealthy black family for granted. That fact alone speaks volumes for how much race relations have changed over time. The visible presence of such a family in an upscale venue like the Four Seasons suggests to white observers that a black person can be among the elite and not just at the bottom of the social hierarchy. As the number of black people like this man and his family increases, better treatment of black people is promoted.

With the presence of black people who possess status, education, cultivation, and dignity, the position of the race in public estimation improves. Indeed, the apparent rise in the fortunes of such African Americans may well have lent credence to the mistaken notion that programs designed to incorporate large numbers of blacks into the occupational structure are no longer necessary. The truth is more complex: black poverty has not been alleviated, but class divisions among blacks have increased. Those who would exhibit their middle-class status must differentiate themselves carefully from their inner-city cousins.

Most blacks, even those holding a cosmopolitan outlook, generally assume that racism persists in American society, and because of this view most of their close friends are black. Yet, in everyday life, social class generally outweighs racial influences, and cosmos move comfortably among both whites and blacks in middle-class circles. They are prepared to minimize the importance of color in their own lives and to make friends from a variety of ethnic backgrounds. At social gatherings they play down ethnicity, or perhaps ignore it altogether. In Philadelphia the cosmo black person is a rare breed. Typically he or she is found in an interracial marriage, or grew up in a biracial family in one of the city's few integrated neighborhoods. A few blacks raised in segregated communities elsewhere come to accept interracial associations in college and professional school.

RICHARD

The most cosmopolitan black Philadelphian I know became firmly attached to the dominant culture in his youth. Richard, now seventy years old, is a retired professor. He was born and lived in the South Bronx, near Colin Powell's old neighborhood, and attended racially integrated schools until the eighth grade, when the tight-knit neighborhood was being abandoned by Italian and Irish immigrants and gangs were beginning to emerge. Seeing the neighborhood deteriorate, Richard's parents searched for an acceptable school. Although not from a privileged background, he was a very good student with exceptional musical interest and talent. During his formative years he studied classical violin and, after excelling in his courses, took more advanced lessons. Later, because his parents could not afford to send him to college, he joined the Army; after serving for two years with assignments in Korea, he attended college on the GI Bill. He went to graduate school at the University of Wisconsin and on obtaining his advanced degree settled in Philadelphia with his wife and two daughters. His interest in classical music persisted, and he became a devotee of the professional music culture of Philadelphia and a supporter of the arts. When they were ready for formal lessons, he enrolled his children in the Settlement Music School, where Richard and I first met.

Part of his attraction to Philadelphia was the fact that many members of his extended family live in the North Philadelphia ghetto, and he has siblings in nearby New Jersey. At the same time, because he is an academic, many of his friends are members of the black middle class. Those factors made Philadelphia attractive to him.

Richard plays the violin as a skilled amateur, and he serves on the board of the Philadelphia Chamber Music Society and on committees of the Philadelphia Orchestra. He has often pressed his colleagues to be more inclusive of minorities and to expand opportunities for inner-city young people to be exposed to classical music. But, while his colleagues say that they would like to have more black people in their audiences at the Kimmel Center or in their programs, he remains one of the few representatives of his race at most performances. A few years ago Richard played a major part in a campaign to bring Marian Anderson's grandnephew to the orchestra in the role of guest conductor. The campaign was a success and was especially meaningful for the city's black community, because representation at this level is rare. Richard says he sometimes thinks that his colleagues prefer it that way, for the exclusiveness of their circle is a testament to their elite status. To Richard, however, the musical heritage of Europe and America is universal.

At periodic recitals at the Settlement Music School, which he continues to support, we became better acquainted and friends. He and his wife attended these recitals to support his young daughters. After arduous work under the careful tutelage of professional musicians who moonlight there, the many young students perform before family and friends on Sunday afternoons. The recital takes place in a former synagogue on Wynnefield Avenue in West Philadelphia. The audience is racially diverse. At recitals African Americans mix with Jews, Italians, Irish, and others, especially at the receptions, where they enjoy apple juice and cookies. One of the most striking sights to behold is that of working-class, and occasionally poor, African American young people competently playing classical music on instruments as varied as the violin, piano, flute, oboe, and marimba. One outstanding immigrant piano teacher who lived in the Russian Jewish community of Philadelphia's northeast, a place in the city known, particularly among blacks, for its intolerance of black people, had numerous black students who became exceptional performers.

From the pews families and friends listen, feeling alternately proud of and nervous for their children. Occasionally, a young person shines brilliantly, and everyone notices and applauds, regardless of race or ethnicity; others fall flat and are comforted by all. In this setting racial-ethnic divisions become blurred, and everyone gets along wonderfully. That is possible because of a critical mass of middle-class blacks and other minority-group members who support the education of their children and, in this endeavor, encounter like-minded white people. In fact, the Settlement Music School has a policy of promoting racial and class diversity through its scholarship programs. The important social lessons learned in this canopy environment are taken elsewhere by the members of the school community.

Still, most black people view the symphony and the theater as "white" places and consider the activities conducted there off limits for black people. Blacks who do attend risk being viewed by other blacks as "not black enough." They may think of themselves as cultured or cosmopolitan, but other blacks may think of them as having sold out or being an "Oreo."[5] Many blacks would not like to deal with the ambiguity about their identity and commitment to the race that would accompany such involvement, so they do not attend. This impression is reinforced by the fact that black people are seldom represented on the stage and in the orchestra. Few blacks are inclined to pay money to see and hear people who don't look like them; when performers are black, black attendance increases dramatically. Moreover, the difficulties and challenges inherent in all excursions into the white ethno space make the prospect of being around so many whites for the afternoon more objectionable than enjoyable. The same reasoning explains blacks' absence from public places where we might expect to see them well represented.

In their technical and service-related jobs, middle-class blacks gain exposure to the wider culture and embrace the need to get along with professional peers. Because of their middle-class position, their child-care arrangements, the schools their children attend, and even their children's play groups tend to be predominantly white, their ethnocentric reservations notwithstanding. Many participate in the home and school association in their neighborhood or magnet school. Through these activities, those blacks who are so inclined may come to know the parents of white children socially, as individuals and not simply as members of a racial category. On occasion cosmos attend the theater with white friends; some even take up pastimes previously exclusive to whites, such as golf or tennis.

Indeed, because of racialized social stratification and the limited number of middle-class blacks in many settings, cosmos are often the only black persons, or among a very few black persons, who attend social affairs hosted by their white colleagues and friends. In these circumstances they become "race ambassadors," a role that some embrace and many others disdain.

Many working-class and poor black people are ethnocentric because they have limited exposure to white people who are not agents of the dominant society in the ghetto. The social isolation they experience encourages them to feel that the wider society is profoundly unreceptive to them and to all black people. This orientation is different from that of the more chauvinistic ethnocentrists, who actively reject assimilation. Similarly, some cosmopolitan black persons genuinely desire to be part of the wider system, while others are passively integrationist, with a primarily instrumental orientation toward the whites with whom they come into contact at work and elsewhere in the city.

Many blacks and whites get along in public by adopting a cosmo orientation in interracial settings and an ethno orientation when they feel more relaxed. Their behavior is dictated largely by the definition of the situation, as they think of it. When their paths cross, blacks and whites politely and carefully accommodate one another. When necessary, both may behave as though they are part of the same social world. This self-presentation is most common under the cosmopolitan canopy, where people come together, engage in mutual reconnaissance, and put on their best social behavior. When they leave these settings, however, they often return to a much more racially segregated, ethnically particularistic social world.

7. | THE BLACK MIDDLE CLASS IN PUBLIC

On the journey from particularistic neighborhood enclaves into the cosmopolitan city, we see telling interactions between blacks and whites. Like many Philadelphians, I use public transit to go downtown and rely on taxis to get around once I'm there. From my home in Chestnut Hill, a racially mixed but predominantly white "suburb within the city," I take the SEPTA (Southeastern Pennsylvania Transit Authority) train from St. Martins station. Typically, a handful of people wait inside the station or on the benches outside and along the tracks. Those who board the train here are most often business executives, lawyers, accountants, professors, and young students, with women and men represented in roughly equal numbers. Apart from Lucy, the African American clerk, I am usually the only black person. This morning two other black people, a middle-aged woman and an elderly man, are waiting on the platform. Everyone is polite, even pleasant. Neighbors greet one another, and those whose faces have become familiar nod hello.

Public transportation reflects the class and racial composition of Philadelphia neighborhoods, which, like many other big-city residential areas, remain racially segregated. Black and white urbanites alike may be put off by the anonymous "ghetto-looking" black male, but there has recently emerged some feeling that because of terrorism perpetrated by Middle Eastern–looking men, a large black man may be a welcome presence to some who were formerly most prejudiced toward black males.

The code of civility that defines the cosmopolitan canopy can break down in various ways on public transportation. People occasionally complain about seating or loud music and can be offended by one another. In particular, when race and gender come together in the presence of the anonymous black male, the ideals of civility and cosmopolitanism are severely tested. Observations on regional trains like the R8 show that the anonymous black male is often the last person others will sit next to. Black men generally agree that they can ride the length of the train line seated alone, unless the train is crowded and seating is scarce. Black men of all social classes understand full well that they are avoided on public transportation. It is common knowledge among black men that they are stigmatized or degraded in public in this way, not just by whites but sometimes by other blacks. The black male may put white people off just by virtue of being black, and the younger he is and the more "ghetto" he looks, the more distrust he engenders. This leads many to the working conception or folk belief that white people, protestations to the contrary notwithstanding, generally dislike black people, especially black males, and seek distance from those they do not know.

As young black men talk about this issue among themselves, it seems as though each man has a story about prejudice and discrimination in public, but especially of police harassment. Being avoided in public is a dominant theme. Whether or not there is truth to this in some objective sense, it is too often believed to be true by the black male, leading him to develop his own sense of group position vis-à-vis the wider society, especially white people. In this respect black men engage in folk ethnography among themselves, comparing notes and developing coping strategies for avoiding such arbitrary treatment in public and salvaging their self-respect.

At times they may attempt to turn the tables. Believing that whites generally wish to avoid them in public, they make the first move to control the situation, or to avoid the "other" first. In truth, other blacks will also sometimes seek to avoid anonymous young black males about whom they are uncertain, though blacks are usually more savvy about distinguishing which black person it is who poses an authentic threat in public; intimately familiar with black life, they are often capable of making finer distinctions than their white counterparts can make.

Around Philadelphia, some black men have taken to devising tests for whites who might face the choice of sitting next to them on public transportation, particularly buses of the city. After spotting an available seating area, including both an aisle and a window, the young man will move deliberately to the aisle seat, and leave the window seat empty, thereby requiring anyone wishing to sit down to pass by him to acquire the window seat, which many passengers view as desirable. Deciding he would rather ride with the seat to himself, he will then adopt an off-putting appearance, displaying looks geared to make others nervous and determined to avoid him. His bet is that most passengers will not want to cross the barrier he has set, but if a white person is willing to request the seat and then to sit down, this person then passes the test. A white person willing to run the gauntlet, as it were, may be judged acceptable and not a "racist." Some black men acknowledge that they are sometimes taken by surprise when a white person does request the seat; then they may welcome the person and even engage him or her in conversation. He or she passes the test.

After buying my ticket, I catch up with Lucy. We've known each other for several years, and when I take the R8 into town we always chat. When other riders approach the ticket window, I move aside. We resume our conversation, but soon the train approaches, and she announces, "Train is arriving!" We say our goodbyes, and I'm off to board the train. The conductors—two African American, one white—direct passengers up the steps. Not many seats are occupied yet, for the train has made only a few stops. Except for the conductors and we three riders, everyone on the train is white, reflecting the makeup of Philadelphia's outer neighborhoods. As the train makes its way through Mount Airy, Germantown,

and North Philadelphia toward downtown, the complexion of the riders changes steadily from white to black. By
the time the train reaches Thirtieth Street Station, the cars
are packed with black and white passengers. The next stop
is Allen Lane in Mount Airy–Germantown. One black man,
two black women, and one white woman enter the car and
seat themselves. A little later another black male enters the
car, approaches me, and without making eye contact, takes
a seat in front of me. The train is beginning to fill, and by
now almost every three-across seat has at least one passenger.
All the passengers seem to prefer sitting by themselves for as
long as they can. On occasion I've bumped into neighbors
or friends on this train and shared my seat with them for the
duration of the trip to town, but not today.

As we proceed into the city, the empty spaces fill. At the
next stop many more passengers, a mix of black and white
men and women, board and move through the train search-
ing for a seat. Riders readjust themselves and their belongings to make room for the additions. The etiquette here
roughly resembles that surrounding the benches in the park
at Rittenhouse Square. If people cannot easily sit alone, they
may opt to sit with a person who they believe looks least likely
to cause them trouble or distress. Generally, people's comfort level with others appears to take priority. Black as well as
white riders behave this way.

As more black passengers board, they sit by themselves,
but as the train becomes more crowded, they find themselves sharing a seat with someone. Black persons, male

and female alike, tend to choose seats where another black person is already sitting. So marked is the avoidance of African Americans by whites that black people often spend an entire regional train ride seated alone. Few treat this as a privilege. Black men experience this shunning most often, but black women voice complaints as well. When the car fills up, a white person might take a seat next to a black person. The two might even become engaged in a brief conversation, though this seldom happens.

When a "better" seat becomes available, the black person might expect the white person to abruptly pick up and move, perhaps seeking to escape an uncomfortable situation, and if he does not move, it may surprise the black person and even become a story that he will later share with his friends. After several more stops on the R8, as more and more riders board the train, almost all of the three-across seats are occupied by two persons, with a rider on either end leaving a vacant space in the middle. Eventually, the middle seats begin to fill up. The train makes a stop, and the white male conductor bellows out, "Tulpehocken," and then opens the door. No one departs, while new passengers board and enter this car. The proportion of blacks to whites increases. My car is now about 60 percent white and 40 percent black. Significantly, all the people of color appear to be African American; not one is identifiably Hispanic, South Asian, or African.

By the time we reach Queen Lane, a stop in close proximity to a public housing project, everyone boarding is black, except for an Asian woman, a white man, and a white woman.

The ridership is now about fifty-fifty black and white. The white middle-aged conductor walks the aisle taking tickets. He makes direct eye contact, smiles, and greets some of the regular passengers he knows. The elderly black man who got on in Chestnut Hill stands in the aisle to stretch his legs and exchanges a few words with other passengers.

People use cell phones freely, but tend to keep their conversations quiet. Across the aisle from me a middle-aged white man types on his laptop. As we approach North Philadelphia, a sign appears just above the station emblazoned with the hand-painted words "City of Brotherly Love." At this point the conductor murmurs, "Thirtieth Street Station will be next." People begin to collect their bags, preparing to exit the train. The public address system comes on for the first time, announcing loudly, "Six to eight minutes to Amtrak Thirtieth Street Station."

By now the disembarking riders have gathered up their stuff and are standing in the aisle. A black male conductor stands outside on the platform and herds us to the station entrance. The departing riders meet and pass those boarding the train, exchanging places in a delicate ballet. Then we crush through the station doorway to begin our descent to the concourse below.

THE THIRTIETH STREET STATION

We are engulfed by hustle and bustle, as travelers pass one another intent on getting to their destination. The station personnel stick to their tasks, working around this throng to get their jobs done. A young white man and a young black woman push their trash carts toward the plastic cans in opposite corners, moving in unison, constantly emptying the bins. Riders seem oblivious as they go on about their business. A few stop and queue up at the newsstand to buy a paper, a sweet treat, or a lotto ticket. More stop at Dunkin' Donuts and get coffee or breakfast before continuing on to work.

All this is happening in a wide, elevated anteroom to the main part of Thirtieth Street Station, a hub for Philadelphia's regional rail. Amid the stream of arriving passengers moving toward the station proper and the outside doors, some people—both black and white—are seated on the benches in the middle of the concourse. One white male rider leads a blind man. A young black man sits down as he answers a call on his cell phone. Another cell phone rings, and the woman answers, speaking to her friend within earshot of a small group of bystanders. A woman groans; it seems that every other person has a cell phone. Passengers heading for the Amtrak trains pull their baggage along, approaching the walkway leading away from the local trains and opening out into the main station.

Some pause to drink their coffee. Others head for the SEPTA ticket window, where they stand and wait. The sound of the trains rumbling in and out of the station penetrates the din. A woman police officer appears, the first I've seen all morning. As we approach the large opening to the vast, high-ceilinged lobby of Thirtieth Street Station, some riders rush past, eager to go outside to catch their taxis and buses and get on with the day's business. I notice an Asian priest, a young woman at his side, heading down the ramp.

Most of this traffic is one-way, from the suburbs to the city; later in the day, this spectacle is reversed. I follow the throng marching along toward the opening to the grand station, less grand than New York's Grand Central Terminal, but nevertheless quite impressive. The Thirtieth Street Station serves as a major interchange for residents, as well as a portal to the city for visitors who arrive via Amtrak. Mass transit in the form of SEPTA, the urban-suburban rail system, extends to the airport and throughout the metropolitan region. The station's massive size, clean, modern lines, cement construction, cavernous ceilings, and stunning art deco interior convey a solidity and spirit of conviction that its history and present state call into question.

Planned in the late 1920s, when the Pennsylvania Railroad epitomized the successes of the corporate system, it was completed in 1933, after the financial panic and depression had shaken confidence in the American economy. Though this grand building is adjacent to the underground subway station, the tunnel between them was closed because of what the city euphemistically described as "concerns" about crime and vagrancy, so one waiting room ends in an oddly blank wall. Still, the place is as lively as any downtown train station.

At the bottom of the ramp, at the far end in the corner, are a flower shop, a busy concourse area leading to Market Street, an Au Bon Pain, a shoeshine stand, then a food court, and, down the way a bit, another newsstand. I make my way through the expanse, past these establishments and the shiny and sparsely occupied wooden benches that resemble church pews, through the mass of humanity milling about waiting for connections, be they people or trains, and past the statue of "the angel." Installed in 1950 to honor the 1,307 Pennsylvania Railroad employees who were killed in World War II, the bronze statue shows the archangel Michael lifting the body of a dead soldier out of the flames of war. Though the monument sometimes transfixes visitors, commuters pass this provocative statue without a second glance.

Immediately outside the doors on the east side of the building is the taxi stand, where would-be riders wait in line. The queue is racially mixed, but contains an overwhelming number of white professionals en route to their meetings and workplaces. It always includes a smattering of black people, almost all of them middle-class.

CANOPIES IN PUBLIC AND PRIVATE

In Center City the concentration of canopies has a synergistic effect that creates a series of cosmopolitan zones in which various kinds of people are on the move or simply hang out. This space outside the canopy is somewhat wilder, without the social controls that encourage common acts of civility and comity.

In those zones diverse people pursue their everyday affairs, navigating the public space largely in small clumps.

The clumps may be formed for protection or simply for company: two white boys here; a white family of four there; a group of four black homeboys over there, all dressed in white T-shirts and making their way about the downtown area. As these clumps navigate the space, they appear as segregated groupings; whites run with whites, and blacks with blacks. The clumps are generally civil to one another, though black clumps can arouse fear in others owing to their reputation for violence.

A hierarchy of comfort can be discerned: white women, black women, white men, and then black men. In public, ethnicity is not always visible and discernible, but color and gender are. When people look for and read visual cues, these characteristics become significant, and even operative, in determining who means what to whom in the public space. White women and their male counterparts may tense up around lone black males, moving away or clutching their pocketbooks. Through such actions, all are taught about what to expect in public. These feelings of discomfort or irritability may dissipate as the noisome agent becomes better known and understood as harmless or nonthreatening.

It would be naive to think that this hierarchy of functional prejudice is left outside the workplace door. The attitude finds its way inside, albeit in a watered-down fashion, through presumptions that may express themselves in the degree or amount of respect or disrespect that people encounter in these settings.

Many of these lessons are drawn from observations of

activities on the outside as people engage in folk ethnography. These observations may generate not only common sense but confusion and misunderstandings. For instance, black males often think whites who avoid them in public are simply racist or worse. Young black males generally walk with a certain swagger, moving about as though they own the downtown streets. This defensive posture is useful in the 'hood, but not necessary downtown. Yet it is employed anyway, often without deliberate thought, even under the canopy.

Middle-aged and older black males tend to be much more polite and solicitous of others, including whites. Black women and men seem to be most helpful to those with disabilities; they display a degree of empathy that is lacking among many. It may well be that because of the long history of their subjugation by the white majority, blacks are generally able to empathize with victims of injustice—just as Jews, because of their history, are often said to empathize with blacks.

Situated between working-class and poor blacks on the one hand and the white middle class on the other, the black middle class occupies an awkward and often uncomfortable position. Members of the black middle class lead a peculiarly marginal existence.[1] The American Dream promises that hard work leads to success, respectability, and social acceptance, but they find that white society still treats them like members of a stigmatized black caste. At the same time, their material success sets them apart from the rest of the black community.[2]

On the streets of Center City, members of the black

middle class are recognizable to those who take the time to observe them by their bearing, grooming, and, most strikingly, dress. They are often dressed fashionably, sometimes with an understated flair. They take style to the nth degree; their white colleagues may appear underdressed by comparison. One reason for this difference is that black people have traditionally been unable to take their appearance for granted. Whether or not this self-presentation actually matters to nonblacks, the impression they make is often uppermost in their own minds. They look for the best they can afford in clothes, cars, and liquor. Expensive and fashionable dress is very often preferred by members of this group, which can set the stage for invidious comparisons among friends and associates. In the predominantly white workplace, black persons at times feel they are "on," a feeling that encourages them to be at their best, but also to be careful to abide by certain rules of propriety. A form of ritualism develops, particularly in the presence of those who could impose sanctions for unwitting violations.

Members of this group prefer to maintain cultural and class distinctions between themselves and other blacks. Reserved and quiet, they dislike situations in which they might come face-to-face with discrimination. When they go out into the world, they are often sensitive to slights and derision of any kind. Signs of a problem discourage them from remaining in the setting and may drive them away permanently. News of a bad experience reverberates throughout the community. Not only may the place be shunned in the future, but the entire class of places like it may be avoided. Blacks look for signs that something is wrong—the fact that no blacks work there, that no blacks hold authority positions, that the place has a "white bread" air—and when they find evidence of such conditions they conclude that the place is not hospitable to black people.

Significantly, blacks take careful and immediate note of welcome signs in social settings. People come to a place once, talk to their friends, family, and others, and return later. Word gets around: this place is good for blacks. Slowly, a penetration begins, and if all goes well the number of blacks who frequent the place grows. At some point a critical mass of black clients is reached and the place becomes known as "Black."

Such black-themed Philadelphia restaurants as Bluezette, Zanzibar Blue, and Warmdaddy's, like their counterparts in other cities around the country, owe their existence both to the growing affluence of black people as a group and to the recent emergence of a black middle class that is increasingly separated from, though not entirely independent of, the traditional black community. Blacks who return to the 'hood do so in order to get in touch with their roots or to get a fix of black culture, since their suburban neighborhoods and predominantly white workplaces permit them very little relaxed contact with other blacks. They gravitate to where blacks tend to congregate to relieve the stress they experience as they navigate through the dominant white society. Such a place provides a refuge where they do not have to be "on" for white folks.

This pattern of sticking with one's own kind is a reaction to the treatment blacks have historically experienced when they have tried to operate in the white-dominated society. Blacks go where they believe they can be safe, congregating in places where they are accepted. They also reward their friends and punish their enemies by giving and restricting patronage. They gather whenever they see visible signs of acceptance, even if they do not really know the other people who hang out there. What matters is that their brothers and sisters generally make them feel comfortable, or at least don't make them feel uncomfortable because of subtle racial antipathy.

Fortunately for today's middle-class blacks, the world is full of options. No one restricts them to this or that place, so they have been granted a certain paradoxical freedom. They can segregate themselves if they choose and "stick with their own kind"; they alone are responsible for this self-imposed separation of the races. Self-segregation is acceptable.

Form and self-presentation are very important to the members of the black middle class. They do not want to come off as bold and boisterous. Because color is still so powerful, when upper-middle-class blacks dress casually, others do not distinguish them from their less successful brothers and sisters. So part of the unconscious—and sometimes very self-conscious—agenda of the black middle class is to target

people who might not be making such distinctions and disabuse them of their misconceptions. Members of the black
middle class work hard to avoid being confused with their
lower-class counterparts.[3] In their actions they make the
claim that they are individual members of an economic class,
not representatives of a racial caste. At the same time they
buy into racial particularism as a defense mechanism. It is
a paradoxical explanation of their failure to stand out from
the black lower classes.

When a black woman appears in an extravagant outfit or
a black man is driving a Lexus, the person's blackness overwhelms the image she or he is trying to project. An expensive
dress or a flashy car means something different when exhibited by black people. The man might be seen as a drug dealer,
the woman as a prostitute. Trappings of the good life aren't
seen as a sign that the individual has been successful in a legitimate business. Middle-class blacks are often unrecognizable
in the general population of Philadelphia, and their invisibil-
ity or mistaken identity often infuriates them. It is bewildering
that they nonetheless allow whites, especially powerful whites
with whom they must consort, to get away with this behavior.
Blacks do not lash out in response but constantly behave and
present themselves in accordance with middle- and upper-
middle-class propriety in order to be seen as worthy of such a
perch. Middle-class blacks are acutely aware of what the wider
society thinks of their poorer cousins, and to some degree
they share these opinions. They are caught in a bind, yet they
lack the perspective to see themselves or their own people in

ways that might lessen their burden. This predicament leads them to avoid not just those settings that are considered to be "too white" but also those that are "too black."

Today anonymous black people on the streets or anywhere in the city could be doctors, lawyers, professors, businesspeople, or the sons, daughters, cousins, or close friends of influential persons. The prestige of those positions has real implications. The people are members not just of a racial but also of an economic class. Their status should by rights affect positively their treatment in public places, but that is not always the case, as the simple act of eating in a restaurant reveals.

THE COLOR LINE IN RESTAURANTS

Race is deeply implicated in eating in the city's downtown restaurants, though not always in the obvious ways that we might assume. In upscale establishments the waitstaffs are mainly white young people; if blacks are there at all, they are to be found in the kitchen among the mostly Latino staff. For the most part the patrons are white. Blacks tend not to eat in such places, not simply because there is a limited culture of eating out among blacks but also because they are put off by the poor service they often receive. Sometimes this becomes a self-fulfilling prophecy: the server fails to give good service because she expects a "bad" tip. Instead, blacks are drawn to moderately priced chains or to restaurants that sell fast food.

On Saturday, Charlene, Rashida, Jamila, and Annette sat together in the Down Home Diner at the Reading Terminal. They were enjoying one another's company, constantly giggling at inside jokes. Their loud laughter annoyed other patrons, but the girls were oblivious to the discomfort they were causing. A number of the other customers paid them close attention, taking in their show. Finally the girls quieted down, but on their own terms. Snatches of their dialogue reveal their anxieties about the restaurant scene: "The best pizza is Chuck E. Cheese's. They put on a show. They got better service." The first pizza brought to their table was unacceptable. The staff brought another pizza and they tried it, but again they found it too oily. "You call this good service?" A white couple commented to themselves about the young black girls' behavior. After hearing as much of this conversation as they could stand, they got up and left, demonstratively rolling their eyes as they made their way to another booth. As the white couple decamped, the young girls laughed as though they had achieved some sort of victory, and in a real sense they had, but at a social cost to other blacks toward whom these people may well express their prejudice.

This incident suggests that a black presence in white restaurants is a socially complicated affair. Surveying numerous restaurants in Center City on successive weekend nights, I found that they present an almost entirely white appearance. Patrons are overwhelmingly white, with a black person or couple present only here and there. Employees who meet the public are also predominantly white. The waitstaff is generally twentysomething, white, and female or gender-mixed. Many are students or actively engaged in the arts, perhaps pursuing a career in the theater. A few Latinos park cars out front, bus tables, or wash dishes in back. Blacks are almost entirely absent. This racial advertisement alone turns off many black people, particularly those with ethno predilections. Some have little taste for "white" food, which they consider too bland. For many, spending upwards of fifty dollars for a meal would amount to foolishness.

Center City restaurant managers have unacknowledged biases against employing African Americans, especially those from the local community. Most hiring is done through the social networks of current employees. When an opening occurs, employees tell their friends about the opportunity, in the process accruing status and expressing their own social power. Most white waitstaff members have few black friends, and the makeup of their networks reinforces the whiteness of the restaurant's workforce. The only blacks who are able to break through these barriers are those who befriend whites, particularly lesbians and gay men. They may be hired and promoted because the particular workplace has a limited pool of whites vying for the available positions.

Many black people are reluctant to patronize a restaurant that fails to hire people who look like them. This concern is a holdover from segregation, when blacks were told that they would not be served or had to enter through the back door. Subliminally or consciously, a question always hovers: how will I be received? When blacks are alive to slights, they can interpret all discourteous behavior as racially motivated. Often the offending person is simply incompetent, but blacks tend to attribute bad behavior to racism. This uncertainty alone makes venturing onto unfamiliar territory risky.

Another consideration is that many middle-class black people have not fully assimilated the habits and values of the privileged class. Eating out requires the ability to feel comfortable rather than self-conscious eating in front of others. Blacks do not have a well-developed culture of eating where they will see and be seen among strangers. Black people tend to think of food as food, not as a form of conspicuous expenditure and a sign of status. Some middle-class black people spend substantial sums at black-themed restaurants. But these are seldom places for elegant dining and tend to attract a class of black people that the very well-to-do would prefer not to be associated with. In sum, the black restaurants are not good enough, and the white restaurants do not attract a critical mass of black people.

When black people are present in upscale restaurants, the waitstaff may adopt a particular attitude toward them. Blacks have a reputation as difficult, demanding customers who don't tip. During their breaks members of the waitstaff share their stories and stereotypes. After all, their day's earnings depend on the clientele. Since black customers are also apprehensive about the service they receive, the situation is often tense right from the start. A server without effective people skills can exacerbate the problem. In the worst case the interaction turns into an argument over the quality of the service. When a tip is withheld, the stereotype is reinforced, damaging relations between black people and the waitstaff. Many upscale restaurants encourage their employees to be solicitous of customers, bending over backward to treat them well. Most interactions turn out just fine. However, the memorable situations are those that are most difficult for all involved, customers as well as waitstaff.

Often enough to arouse suspicion, blacks receive the worst tables in restaurants. Typically, when a black couple are seated next to the bathroom or kitchen door, they complain and ask to be seated elsewhere. When the person doing the seating says, "We don't have any other tables," the couple point to other unoccupied tables, and the person responds, "Those are reserved." The couple may become indignant. They reason, often rightly, that they had reservations, so how do people who have not shown up rate higher? Why does this server see fit to inconvenience people with whom she has a face-to-face relationship in order to favor people she has not even met? As they do their mental calculations, the blacks become more upset, believing firmly that they have been victims of racial discrimination.

What has happened here involves misunderstandings on both sides. People who seem to the server to carry little social significance have confronted her. Initially, she may not have had any racial animus, but the diners have the impression that their black skin color has marked them as outsiders, people with little moral authority, which allows her to treat them any way she wants. The fact that they are upset means little to her, except that they might make a scene and she might lose her tip. The diners interpret her behavior as racially motivated. They imagine the server thinking to herself that "people like this"—that is, black people—should feel good just to be allowed inside such a fine dining establishment. Most of their kind are locked away in the ghetto, out of work and having baby after baby, or in prison. This is unlikely to be the waitstaff's conscious reasoning process, but black patrons attribute this sort of thinking to the server.

The black couple, having been victimized repeatedly by similar events at too many other restaurants, know the whole routine and can recite it chapter and verse. They say to each other, with a roll of the eyes and a knowing look, "Here we go again." The black patrons feel certain in their interpretation of what just happened. A neutral observer, giving the white server the benefit of the doubt, may have the contrary impression, suspecting that this sort of thinking is alien to her, since she is concerned mostly about how hard she has to work to make decent tips. The server would have difficulty recognizing the racial dimensions of the problem, even if she means well and is open to compelling evidence that a wrong has been committed against the black couple. The confrontation between the black patrons and white server arises from this profound mutual misunderstanding.

Other customers and waitstaff begin to notice, even to stare. Too often the situation is viewed as "a black couple causing trouble," because onlookers rarely experience such repeated slights. The black customers, on the other hand, feel that they have to campaign for rights that people with white skin take for granted. This campaign requires great energy as well as constant vigilance. In these circumstances courtesy evaporates; the tip is forfeited. For white waitstaff, the negative reputation of black diners grows. For blacks it is once again more than enough; they may not go to an upscale, "white" restaurant for a long while. Instead, they seek out restaurants that cater to black people, or those that have been tested and found acceptable. In mainstream restaurants, however, the situation is always fluid. The welcome that blacks receive may be undermined or supported by caring or uncaring waitstaff, whose behavior directly affects whether blacks choose to be present. Most often, they choose not to be.

THE TROUBLE WITH LARRY

It was a warm Tuesday evening in April, and I was set to meet my seminar students for our end-of-semester dinner at the Campus Café. Convenient to the Penn campus, the place is a favorite of many faculty. I had developed the habit over the years of taking my class there to have a meal together and conduct our last seminar around the table. When I called ahead for a reservation, I specified the desired room, which is conducive to conversation. At 6:30 sharp I walked through the doors and into the bar, which is adjacent to the restaurant, and passed through the usual happy-hour crowd of Penn law students, grad students, and other young professionals. I continued past the bar and on to the reception desk for the restaurant.

After standing there for a few minutes, I encountered Larry, the host. We exchanged greetings. I'd known Larry for a while, and he'd booked reservations for me before. But this time as he looked down the reservation list while I waited, a puzzled expression came over his face. "There seems to be some sort of mix-up," he said. "Well, I certainly made a reservation," I said, and mentioned the room I usually sat in with my class. "Yes, I see," he agreed, acknowledging that my reservation had actually been logged. His brow furrowing, he stared down at the list. He then looked up at me, and his eyes wandered off into the distance across the room, panning the gathering dinner crowd. "Well, I'm going to have to give you another space. You can have the space over there," he said, pointing to an open area surrounded by other diners. "That won't do," I complained. "I had reservations, and we were really counting on the side room." "Yes, but it looks as though someone promised that room to another party."

"So the other party is already there?" I asked. He looked down at his watch. "No, they're scheduled to arrive at seven." "Well, it is now six-forty-five, and I'm already here," I argued. "Yes, I know, I'm sorry, but that's how it is," he said. "This is strange," I said. "It seems so arbitrary." "No, no," he said, becoming increasingly indignant and defensive, catching my drift. Suddenly my skin color became highly significant to both of us. He tried to explain why we should be inconvenienced while the prospective guests should not, but his explanations were illogical and amounted to "Because I say so." By now my whole class, mixed black and white, had gathered at the reception desk and wondered what was going on. Ultimately, we had no choice and wound up taking the much less private space. As we conducted the class, some of the students wanted to use this experience as a teaching moment, particularly as we ate and observed the all-white party that had "bested" our group.

IMMIGRANT TAXI DRIVERS AND BLACK FARES

The quick judgments made by whites are also made by others. The cab drivers who congregate outside the Thirtieth Street Station have a finely tuned ethnographic sense. Coming from distant, culturally different lands, they must interact with diverse elements of a global American city. In adapting to this new and provocative situation, the cabbies' mobile workplace blends both ethnocentric and cosmopolitan realities. During their down time they gather at urban central places and form a sort of cosmopolitan canopy among themselves.

Taxi drivers' daily experience in traversing the city exposes them to a wide diversity of passengers and provides them a unique local knowledge of Philadelphians as well as the neighborhoods in which they live. Through work, including their daily travels and repeated encounters with locals, they develop exquisite "cognitive maps" of the city's social geography.[4] The occupation is a trying one, highly dangerous and only minimally rewarding, but always challenging and edifying. The taxi driver stays in constant touch with the everyday public life of the city, and in this special respect, through this exposure and the resulting sophistication, he adopts an intimate yet cosmopolitan perspective toward the wider social world at large.

Taxi drivers and Philadelphians alike use their cognitive maps to understand the various groups that make up the city and where they reside, influencing their interactions. The conventional ethnographic wisdom of the city states that the Italians were understood to occupy and control this neighborhood, the Irish that neighborhood, the Jews another, the Latinos pockets of Northeast Philadelphia; blacks generally resided in wide swaths of ghetto communities from Southwest to West Philadelphia, North Philadelphia, Gray's Ferry, and Cobbs Creek. Recently a large influx of immigrants of color from all over the world has upended the local employment structure. Given their extra amounts of social and human capital, immigrants compete very effectively with the most disadvantaged element of the urban labor force—the impoverished young black male.

The goal of the taxi driver is to stay alive while making a living. As he goes about his day, the tension in his work life centers on his relationship with the public, with traffic, and with the police. An important part of his work culture involves distinguishing "good" people from "bad," prospective customers from those who would give him trouble. In order to accomplish this, he pays close attention to the signs they display, reading them carefully and trying to behave accordingly. He employs his own peculiar form of folk ethnography to judge the people and places he encounters each and every day. A big city like Philadelphia, which has been powerfully shaped by the social forces of ethnicity, race, and class and which has also recently experienced historic levels of street crime and murder, presents a special challenge for him.

Whenever possible, but especially before allowing a passenger into his cab, the taxi driver sizes up his prospective fare. As much as possible, he wants to know whom he's dealing with. He focuses on whether this person is likely to be law-abiding and safe or dangerous, as well as how likely it is that the customer will pay him. In addition, the taxi driver is ever watchful for the police. He worries especially about what he considers the arbitrary application of the law, which sometimes leads to exorbitant fines and lost time, not just on the street but also in the courtroom, where he is required to defend his rights, often without legal counsel. Any trial can become discouragingly and prohibitively expensive; a chance encounter with the wrong cop can be ruinous.

One Thursday evening Arash, an Iranian taxi driver, picked me up in Center City. As we rode along, I asked him about his job. His opening comment was "This is the worst job in the world." My immediate response was to ask why he felt that way.

It is just that you feel used and abused by everyone, the police, the PPA [Philadelphia Parking Authority], and the

*public. I mean, you gotta watch who you pick up all the
time. People are getting robbed left and right, so you've
gotta be very careful and lucky to survive at all out here. You
can't really make any real money out here without working
almost all your waking hours. It's a grind. Then you got the
PPA breathing down your back with all their rules and regu-
lations that make little sense. And you gotta deal with the
police, who are just out to mess with people.*

*A few weeks ago, I had a problem with a lady and a man
who wanted to be let off in the street, so I did. A cop saw it,
and in the middle of traffic he pulls me over and gives me
a citation. I pleaded with him, and he gloated at me. It was
illegal, but it wasn't really my fault. The cop said he couldn't
take the ticket back, because he had already written me up.
So I called his supervisor. Well, the supervisor calls him up,
and he comes back to me and gives me another ticket. How
am I supposed to fight all this? They're just out to get the
foreigners who drive the taxis. You just have to really watch
out for the cops, man. Then on top of all that you gotta
watch out for who you pick up. You can take this job and
shove it. I'm quitting as soon as I can find something.*

Philadelphia has a number of places where taxi drivers
hang out, take a break from the stresses of the streets, or
simply queue up and wait for a guaranteed fare. They may
be out of commission for hours. But they are also recharg-
ing their batteries and socializing with their ethnic brethren
and others under the canopy. In these settings the drivers

come together and talk over their problems of daily living and compare notes on how to deal with life in the new land. Many are recent immigrants from the Middle East or from Africa. Some are still experiencing culture shock in their new home, although others have been in America for as long as two decades.

One day, as Abdul, a West African immigrant, took me on a roundabout way from the Thirtieth Street Station to Rittenhouse Square, I introduced myself as a professor writing a book on cosmopolitan places in the city. Telling him that I was particularly interested in taxi driving in Philadelphia, I secured his consent to be tape-recorded.

Abdul and I spent the next two hours together discussing the ins and outs of taxi driving while he showed me the drivers' special hangouts. He began, "I'm from the Ivory Coast." But taxi drivers all help one another, especially when they face difficulties with the federal immigration authorities. "West Africans, Jews, Arabs, Pakistanis—everybody helps everybody. Jew or Arab, don't matter. Sunni and Shiite, Arab and Christian, they all come together here. Muslim and Christian may have some kind of problem in the Ivory Coast, but here we just joke about it. It does not matter. Here it is different. We make a joke about it here. We come together as one. I've never seen such strife here, and I've been here fourteen years.

"Cab driving is a good way to make a living. If you don't have anything else when you come here, it is a good way to get started. An easy way to survive is to drive a cab. It is dangerous, though." Cab drivers try to reduce the risks by avoiding neighborhoods known as dangerous.

"If you call a cab from North Philly—that's a black neighborhood—you'll never get a cab. In a white neighborhood like Rittenhouse Square, you'll have a cab in five minutes. North Philly or Southwest Philly, you'll never get one. We know the dangerous areas. If a black man stop me or a white man stop me, even though I'm black, I'd rather pick up the white man. And that's not only me! You're afraid for your life. See, the African Americans, they think we Africans are from the jungle. He's my brother, though; we both black. I mean I can raise the barrier up, but he can come around and shoot me from there. Last year it was four cab drivers who got killed. One Jamaican, one Asian, one white, and one African American. Either way he can still get you. Unbelievable." "So the four drivers who were killed were killed by black guys?" I asked. "Of course," Abdul replied, not missing a beat. "I've been driving for eight years, and something tells me, 'Don't pick up this guy.' I know who to pick up, and who to avoid. It is about staying alive, I promise you.

"Some people can offer you a hundred dollars to buy drugs. And I never smoke in my life; I don't know where to buy drugs. I might get shot. For what?! They'll try to get you to go this neighborhood or that one. I might get shot over there for a hundred dollars. Sometimes white people want to go into a black neighborhood to buy drugs. If I don't know the person, why should I pick him up? Might be spies, might be FBI, I don't know. You must be careful. You have to know where to go. See, every day, I read the newspapers, been learning a lot. See, the new people just learning to drive, they don't know. I'm learning every day.

"When someone is getting killed, ninety percent of the time it is in North Philly. It used to be only at nighttime, but now it is in broad daylight. It is a shame. You black, I'm black. It is a shame to say it. Danny Glover, the actor, had a hard time getting a taxi in New York. Nobody wanted to pick him up, so he filed a complaint against the city."

I asked Abdul specifically about relationships between Africans and African Americans. "That's a difficult one," he replied. "They think we are jungle people, and some simply don't like us. And some like us a little bit. See, the problem is this. Only two percent of the cab drivers are African American. See, to be able to drive a cab, you have to have a cab certificate. Everything is so critical now for your application. You have to have a blood test, a background check. I'm a cab driver, right? I could take you someplace and rob you. So, I've got to have a clean background, right? Ninety percent of the African Americans don't pass the background check. Don't get me wrong, there are some good people who are African American. There's just a lot of tension. See, Asians, Africans, they come here for something. Like my father, he is sick, and I'm helping him. Everybody's taking care of his family. My siblings, I'm taking care of them, sending money home. So I cannot play around. Many African Americans don't have the same mentality as me. But African Americans are very difficult."

Immigrants from diverse cultures may forge a new sense of identity as they find out what they have in common and what differentiates them from others. In this way the taxi stand is a mini–cosmopolitan canopy. Yet drivers' conversation includes many accounts that reinforce negative stereotypes of black people. As the taxi driver listens to his fellow drivers talk about their experiences and as he interacts with the fares he picks up, he tries to place customers in comprehensible categories. Both his income and his safety depend on making the right decisions about whom to pick up or how to treat passengers. What emerges are largely stereotypes concerning the "black man," the "white man," the "white lady," the "black lady," the "black teenager," and so on. For the time being, these stereotypes work to keep him out of harm's way—or so he hopes. Black people who are seen as a threat are not allowed into his taxi, confirming black Americans' worst fears about racial discrimination.

The practices of taxi drivers in Philadelphia illustrate a key feature of urban life: the necessity of watching other people and making split-second decisions about them on the basis of apprehensions of danger. For the cab driver, black or white, immigrant or native-born, decisions about potential fares can be a matter of life or death. Alone in his car, he is especially vulnerable to robbery or violence. For relative newcomers recognized stereotypes, reinforced by accounts of actual experiences, are an all too easy way to learn how to be—or at least to feel—safe on the streets. But the racial profiling that results, demonizing the young black urban male, slides over into suspicion of all blacks and contributes to widespread prejudice. The casual ethnography that leads the cabbie to discriminate becomes an item in African American folk ethnography and shapes an experience of race for both groups that is divisive and predominantly negative.

In the next chapter, we step out of the car to see what happens when these kinds of split-second decisions are made in the presence of a diverse crowd.

8. THE "NIGGER MOMENT"

Shawn was one of a handful of black students attending a prestigious law school in Washington, D.C. He came from inner-city Philadelphia but was able to attend an elite private high school on scholarship, where he did very well, and went on to graduate from college. Accustomed to associating freely with peers from diverse backgrounds, he aspired to become a lawyer and won admission to an institution in the nation's capital. He and a few other black law students were the only nonwhite residents of the adjacent affluent neighborhood. One evening after classes, Shawn was waiting for a bus to go home. His apartment was only a ten-minute walk away, but he had stopped by the store and had groceries as well as books to carry. He decided to take the bus that stopped just across the street from the law school. Talking to his girlfriend on the phone while he waited, Shawn noticed a police car drive slowly by. Then it drove by again, and circled a third time. On the fourth pass, the officer pulled up behind him and sat for approximately three minutes, with the car's floodlight shining on the bus stall in which Shawn sat.

Shawn was startled to hear the officer's voice on the loud-speaker order him to put his hands out where they could be seen and to turn slowly toward the light. Shawn did so, with his phone still in his hand. As he turned toward the officer, who had stepped out of the cruiser, he saw that the cop was reaching for his holster and drawing his gun. Another law student, a white female whom Shawn did not know but who had also been waiting for the bus, yelled out to the officer that what Shawn had in his hand was only a cell phone. The officer yelled for Shawn to drop it, which he did. Ordering Shawn to place his hands against the wall and not move, the officer immediately handcuffed and frisked him.

Shawn asked what was happening and explained that he was a student at the law school just across the street and was waiting for the bus to go home. The cop ignored his expla-nation and continued frisking him. By then approximately seven other police cars had arrived and had blocked off the street to traffic. Students and professors from Shawn's law school began to form a crowd across the street, but no one made a move to assist him. He was humiliated. The police cursed at him and yelled at him to cooperate. He did, but felt confused by what was going on. They repeatedly kicked at his ankles, forcing his legs farther and farther apart until he was spread-eagled. They kept pushing his face against the wall or down toward his chest, telling him to stop resisting. He was frisked two more times, and his wallet was taken. His schoolbooks and laptop were dumped out on the sidewalk; his grocery bags were emptied. Shawn was restrained by three officers who held his handcuffed wrists together with the slack from the back of his shirt and pants to prevent him from running away. They questioned him roughly, showing no respect for him as a law-abiding citizen.

When Shawn again asked what was going on, he was told he fit the description of someone involved in a shooting a few blocks away. Just then, one of the officers' radios crackled, "Black male, five-foot-eight, blue button-down shirt, khaki tan dress pants, brown dress shoes." The description fit Shawn exactly. Having heard himself being described over the radio, he was convinced he was going to jail. After ten minutes of being forced to stand straddled, physically restrained and handcuffed, in front of his peers and professors, another radio announcement let the officers know that the actual suspect had been apprehended elsewhere.

Shawn was uncuffed and told to have a seat. The cops who had been standing around returned to their vehicles and drove off. The officer who made the initial stop remained and took down Shawn's information for the police report. As he filled out the form, he attempted to make small talk. Shawn answered his direct questions politely, but otherwise remained silent. He felt mortified and was still afraid, but mostly was angry at the lack of respect he had received and the clear racial profiling that had just taken place.

During the commotion, a group of neighbors had congregated on an adjacent corner behind the police car barricade. As the officer was writing down Shawn's information, a neighbor came up and, in front of Shawn, asked if Shawn was "the guy." The officer replied that, no, it turned out to be someone else. The neighbor, whispering within Shawn's hearing, offered to follow Shawn home to make sure. The officer said that that would not be necessary. Shawn later learned from local news that the actual suspect was the victim's college roommate, who had been playing around when he accidentally discharged the gun. He was a white male.

Shawn realized that it was the neighbors who had called the cops and furnished his description. They had heard that there was a shooting in the neighborhood, and when they saw Shawn, they concluded that this black male must be the suspect. Every day for three years they had noticed him, avoiding eye contact as he walked by them on his way to and from law school.[1] This incident of racial profiling, then, began not with the police but with his own neighbors.

Today, five years after this ordeal, Shawn has completed law school, returned to Philadelphia, and taken a position with a Center City law firm. Although he says that he has "moved on" from this experience, he comments, "Never does a day go by that I don't think about what happened back then. That incident was traumatic for me, and now I feel somewhat jaded. It has taken me a while to get over what happened. The incident was part of my education as a young black man. Now, I'm not so quick to trust [white] people, and the incident continues to color my view and my feelings of what is and is not possible for a young black man."

Shawn's trauma and disillusionment are not the only consequences of this incident. Personal stories of racial injury circulate within the black community and, as they percolate, reinforce preexisting suspicions and distrust of the wider white society.

There comes a time in the life of every African American when he or she is powerfully reminded of his or her putative place as a black person. Among themselves, black people often refer to this experience after the fact in a lighthearted manner and with an occasional chuckle as the "nigger moment."[2] It is something of an inside joke. At the time it occurs, however, the awareness of this act of acute disrespect and discrimination is shocking; the victim is taken by surprise, caught off guard. The affront very often takes place in a trusted social space or public environment like the cosmopolitan-oriented canopy, where a certain level of decorum and goodwill is ordinarily expected. Emotions flood over the victim as this middle-class, cosmopolitan-oriented black person is humiliated and shown that he or she is, before anything else, a racially circumscribed black person after all.[3] No matter what she has achieved, or how decent and law-abiding she is, there is no protection, no sanctuary, no escaping from this fact. She is vulnerable. Whatever the educated and often professionally successful person previously thought her position in society was, now she is challenged, as random white persons casually but powerfully degrade her. This moment is always insulting, and even a relatively minor incident can have a significant impact.

THE LEGACY OF CASTE

In public canopies like the Reading Terminal Market, Rittenhouse Square, or the lobby of the Four Seasons Hotel, the presence of black people is generally accepted without remark. As I discussed earlier, the civil rights movement, which culminated in civil disorder in major cities around the country, set in motion a process of racial incorporation. It was aided by "affirmative action" and "set asides" for black Americans and resulted in significant inclusion of black people in various areas of American life.[4] The racial incorporation process changed not only the complexion of the workplace but also of public settings that we can recognize today as cosmopolitan canopies; such settings now upset previously held expectations of who would be found there. Today, after forty years of such inclusion efforts, the process has borne serious fruit. Many, many black people have moved away from the segregated black ghetto community, integrating residential, occupational, and social spaces that were once completely off limits to members of their race. Black people appear almost everywhere, and are often apparently well received according to their station and educational levels.

Yet the simultaneous existence of impoverished inner-city neighborhoods complicates the situation. Over much of U.S. urban history, whites sought to contain the problems that black people represent by confining them to ghettos.[5] The fact that there remains a large, distressed urban community that is black and associated with poverty and crime means that black people continue to be strongly associated with the "iconic ghetto," regardless of their actual connection to that ghetto. And from this association there persists a certain apprehension toward anonymous black people who appear in public places.

Hence, the anonymous black person carries historical and social baggage, and thus may move somewhat self-consciously when in mixed company. Far too often, the treatment black people receive in public is based on negative assumptions, as strangers they encounter fall back on scripts, roles, and stereotypes that raise doubts about the black person's claims to decency and middle-class status. Today, when blacks appear in public places that are relatively diverse, they may often be assumed to be from the ghetto even when they are not. Every black person must work hard in public to disabuse other people of this presumption. But all too often, people make such judgments and act before they know better.

Many Americans feel apprehensive about encountering anonymous black people in public places. A strange black male can be viewed as criminal or crime-prone until he can prove he is not, which is difficult to do in the split-second interaction that typically occurs in public spaces. Based on these invidious assumptions, other people enact scripts that negate the black person's claims to decency and middle-class status.[6]

When the black person is not given his proper due and the transgressor is white, the slight is interpreted as racial. Such slights happen all the time. They may be large or small, but when they become racialized they grow in significance. Because of the history of racial injury in America, black people have developed a heightened sensitivity to insults. Although some incidents arise from mutual misunderstanding, the underlying dynamic is indicative of the current unstable state of race relations.

Hence, the "nigger moment" turns on the issue of social place. The civil rights movement and the incorporation process that followed have allowed black people to move more freely, to work in places from which they were formerly excluded, and to hold high-status positions people who look like them have never held before. This situation creates dilemmas and contradictions of status that complicate social interactions.[7] Although African Americans no longer comprise a lower caste or monolithic underclass, educated, middle-class black professionals find that their skin color still prompts others to misperceive them. The "nigger moment" occurs because others have not assimilated, or do not fully accept, the implications of these recent social changes.

The racial slight that morphs into the "nigger moment" often occurs in circumstances where whites do not expect to encounter blacks. If a black person is present, whites may assume that he or she does not belong there, or has some status deficit by virtue of color and is therefore unworthy of regard or respect—or, at least, many blacks believe this to be their assumption. In settings defined as "white," black people are highly conscious of their racial difference and tend to think of themselves as outsiders. The white people whom blacks expect to encounter in such settings command a certain degree of respect, or at least deference. Black people, because of their association with the ghetto and their history as a subjugated class, are often unable to command such respect, especially from people who operate with a self-enhancing view that encourages them to think of themselves as being above black people.

Significantly, black people who are accustomed to catering to white patrons in prestigious places may also be surprised to find themselves catering to black patrons. Black people sometimes have trouble commanding respect from other blacks, who feel that they lose something by working for blacks instead of for elite whites. In this zero-sum equation, all black persons are assumed to be of low status, so anyone who defers to them suffers a diminution of his or her own status.

When a black person appears out of his or her conventional social place, others have to deal with a situation of cognitive dissonance, for the person's color does not seem to comport with his or her class status. Since black people are "causing" the dissonance because of their presence, "correction" often begins by focusing on them. Strikingly, the white people who respond this way are most frequently insecure about their own social positions. As blacks move into the middle class, some people are prepared to stop them at the door. Those whites who try to forbid them entry often view the advance of black people as a threat to their own well-being. Significantly, many of them have only just arrived socially and economically and are aware that they are barely hanging on to their middle-class positions; being "above blacks" is key to their sense of status. They collaborate to prevent blacks from enjoying the full rights, obligations, and perquisites of their positions and are prepared to frustrate, if not entirely stop, blacks' upward mobility.

In rudely putting blacks "back in their place," insecure whites often become the major actors in constructing the "nigger moment." Yet others commit similar blunders. A person with black skin is viewed as black long before he or she is viewed as a doctor, lawyer, or professor. Blackness is a "master status" that supersedes whatever else a person may claim to be; he or she is viewed as a black doctor, a black lawyer, or a black professor, whatever that adjective might mean.[8] Black professionals become outraged, for only their credentials and expertise are supposed to matter.

The rising black professional class attracts both scrutiny and disdain, particularly from whites who feel that their own rights have been abrogated by the advancement of blacks. Because of the low place assigned to black people historically, any advancement on the part of an individual black person can be viewed as having been made at the expense of a more deserving white person. People assessing the situation from this perspective tend to be socially comfortable with the privileges that are accrued by white skin and the absence of blacks from their daily lives. The contemporary workplace is particularly prone to incidents of racial slight.

In calling these and other types of racial slights "nigger

moments," blacks express their anger at whites' deprecation of their social status. Since the term "nigger" is so nasty and loaded, it makes a powerful point. In effect, the black person says that this white person who has just tried to put him in his place is a racist who has just called him a "nigger." The "nigger moment" is a stark drawing of the color line that diminishes everyone it touches.

Shawn's experience reflects the fact that his white neighbors failed to accept him as a member of their community, his presence provoking their suspicion and apprehension. In their eyes, Shawn must have been the perpetrator of the nearby shooting, for why else would he be in the neighborhood? The fact that Shawn was young and across the street from a law school did not hold sway in the minds of the neighbors who called to report his presence among them.

JESSE'S DISILLUSIONMENT

Jesse, a thirty-nine-year-old man, grew up in the North Philadelphia ghetto. After graduating from college and trying law school, he decided to become a paralegal. He has worked in a Center City law firm for the past seventeen years. He moved out of the ghetto and bought rental properties around the city, which he manages. Jesse is also a minister for several black congregations. Married with three teenaged children who attend private school, he belongs to the city's growing black middle class.

When he was just starting out at the law firm, he met with

an incident that tested him. He had been happy in his new job, attending meetings with his colleagues, enjoying being invited to their parties, and getting along quite well with them. He was about to take a vacation trip to Lima, Peru, when one day a senior white partner gave Jesse some advice in front of other white partners: "When you get to Peru, don't hang out too much with the banana-eating monkeys! And don't hang out too much with the drug dealers." There was an uncomfortable silence and then nervous chuckles from the group. But Jesse wasn't laughing—he was stunned. He was not only deeply offended by the behavior of this principal but also shaken by the others' accommodating reactions.

He left the gathering feeling demoralized. In thinking over the incident, he became confused. He didn't know what to do, but he knew he needed to make things right. All he could think of was that he was owed an apology. Jesse asked the offending party to apologize, but to no avail. In a few days, the other white partners apologized to him on their senior partner's behalf but indicated that Jesse should not expect an apology from him. Jesse considered suing the firm, but a young black female lawyer talked him out of this idea. She and other colleagues tried to show support for Jesse, and finally the situation calmed down. But things were never really the same for him at the firm.

Jesse was disillusioned. Were they all this way? He wondered, is this how they really feel about me? He couldn't help having such doubts. But he enjoyed his profession and wanted to make the best of it. He developed a strategy of managing his workplace. He no longer attends his colleagues' social functions. In their presence, he is careful and circumspect, rather than spontaneous. He no longer trusts all his co-workers and sees the firm more cynically. He puts in his time at the workplace and then leaves his job behind. His realism has found its way into the advice he gives to younger blacks who are hired by the firm.

Over the years, numerous incidents have provided compelling evidence for his stance. Recently Jesse, who has a passion for expensive clothes and is considered to be a fine dresser, was lauded in the local newspaper. When the article appeared, his colleagues were impressed and complimentary. Weeks later, on a casual-dress Friday at the firm, Jesse decided to go to work "dressed down." He says he usually avoids casual dress on these days, for it always seems to be a bad omen; something bad happens to him when he goes to work without his "protective coloration."

That Friday, Jesse dressed in designer shorts and arrived at work in his new $70,000 BMW convertible. As he parked in the company lot, he sidled up next to a new Volvo, which he was careful not to bump. After getting out, he noticed one of the white partners behind the wheel. He nodded a greeting and proceeded to the building. The day passed uneventfully. But a few days later, the white partner called Jesse into his office for a talk. He asked, "How can a man like you afford a car like that? And how can you afford to dress the way you do?" Jesse was taken aback by these questions but had come to expect such behavior from some of his white colleagues.

He replied, "Can we talk as men?" The partner replied, "Yes, we can." Then Jesse said, "I'm a married man. I don't have vices like chasing women, don't drink, don't smoke, don't gamble. Clothes are my passion. And I love my automobile. Also, I have a variety of revenue streams. This is not my only source of income. I am a minister. I have apartment buildings and other rental properties. Furthermore, you have no right to question me like this." During this conversation, the partner began to show discomfort, realizing that he had crossed a line and should never have broached the subject. The conversation soon ended.

This set of interactions told Jesse that things were not what he thought they were. He realized that he is not who his colleagues think he is and that some of his white colleagues are not who they pretend to be. The situation becomes unavoidably racial. At that transformative moment, the black person discovers that he or she is utterly unequal, not accepted as normal but racially circumscribed. For many African Americans, although this realization is not entirely a surprise, to come face-to-face with it is a shocking setback, at times even a defeat.[9] This moment of acute discrimination is unusual, which makes it especially powerful when it occurs. Until this moment, the black person simply went about his business; when the line is drawn, the situation becomes painfully clear.

Over generations blacks have become strongly motivated to avoid such moments, largely by developing a strategy of avoidance. In the past, the situation was easier to manage interpersonally; today, professional and social contact between the races is inevitable. Blacks' adoption of a defensive stance has profound implications for their relations with whites as well as for the way they coach others about how to deal with white people. The fact that whites collectively hold the power to enact this socially constructed "nigger moment" sets the stage for a deferential, rather than mutually respectful, scenario in interactions between blacks and whites. This dynamic intensifies the racial divide.

Paradoxically, despite the subterranean and local knowledge about race relations that African Americans share, when the dreaded "nigger moment" does occur, the black person is often incredulous. "How could this be happening?" "Don't they know who I am?" The black person is left feeling that whites have had enough of his "shit," his uppity behavior. He is ready to say, "They don't know who they're messing with!" In a real sense, whites do know. Black people who live in a land dominated by whites undergo a series of little humiliations at the hands of their white counterparts day in and day out.[10] Some slights are deliberate, but others are unintentional.

Sometimes the offense is simply a misperception of a stranger. But the black person may take the white person's misperception as an insult, especially since he or she has had to endure a lifetime of similar incidents. Many blacks complain that in the office buildings where they work, whites who do not know them personally often mistake them for a cleaning lady or janitor or for someone else of lower rank. They assume that no black person occupies a position of status in the workplace. The black person assumes that the white person meant the offense as a racial insult. The white person is offended that his behavior is taken as racist, rather than as a simple mistake. Thousands of little cuts like this must be endured in everyday life. If the black person made something of each and every incident, she would soon become unable to function at all. In response blacks develop thick skin and try to rise above the situation, even to laugh it off. Conventional middle-class culture is not kind to the wronged and the embittered. "Never show blood," the saying goes; deal with such insults in ways that do not attract sharks.

Yet when a person has been cut, he cannot help but bleed. These moments are anticipated with dread, even when the cosmopolitan black person understands that many comments are not racially motivated. When these incidents do involve race, they are dreaded all the more. The question of whether a white person is racist is not rhetorical, and the answer is never entirely predictable. For blacks, any unfamiliar person might cause a "nigger moment," so he or she must be watched carefully.

In order to deal with this problem, black parents try to socialize their children to stay out of harm's way. They instruct them to avoid trusting relations with white people, or they risk being hurt. But as American society becomes increasingly multicultural, avoiding close relations with members of a specific group is no longer feasible. For the middle class or those who aspire to upward mobility, avoidance is impossible or self-defeating. The protection that parents provide for their children is inevitably punctured by momentary but repeated racial insults. As these indignities mount up quantitatively, they change a young life in a qualitative manner. When the youth experiences what amounts to his first "nigger moment," he reacts in a way that is quite profound. First and foremost he begins to rethink his relationships with white people, or to consider them with greater care.

NATHAN'S MOMENT

Thelma, a middle-aged African American, was raised in Philadelphia's racially segregated neighborhoods but now lives with her husband in a racially mixed section of the city. In her work as a real estate broker, she regularly witnesses racial discrimination in housing. She and her husband struggled to teach their son, Nathan, not only to be respectful of all people but also to value his particular background. While providing him with a cosmopolitan upbringing, they made him aware that black people are still victimized by racism. Thelma always sought educational opportunities for her son, which often landed him in environments where he was the only black child. For instance, she encouraged him to take up tennis, a traditionally "white" sport. She tells this story.

Nathan started in an all-black private school and then went to an all-black public school in the neighborhood. His junior high school was mixed, fifty-fifty. First time he was exposed to whites. I signed him up for tennis. One day when he was twelve or thirteen, we had a conversation about race when I picked him up from school.

Nathan said to me, "Mom, why is it that the black kids start all the trouble?" I asked him what he meant. He described how this one young man was always starting trouble in school; he sounded like a bully. I tried to explain that sometimes people have difficult home lives and that he probably brought some of that tension to school. But I said, "Nathan, I want you to understand that ignorance comes in any color." So we began to talk about race. As I was driving him to Arthur Ashe [Youth Tennis Center] in Roxborough, the conversation got kind of heated. He said, "Mommy, I think you're a racist." I said, "No, I'm not a racist, I'm a realist." Because I was pointing out what blacks had gone through. I was really advocating the black experience. Maybe he thought I was putting down white people, I don't know. But I just wanted him to know that ignorance comes in any color. "You'll see this as you grow up." I just remember what he called me. I was really just trying to give him a sense of our history.

I don't know how long it was after that, but it was very close in my mind, and he could remember this discussion very clearly, he had this confrontation at tennis. A group of students was bussed in to play. They were all white. It was kind of strange. I had never seen this before. The coach had grouped Nathan and this other young fellow to play doubles in the little tennis match. He was quite good, so the coach put them together. Then Nathan missed the ball, and this Caucasian young man called him a bunch a nasty, dirty words. I couldn't hear it because I was up in [the stands]. But I could tell by his body language, and I could tell by my son's face. He was just stunned that these words were coming out of this young man's mouth. He looks up at me up on the platform, and I just looked at him to say, "You handle it—I'm not gonna handle it!" He then looks at the coach to handle it, but the coach didn't handle it. So it was left that way. If you know my son, he shows everything on his face. He was just stunned. He was paralyzed. As he came up the steps, I just looked at him. And my words [to him] were, "Ignorance comes in any color." He began to tell me what the young man said. It was incredible. He was cursing Nathan, calling him dumb, a lot of crazy adjectives—I don't even know [them all]. That began to open his eyes. It was clearly racial. The boy just thought he could run over him. My son was the only black person, and this was what came out. About a month later, when they were playing, this kid came with this same kind of aggressiveness. This is when Nathan began to be exposed. He had learned what was expected of him. He learned who he was at that time.

Nathan was on his way to becoming cosmopolitan, but this experience gave rise to doubts and second thoughts.

If a young person once disregarded the entreaties of more ethnocentric black people, he or she may now listen to their opinions. A youth who had doubted the warnings of the old heads—mature black men and women who pass on their painfully accumulated wisdom to the next generation—may give their advice more respect. In his imagination, these voices all chime in, "We told you so." In the heat of this moment, he must recalculate both the consonant and the discordant sounds. A few simple messages begin to resonate for him: "Don't trust white people"; "Choose white friends and associates with care." Not only does he begin to give ethnocentric arguments more weight, but he also develops a certain black consciousness. His wariness around whites may begin to show, and his white friends may now discern a certain swagger in his step and a chip on his shoulder.

In such tense circumstances, the most unsophisticated young brothers are ready to blow up whenever they perceive a slight. Many a life has been turned upside down or ruined by such haste. The young brother risks calling forth the stereotype of the angry black man, all too easily dismissed by his white counterparts. The old heads caution him to "suck it up" and to learn from and build on this traumatic experience. They say, "Pick your battles" or "All races have good and bad people." He listens and tries to learn patience.

It is very difficult for many people to come to terms with what has happened to them. It is equally difficult to normalize it, seeking out a universalistic explanation, denying the role of racism, and asserting that blacks and whites are really equal. "No, this would not have happened to a white man in a similar situation," he argues. These are the lessons of the brothers and sisters who have survived a succession of "nigger moments" and have developed the insight and strength to carry on.

The victim in a "nigger moment" may, in turn, identify his or her abuser as a racist—the most powerful verbal weapon in the black person's arsenal. This label is a potent epithet that can be irreparably damaging. In turn, the labeler may be accused of "playing the race card," a phrase that has become a rival epithet directed at blacks. Blacks and whites continue to parry one another as public spaces and relationships are perpetually renegotiated.

While avoiding the "nigger moment" is foremost in the minds of many African Americans and keeps them from fully trusting white people, the potential use of the epithet "racist" makes many whites apprehensive about having closer relations with blacks. These concerns are at the heart of the anxiety and insecurity experienced on both sides of the color line. In today's professional work settings that involve interracial interaction, no one wants to be accused of racism or of acting in ways that are racially motivated. Conservatives as well as liberals seek to avoid this appellation, which all acknowledge is seriously damaging. The term "racist" possesses immense power.

When this label is applied, a degradation ceremony begins immediately, whether or not the party is guilty or his conduct has even been investigated.[11] The person on the receiving end of the epithet is being called out on a charge many are prepared to believe. Although a contest may ensue, the label is so powerful that accusations alone may destroy the person's reputation. Media commentators have lost their jobs and managers of large organizations have had to forfeit their positions.

Whether institutional racism is due to sins of commission or to those of omission does not matter, for the result is the same. From the ghetto wastelands in urban centers to the pervasive racial disparities in income, wealth, health, and educational achievement, the bitter fruits of white privilege and black disinheritance are visible. The beneficiaries of this weighty history are also in plain sight. White persons, no matter how humble their origins, are still favored by the legacy of slavery and segregation that pervades contemporary society. Some observers have called this American apartheid.[12]

In the past, the color line in most American cities was painfully clear. Black people "knew their place"—and they did their best to adapt and work around this reality.[13] Over the past forty years, as the racial incorporation process has led to the emergence of a large black middle class, the color line has begun to blur. In some places, at some times, it seems nonexistent. Yet it can still be drawn at any moment. As blacks and whites interact in public, each takes the other's reaction into his calculation of what he expects and can get away with. Navigating the unstable terrain demands unusual poise and forbearance, as assumptions of equality and inclusiveness can suddenly be called into question.

All these dilemmas and contradictions of status figure into race relations today. In our pluralistic society, most Americans have attained a degree of cosmopolitanism. Yet everyone has a mixture of cosmo and ethno elements in his worldview. The public space of the cosmopolitan canopy encourages us to express our better selves and reminds us to keep our ethnocentric feelings in check. Ethno-leaning people can practice acting cosmopolitan, even if they need to put on gloss to give a convincing performance. When ethnocentrically oriented people are in the company of like-minded others, they may drop their pretenses of tolerance and reveal their ethnocentric sides.

The cosmopolitan canopies of the city can be likened to little islands of civility, peaceful settings in which denizens of the urban environment can call time-out from the hustle and bustle of city life. Usually these are settings of utter diversity, and visitors are attracted here in part because these settings are open to everyone. And when people visit, they are inclined to study and observe one another and the goings-on around them—and they generally strive to get along. But they can also be defensive here, becoming engaged in a kind of social reconnaissance, checking out the other, scrutinizing interesting but unknown others—people they otherwise would never encounter up close—in circumstances uniquely afforded by the canopy, and, at times, holding one another accountable. Social life is not always about comity and goodwill under the canopy, but most often it is a pleasant environment, and civility is the usual order of the day.

Stigma underlies the "nigger moment" for blacks under the canopy; in sociological terms, "nigger" can be taken as a metaphor for outcaste status, but this is subject to negotiation depending on situations and social context. At times older people, poor people, white women (as well as white men on occasion), Jews, Muslims, Indians, Latinos, and other people of color are, unfortunately, negatively impacted by this dynamic.[14] Virtually anyone with provisional status may experience a "nigger moment" at any time because issues such as sexual preference, poverty, gender, age, and skin color can and do tear the canopy from time to time.

Of these threats to the canopy, "nigger moments" are the most dangerous and potentially destabilizing. As I've indicated, the canopy is ordinarily an amazing place that privileges diversity by encouraging its denizens to express their more cosmopolitan sides, while encouraging people to keep their ethnocentric feelings in check. In those circumstances in which the canopy is torn, when there is such an interactional crisis of sorts, prevailing conditions most often, but not always, deter people from responding to others in a truly hostile manner. Individuals like Shawn, Jesse, and Nathan will forever be scarred by their "moments," and there is no escaping the harm that these moments inflicted on them and, by implication, their communities.

Such moments represent points of profound tension, when the scales fall from the victim's eyes and he realizes that his racial assumptions about his immediate environment are untrue. There is often a shock of recognition and a painful personal crisis. Meanwhile, everyone observing the incident is interested in what will happen next; all stakeholders are intently focused on what has happened and what then will

be done about it. No one takes more interest in such transactions than young people, as they appear eager to learn
by example and precedent, waiting in the wings to succeed
their elders. The outcome of the incident naturally weakens
or strengthens the canopy, determining its ultimate health
and integrity.

But the canopy is an ongoing concern, and, as Everett
Hughes, the great University of Chicago sociologist, would
have appreciated, a unique urban institution whose hallmark
is a certain resilience and change as it goes about meeting the
exigencies of its everyday environment.[15] As parties recover
and regroup, come together, continue to model civility in
public, and are constantly exposed to one another's humanity, life goes on. For better or worse, people's observations,
and the folk ethnography in which they engage, serve as a
cognitive and cultural base for new modes of behavior, as
they adopt appropriate interactional glosses that help them
through emergent conditions, situations, and circumstances.
Differences in race, ethnicity, gender, or sexual preference
may surface to upset the social balance found there, but they
never rend the canopy beyond repair. The simple provoca-
tions, revelations, and pleasures diverse people find in one
another's company induce them to return to the cosmopolitan canopy again and again. It is through such ongoing activity, the goings-on of everyday life in public, that the canopy
renews itself.

9. | CONCLUSION

Like many older metropolises, Philadelphia remains largely a blue-collar city with a significant number of white-collar residents and more affluent neighborhoods located in the suburbs. Over the past century European immigrants from Germany and Ireland were joined by African American migrants from the South.[1] Today Asian, Hispanic, and African immigrants add diversity to the racial-ethnic mix. By the 2000 census, members of minority racial groups outnumbered white residents. Historically, despite William Penn's vision of a "City of Brotherly Love" in which people of all cultures and creeds were accepted, most Philadelphians have lived in racial-ethnic enclaves. Today, although many neighborhoods have changed from white to black as the ghetto has expanded, segregation persists. Indeed, Philadelphia "ranks highest in the nation [in terms of] segregation between whites and Hispanics" and remains highly segregated between non-Hispanic whites and blacks.[2] And the public spaces of the city are more racially, ethnically, and socially diverse than ever. Social distance and tension as expressed by a wariness of strangers are the order of the day.

Yet, Center City is dotted with cosmopolitan canopies. The atmosphere is usually calm and relatively pleasant, as a diverse mix of people go about their business, at times self-consciously on good or "downtown" behavior, expressing civility to the next person they encounter. Here they sit, eat, and walk, sometimes bumping into people they know or making new acquaintances. Denizens return from time to time to conduct their business, while becoming more familiar with one another as well as with the social ambiance of the setting. In time, they come to "know" the regular people without ever having met them. People at times can be solicitous and helpful to complete strangers.

Such neutral social settings, which no one group expressly owns but all are encouraged to share, situated under a protective umbrella, a canopy, represent a special type of urban space, a peculiar zone that every visitor seems to recognize, appreciate, and enjoy. Many visit not only for instrumental reasons—to have a meal or just to be "out and about"—but also for the experience of being among the social types they find here. In navigating the quasi-public spaces here, there is little sense of obligation to the next person other than common civility. Visitors leave with the memory of a good experience and are likely to return another day, perhaps to relive an otherwise uneventful and pleasant time. This kind of exposure to a multitude of people engaging in everyday behavior often humanizes abstract strangers in the minds of these observers.

As canopies, the Reading Terminal, Rittenhouse Square, and other places not discussed in detail, such as Thirtieth Street Station, the Whole Foods Market, and various sporting events, certainly do not provide an identical social experience. But they do all provide an opportunity for diverse strangers to become better acquainted with people they otherwise seldom observe up close. The existence of the canopy allows such people, whose stronger reference point often remains their own social class or ethnic group, a chance to encounter others and so work toward a more cosmopolitan appreciation of difference.

As urbanites, they discover people who are strangers to them, not just as individuals but also as representatives of groups they "know" only in the abstract. The canopy can thus be a profoundly humanizing experience. And when people exposed to all this return to their own neighborhoods, they may do so with a more grounded knowledge of the other than was possible without such experience. In this way the generations may establish new social patterns.

To be sure, people may develop new stereotypes or hold on to the ones they have previously formed. Yet they will have been exposed to members of a heretofore unknown other. If nothing more, through constant exposures, such environments can encourage the practice of common, everyday taken-for-granted civility toward others who are different from oneself. Moving about through the major canopies such as the Terminal as well as the more intimate ones in restaurants and bars, people can have a sense of being out and about in a cosmopolitan setting. As canopies proliferate, such neutral territories become established elements of the city.

With the urban environment becoming increasingly diverse, the cosmopolitan canopy becomes ever more significant. A model of civility is planted in such settings that may well have a chance to sprout elsewhere in the city. People are repeatedly exposed to the unfamiliar and thus have the opportunity to stretch themselves mentally, emotionally, and socially. The resulting folk ethnography serves as a cognitive and cultural base on which denizens are able to construct behavior in public. And often, though certainly not always, the end result is a growing social sophistication that allows diverse urban people to get along.

Physical separation from the surrounding streetscapes and freedom of movement through the space it encloses are defining characteristics of the cosmopolitan canopy. Reading Terminal is the best model. The place is so crowded and the aisles so close together that people have to watch others in order to avoid bumping into one another. Inevitably, their bodies are on the line, and as they pass, denizens and shoppers look in each other's faces. Also important, eating good food in public appears to break down barriers. Moreover, the resulting intimacy of this space helps make people feel connected. Although less dense and more fluid, Thirtieth Street Station is also an enclosed space. Many come to shop and people watch, and to travel. Public relations are fleeting, but certain stalls and kiosks have encouraged hangers on and regulars, including some homeless people. But generally, public encounters are not so close and the sense of communion is not as powerful as in the Reading Terminal Market.

Canopies vary according to scale. A canopy can be a compact public place, a city street, or an entire neighborhood. Even the city itself might be imagined as a cosmopolitan canopy. The distinction lies in the degrees of separation created by distance. When a space is not quite as intimate, the character of the place is affected.

Canopies also differ in their image and social definition. The Gallery is a black-identified place; people who are not black may feel uncomfortably like outsiders there. Given the prevalence of racial segregation in the early twentieth century not only across the South but also in Philadelphia, spaces that are defined as black carry the implication that they are off limits to whites. This perception is widely shared; though no longer engraved in stone, it is enforced by customs and rules that individuals are reluctant to violate. When blacks are present in force, whites tend to stay away, and vice versa. Some Asians and Latinos partake of the Gallery, as do some white people, including tourists who may wander in unaware of the local definition of the place. In prosperous downtowns, more particularistic central places of commerce and social activity are now the exception rather than the rule.

The cosmopolitan canopy is peculiar in that people of

diverse backgrounds feel they have an equal right to be there. In this space, they can observe and be observed by others, modeling comity unwittingly. Through somewhat natural observation of myriad interactions, they get used to the setting and sometimes learn to appreciate different kinds of people, including those whom in other circumstances, they would have little chance of encountering at all. Typically, there is no violence and little intentional rudeness in such settings; people are usually on their best behavior. Decorum is maintained by common consent. In their own neighborhoods, people may be more possessive about space—my stoop, my parking spot, my corner—but here proprietary concerns are set aside: people who participate in public life may become more cosmopolitan simply by being exposed to others and learning this peculiarly urban experience, and complicating one's point of view.

What must we do to ensure that the cosmopolitan canopy is not suddenly rent by a person drawing the color line but encompasses everyone who moves through the public spaces we share? Over a century ago, in *The Philadelphia Negro*, W. E. B. Du Bois spoke eloquently of the duties of black and white city dwellers toward one another. He was particularly concerned that African Americans, newly arrived in the city from the rural South, interacted mostly with the worst elements of the white lower classes rather than with respectable and well-educated white people. Consigning blacks to the slums would degrade both races, he warned, and risk serious deterioration in the city's social fabric.[3]

Today members of the burgeoning black middle class interact with whites at work and in public, though many black city dwellers remain impoverished and isolated in the inner city. The image of the ghetto shadows blacks of all classes as they traverse the urban landscape, falling with special power over younger males. All black men are required to pay a sort of "tax" and prove they are not who others fear they are. While whites are free to be themselves, blacks must take special measures to distance themselves from the ghetto image by their dress and demeanor. The burden of proof rests upon the black male; it is up to him to make whites comfortable in his presence. Whites who find themselves in mixed company are more inclined to be preoccupied with their own discomfort than with putting others at ease. No matter how carefully the black man tries to avoid arousing apprehension, his mere proximity is taken as a problem.

In contrast, the cosmopolitan canopy offers people an opportunity to express themselves as individuals, each with his or her own style of dress, speech, and movement. It allows complete strangers to observe and appreciate one another, and even communicate for a moment or two. The pleasure that people find in these encounters draws them back to the canopy repeatedly. Over time, they may develop a level of comfort with those who are different from themselves. The canopy offers the promise of edification for all who enter. Exposure to others' humanity generates empathy; fears dissipate, and grounds for mutual appreciation appear.

What personal responsibility do those who interact under the canopy have for ensuring that it covers everyone and for extending it across the cityscape? Keeping an open mind means extending to others the benefit of the doubt and welcoming surprises, even if they are unsettling. It means seeking to make others comfortable, rather than withdrawing from the unfamiliar. Finally, it requires us to treat what happens under the canopy not as "time out" from normal life but as a model for what social relationships could become. Ultimately, lessons learned under the canopy can be carried home to neighborhoods all across the city.

The canopies that have emerged in Philadelphia do not yet encompass the whole cityscape or embrace men and women of all racial groups. Much of the city remains segregated and economically unequal, which reinforces social boundaries. And even under the canopy, those who personify the iconic ghetto are often met with suspicion and avoidance. The challenge of developing a more inclusive civility that extends beyond these magical but bounded settings involves changing what transpires in neighborhoods and workplaces as well as in public.

Under the cosmopolitan canopy, city dwellers learn new ways of interacting with people they do not know who are visibly different from their own group. They become more comfortable with diversity and discover new ways that people express themselves in public. These experiences may lead people to question and modify their negative presuppositions about others. Even if they do not want to know those others intimately, they practice getting along with everyone. The canopy offers a taste of how inclusive and civil social relationships could become. That people find such pleasure in diversity is a positive sign of the possibilities of urban life in the twenty-first century.

ACKNOWLEDGMENTS

I began doing ethnographic research in Philadelphia over thirty years ago, early in my career at the University of Pennsylvania, and I have incurred numerous debts along the way. During the course of my fieldwork, I have encountered innumerable city dwellers who invited me into their homes, workplaces, and social gatherings. Many of these folks endured my close observation of their activities and unhesitatingly provided me with accounts and experiences that either helped me to generate hypotheses or contradicted my misconceptions. I want to express my deep gratitude to each and every one of these ethnographic "subjects," who must remain anonymous.

I also want to thank the Charles and William L. Day family, the generous benefactors of my Distinguished Professorship while I was a member of the standing faculty of the University of Pennsylvania. This chair has provided me with financial support, including the critical "gift of time" to pursue my ethnographic work through the years. At Yale University, whose faculty I joined in 2007, I am grateful for the William K. Lanman, Jr. Professorship, which has enabled me to continue my ethnographic research and to establish the Yale Urban Ethnography Project.

Additionally, I'm grateful for friends and colleagues who have helped me in all sorts of ways, from reading drafts and providing invaluable feedback and editorial comments to research assistance and moral support. These folks include: Alison Anderson, Bernard Anderson, the late David E. Apter, Jacob Avery, Howard S. Becker, Harold J. Bershady, Thomas Blackburn, Charles Bosk, Scott N. Brooks, the late David Cass, Randall Collins, Cara Crosby, Martina Cvajner, Murray Dubin, Waverly O. Duck, Mitchell Duneier, John Eldred, Kai T. Erikson, Judith Fisher, Oliver St. Clair Franklin, Renee C. Fox, Tom Gavin, Patrick Gavin, Judith Gordon, Peter R. Grahame, Richard Greene, Raymond Gunn, Leighton Hull, Robert Inman, Gerald D. Jaynes, Nikki Jones, David Kairys, Philip Kasinitz, Jack Katz, Michael B. Katz, Karen Kauffman, Esther Kim, Samuel Z. Klausner, Abigail Kolker, James Kurth, Massimo Lavelle, Patricia Lavelle, Tim F. Liao, Victor Lidz, Joe Looby, Hilary Lopez, Isaac Lucas, Kimberly McClure, Omar McRoberts, Wayne A. Meeks, Harvey L. Molotch, Acel Moore, Linda Wright Moore, Bob Mueller, Arthur E. Paris, Lynwood Pettie, Joe Procopio, Giuseppe Sciortino, James F. Short, Jr., Marty Spanniger, Gerald D. Suttles, Christine Szczepanowski, Ivan Szelenyi, Bob

Washington, Richard Weishaupt, William Whitworth, Paul Willis, and Tukufu Zuberi.

At the later stages of this project, my administrative assistants, Joellen Adae and Lesley Kent, served as very able proofreaders. I am grateful to Erika Storella and also to Grey Osterud for her critical editing skills. Also, I want to thank my editors at Norton, Tom Mayer and Otto Sonntag. And finally I express my deepest gratitude to my wife, Nancy Anderson, and to my children, Luke Anderson and Caitlin Anderson, all of whom provided their thoughtful comments on this manuscript as well as support for me.

NOTES

PREFACE

1 The concept of the cosmopolitan canopy carries no reference to "the sacred canopy" discussed in Peter L. Berger, *The Sacred Canopy: Elements of a Sociological Theory of Religion* (New York: Anchor Books, 1967).

2 For a complementary theoretical perspective that explores the issue of solidarity in public life more generally, see Jeffrey C. Alexander, *The Civil Sphere* (New York: Oxford University Press, 2006).

3 My previous ethnographic studies of Philadelphia include *Streetwise: Race, Class, and Change in an Urban Community* (Chicago: University of Chicago Press, 1990), *Code of the Street: Decency, Violence, and the Moral Life of the Inner City* (New York: W. W. Norton, 1999), and, as editor, *Against the Wall: Poor, Young, Black, and Male* (Philadelphia: University of Pennsylvania Press, 2008).

4 Victor Lidz has drawn a distinction between "the participant observer" and "the observing participant" with respect to the quality of the field-worker's experience. Typically, an ethnographer begins as a participant observer, but over time, with growing familiarity and involvement with the subjects, approaches the status of observing participant. See Lidz, "The Sense of Identity in Jewish-Christian Families," *Qualitative Sociology* 14, no. 1 (1991): 77–102.

5 See Clifford J. Geertz, *Local Knowledge: Further Essays in Interpretive Anthropology* (New York: Basic Books, 1983).

6 In 1863, Charles Baudelaire wrote an essay titled "The Painter of Modern Life," in which he coined this term: "For the perfect *flâneur*, for the pas-

sionate spectator, it is an immense joy to set up house in the heart of the multitude, amid the ebb and flow of movement, in the midst of the fugitive and the infinite." Baudelaire, *The Painter of Modern Life and Other Essays*, ed. Jonathan Mayne, trans. P. E. Charvet (New York: Phaidon, 1995), 496.

7 Gerald Jaynes, "Immigration and the Social Construction of Otherness: 'Underclass' Stigma and Intergroup Relations," in *Not Just Black and White: Historical and Contemporary Perspectives on Immigration, Race, and Ethnicity in the United States*, ed. Nancy Foner and George M. Fredrickson (New York: Russell Sage, 2004), 100–116.

CHAPTER 1: A CENTER CITY WALKING TOUR

1 Louis Wirth, "Urbanism as a Way of Life," *American Journal of Sociology* 44, no. 1 (1938): 1–24, and Georg Simmel, "The Metropolis and Mental Life" (1903), trans. Kurt H. Wolff, in *The Sociology of Georg Simmel*, ed. Kurt H. Wolff (Glencoe, Ill.: Free Press, 1950), 409–24. For further development of these classic themes, see especially the illuminating and provocative works of Jane Jacobs and Sharon Zukin.

2 See Herbert J. Gans, "Urbanism and Suburbanism as Ways of Life: A Reevaluation of Definitions" (1962), reprinted in *People, Plans, and Policies: Essays on Poverty, Racism, and Other National Urban Problems* (New York: New York University Press, 1994), 51–69, and Gans, *The Urban Villagers: Group and Class in the Life of Italian-Americans* (Glencoe, Ill.: Free Press, 1962). Claude S. Fischer reexamined Wirth's theories in "Toward a Subcultural Theory of Urbanism," *American Journal of Sociology* 80 (1975): 1319–41. Lyn H. Lofland, *A World of Strangers: Order and Action in Urban Public Space* (New York: Basic Books, 1973).

3 For an extended discussion of the concept of social borders and its relevance for urban studies, see Jennie-Keith Ross, "Social Borders: Definitions of Diversity," *Current Anthropology* 16, no. 1 (1975): 53–72.

4 In public places like restaurants and in taxis, the black middle class suffers from the utter confusion of social class with race as exemplified by skin color. Here, the working-out of the "master status" characteristic means that color trumps or supersedes all other characteristics of the black person on display. Given prevailing assumptions, white skin color often operates in similar ways. Although on second thought a more sophisticated approach may take hold, in the instant in which interracial interaction occurs the damage has already been done. See Erving Goffman, *Stigma: Notes on the Management of Spoiled Identity* (Englewood Cliffs, N.J.: Prentice-Hall, 1963); Glenn C. Loury, *The Anatomy of Racial Inequality* (Cambridge, MA: Harvard University Press, 2002).

5 See Elijah Anderson, "Against the Wall: Poor, Young, Black, and Male," in *Against the Wall: Poor, Young, Black, and Male*, ed. Anderson (Philadelphia: University of Pennsylvania Press, 2008), 1–27.

6 For an illuminating perspective on cosmopolitanism as a philosophy of ethics applied on a global scale, see Kwame Anthony Appiah, *Cosmopolitanism: Ethics in a World of Strangers* (New York: W. W. Norton, 2006).

7 Erving Goffman, *The Presentation of Self in Everyday Life* (New York: Doubleday, 1959).

8 Leonard L. Richards, *"Gentlemen of Property and Standing": Anti-Abolition Mobs in Jacksonian America* (New York: Oxford University Press, 1970).

9 See Goffman, *Presentation of Self*.

10 Robert E. Park, Ernest W. Burgess, and Roderick D. McKenzie, *The City: Suggestions for Investigation of Human Behavior in the Urban Environment* (Chicago: University of Chicago Press, 1925).

11 Elijah Anderson, *Code of the Street: Decency, Violence, and the Moral Life of the Inner City* (New York: W. W. Norton, 1999).

12 See the classic article by Herbert J. Blumer, "Race Prejudice as a Sense of Group Position," *Pacific Sociological Review* 1 (1958): 3–7.

CHAPTER 2: THE READING TERMINAL: A COSMOPOLITAN CANOPY

1 In a personal communication, Acel Moore, a *Philadelphia Inquirer* reporter and lifelong Philadelphia resident, recalled hearing his parents and grandparents discuss the Reading Terminal Market in the 1940s and 1950s. They described it as a place where blacks could go and "not be messed with," as a relatively safe place for them to be seen in public where they could expect decent treatment.

2 All personal names used in this book are pseudonyms.

3 For an ethnographic study of bar behavior that has implications for understanding social transactions at the Reading Terminal, see Sherri Cavan, *Liquor License: An Ethnography of Bar Behavior* (Chicago: Aldine, 1966).

4 Herbert J. Blumer, "Race Prejudice as a Sense of Group Position," *Pacific Sociological Review* 1 (1958): 3–7.

5 Georg Simmel, *On Individuality and Social Forms: Selected Writings*, ed. Donald Levine (Chicago: University of Chicago Press, 1971).

CHAPTER 3: THE GALLERY MALL: THE GHETTO DOWNTOWN

1 In the early 1990s, the Pennsylvania Convention Center Authority revitalized the Reading Terminal Market as a grand entranceway to the new Convention Center.

2 For an excellent illumination of this process, see Malcolm Gladwell, *The Tipping Point* (Boston: Little, Brown, 2000).

3 For a detailed discussion of the extended primary group, see Elijah Anderson, *A Place on the Corner*, 2nd ed. (Chicago: University of Chicago Press, 2003). Also, see Mitchell Duneier, *Slim's Table: Race, Respectability, and Masculinity* (Chicago: University of Chicago Press, 1992).

4 Erving Goffman, *The Presentation of Self in Everyday Life* (New York: Doubleday, 1959).

5 Georg Simmel, "The Metropolis and Mental Life" (1903), trans. Kurt H. Wolff, in *The Sociology of Georg Simmel*, ed. Kurt H. Wolff (Glencoe, Ill.: Free Press, 1950), 409–24.

6 Bill Wasik, an editor at *Harper's Magazine*, created the "flash mob" concept. In the summer of 2003, his Mob Project used chain emails to gather "inexplicable mobs" of people at various sites in Manhattan for ten minutes or less as a form of performance art. See Bill Wasik, *And Then There's This: How Stories Live and Die in Viral Culture* (New York: Viking Press, 2009).

7 Everett C. Hughes, "Dilemmas and Contradictions of Status," *American Journal of Sociology* 50 (1945): 353–59. See also Gerald Jaynes, "Immigration and the Social Construction of Otherness: 'Underclass' Stigma and Intergroup Relations," in *Not Just Black and White: Historical and Contemporary Perspectives on Immigration, Race, and Ethnicity in the United States*, ed. Nancy Foner and George M. Fredrickson (New York: Russell Sage, 2004), 100–116.

CHAPTER 4: RITTENHOUSE SQUARE: THE PRACTICE OF CIVILITY

1 See Clifford J. Geertz, *Local Knowledge: Further Essays in Interpretive Anthropology* (New York: Basic Books, 1983), and Jane Jacobs, *The Death and Life of Great American Cities* (New York: Random House, 1961).

2 For an earlier discussion of this process, see my discussion in *Streetwise: Race, Class, and Change in an Urban Community* (Chicago: University of Chicago Press, 1990).

3 For an insightful ethnographic analysis of white doormen in New York City, see Peter S. Bearman, *Doormen* (Chicago: University of Chicago Press, 2005).

4 Louis Wirth, "Urbanism as a Way of Life," *American Journal of Sociology* 14, no. 1 (1938): 1–24, and Georg Simmel, "The Metropolis and Mental Life" (1903), trans. Kurt H. Wolff, in *The Sociology of Georg Simmel*, ed. Kurt H. Wolff (Glencoe, Ill.: Free Press, 1950), 409–24.

5 W. E. B. Du Bois, *The Philadelphia Negro: A Social Study* (1899; reprinted

with a new introduction by Elijah Anderson, Philadelphia: University of Pennsylvania Press, 1995).

CHAPTER 5: THE COLOR LINE AND THE CANOPY

1 W. E. B. Du Bois, *The Souls of Black Folk* (Chicago: A. C. McClung, 1903; reprinted New York: Vintage Books, 1990).

2 See Herbert J. Blumer, "Race Prejudice as a Sense of Group Position," *Pacific Sociological Review* 1 (1958): 3–7, and Nathan Glazer, *Affirmative Discrimination: Ethnic Inequality and Public Policy* (Cambridge: Harvard University Press, 1987).

3 See William Julius Wilson, *The Truly Disadvantaged: The Inner City, the Underclass, and Public Policy* (Chicago: University of Chicago Press, 1987).

4 See Allan H. Spear, *Black Chicago: The Making of a Negro Ghetto, 1890–1920* (Chicago: University of Chicago Press, 1967), and Douglas S. Massey and Nancy A. Denton, *American Apartheid: Segregation and the Making of the Underclass* (Cambridge: Harvard University Press, 1993).

5 Pew Charitable Trusts, *Philadelphia 2009: The State of the City,* available online at www.pewtrusts.org/our_work_report_detail.aspx?id=50478 (accessed July 23, 2010). See also Pew Charitable Trusts, "Philadelphia: The State of the City—A 2010 Update."

6 On the social effects of the spatial concentration of poverty, see Wilson, *Truly Disadvantaged.*

7 In an episode of his *Boondocks* cartoon television series that aired on November 27, 2005, Aaron McGruder introduced his concept of "the nigga moment," which he defined as "a moment when ignorance overwhelms the mind of an otherwise logical Negro man, causing him to act in an illogical, self-destructive manner." This concept is not synonymous with my use of the term "nigger moment," which refers not to irrational behavior on the part of blacks but to a situation in which a black person is made to feel his provisional status most acutely. My black middle-class informants use this term to describe moments when they or those they know experience a dramatic failure of white people to treat them with the respect they have come to expect. When this happens, they figure that the white people thought of them as a "nigger" all along, the whites' protestations notwithstanding. To view the episode of *Boondocks,* go to www.youtube .com/watch?v=0B9QGrpdu5Y. For a definition, see the Urban Dictionary, at www.urbandictionary.com/define.php?term=nigga%20moment.

8 For an enlightening treatment of the daily frustrations of middle-class blacks, see Ellis Cose, *The Rage of a Privileged Class* (New York: HarperCollins, 1993).

9 See Everett C. Hughes, "Dilemmas and Contradictions of Status," *American Journal of Sociology* 50 (1945): 353–59. See also Gerald Jaynes, "Immigration and the Social Construction of Otherness: 'Underclass' Stigma and Intergroup Relations," in *Not Just Black and White: Historical and Contemporary Perspectives on Immigration, Race, and Ethnicity in the United States*, ed. Nancy Foner and George M. Fredrickson (New York: Russell Sage, 2004), 100–116.

10 See Clifford J. Geertz, *Local Knowledge: Further Essays in Interpretive Anthropology* (New York: Basic Books, 1983), and Blumer, "Race Prejudice."

11 Despite the generally positive atmosphere of the canopy, where "the better angels of our nature" are often summoned and allowed free expression, these self-presentations may be thought of as a form of "gloss," a façade that deflects scrutiny, allowing the person to pass close inspection by more established members of the group he or she may be trying to join. By displaying this gloss, the person may play for credibility, which is useful in negotiating and managing provisional status. In this sense, gloss is a form of dissembling, commonly enacted in polite smiles, warm greetings, handshakes, and small talk. My conception of gloss in race relations, especially as black and white employees maneuver to get past one another in the workplace, builds on Goffman's notion of physical performance to encompass conversational tools and appearance. See Erving Goffman, *Relations in Public: Microstudies of the Public Order* (New York: Basic Books, 1971), 128–38.

12 Louis Wirth, "Urbanism as a Way of Life," *American Journal of Sociology* 44, no. 1 (1938): 1–24.

13 Hughes, "Dilemmas and Contradictions of Status." Also, see Crenshaw, Gotanda, and Peller's discussion of "a provisional concept linking contemporary politics and postmodern theory." My notion of "provisional status" is ethnographic and has to do with the manner in which "provisional status" is related to social interaction and stigma. Kimberlé Crenshaw, Neil Gotanda, and Gary Peller, *Critical Race Theory: The Key Writings That Formed the Movement* (New York: New Press, 1995).

14 Alexis de Tocqueville, *Democracy in America* (1835–40), trans. Arthur Goldhammer, ed. Oliver Zunz (New York: Library of America, 2004).

15 Erving Goffman, *Stigma: Notes on the Management of Spoiled Identity* (Englewood Cliffs, N.J.: Prentice-Hall, 1963).

16 In *Living with Racism*, Joe Feagin and Melvin Sikes discuss how many black employees become segregated in "ghettos" within the corporation—that is to say, jobs designed for black employees, such as an equal opportunity officer or director of human resources, with a special role in hiring and managing black employees. Typically these positions have little decision-making power and offer little opportunity for advancement. Feagin and Sikes explain that these employees may serve as "fire insurance" for the company, a preven-

tative against possible discontent among black workers and accusations of discrimination in employment practices. See Feagin and Sikes, *Living with Racism: The Black Middle-Class Experience* (Boston: Beacon Press, 1994).

CHAPTER 6: ETHNOS AND COSMOS

1 Drawing on a long line of sociological thinkers including Tönnies, Simmel, Cooley, Weber, and Durkheim, Robert K. Merton distinguished between "locals" and "cosmopolitans" on the basis and breadth of their views. Here I introduce a typology that distinguishes between "cosmopolitan" (cosmo) and "ethnocentric" (ethno) perspectives held by black urbanites. Significantly, this divergence is not unique to black people but can be observed among other groups defined on the basis of such particularistic factors as ethnicity, gender, and sexual preference. See Merton, "Patterns of Influence: Local and Cosmopolitan Influentials," in *Social Theory and Social Structure* (New York: Free Press, 1968), 441–74.

2 The ethno orientation is to be distinguished from ethnicity and from behavior, dress, language, and other forms of self-presentation that express ethnicity. The term "ethno" derives from ethnocentrism, rather than ethnicity, and indicates a perspective on social interactions that is strongly particularistic and values one's own group over others. A person with a strong ethnic identity may have a very cosmopolitan orientation, while someone who does not display outward signs of a particular ethnic group may be very ethnocentric in his or her worldview. Ethnos can be members of any race.

3 "Code-switching" has a long history as a term used to describe the practice of moving back and forth between two or more languages or dialects. In *Code of the Street* (New York: W. W. Norton, 1999), I use it to describe the alteration of behavior between "decent" and "street" codes. Code-switching between cosmo and ethno describes a behavioral transition depending on the "definition of the situation," and may or may not include language modification. For more on the definition of the situation and its implications for symbolic interaction, see William I. Thomas, *The Unadjusted Girl* (Boston: Little, Brown, 1923), George Herbert Mead, *Mind, Self and Society: From the Standpoint of a Social Behaviorist* (Chicago: University of Chicago Press, 1934), and Herbert J. Blumer, *Symbolic Interactionism: Perspective and Method* (Englewood Cliffs, N.J.: Prentice-Hall, 1969).

4 The concepts of cosmo and ethno serve as what Max Weber referred to as "ideal types," necessary conventions for the interpretation of human interaction. Ideal types are analytical constructs that form the basis of comparative study—in this case, to illustrate opposite ends along a spectrum of racial perspectives. See Max Weber, "Objectivity in Social Science and

Social Policy" (1904), in *The Methodology of the Social Sciences*, ed. and trans. Edward A. Shils and Henry A. Finch (Glencoe, Ill.: Free Press, 1949).

5 The term "Oreo" refers to the Nabisco cookie of the same name: a chocolate cookie with vanilla crème filling. It suggests that someone is black on the outside but white on the inside, that the person has "sold out."

CHAPTER 7: THE BLACK MIDDLE CLASS IN PUBLIC

1 For a thoughtful examination of the lives of affluent black suburbanites, see Karyn Lacy, *Blue-Chip Black: Race, Class, and Status in the New Black Middle Class* (Berkeley: University of California Press, 2007). See also Joe R. Feagin and Melvin P. Sikes, *Living with Racism: The Black Middle-Class Experience* (Boston: Beacon Press, 1994). Also, see E. Franklin Frazier, *Black Bourgeoisie* (New York: Free Press, 1957) and Bart Landry, *The New Black Middle Class* (Berkeley: University of California Press, 1987).

2 In *Black Picket Fences*, Mary Pattillo-McCoy explores class differences among blacks in a gentrified neighborhood of Chicago. She illustrates how middle-class blacks function as brokers between the poor and the elite, serving as a bridge between the underserved and the public institutions they petition. See Mary Patillo-McCoy, *Black Picket Fences: Privilege and Peril among the Black Middle Class* (Chicago: University of Chicago Press, 1999).

3 For a provocative exploration of the psychological hurt associated with persistent lower-class status among whites, see Richard Sennett and Jonathan Cobb, *The Hidden Injuries of Class* (New York: W. W. Norton, 1993). In contemporary society, issues of racism often become powerfully intertwined with issues of class. When black skin is confused with low class status, racial discrimination becomes a more complicated affair.

4 See Kevin Lynch, *The Image of the City* (Cambridge: MIT Press, 1960).

CHAPTER 8: THE "NIGGER MOMENT"

1 Randall Collins finds that the more police that show up at a scene, the more likely there is to be police violence. When they call for backup, rumors circulate that the suspect is armed and dangerous and will not give himself up without taking someone out. See Collins, *Violence: A Microsociological Theory* (Princeton: Princeton University Press, 2008).

2 All ethnic groups—Asians, Hispanics, Jews, Irish, Italians, and others—have experienced this moment in some way. So have women of all racial-ethnic backgrounds. Black women encounter a particularly loaded combination of racism and sexism. See Randall Kennedy, *Nigger: The Strange Career of a Troublesome Word* (New York: Random House, 2002). And on the concept

of labeling, see Howard S. Becker, *Outsiders: Studies in the Sociology of Deviance* (New York: Free Press, 1973). Also see Bertram Wilbur Doyle, *The Etiquette of Race Relations in the South: A Study in Social Control*, 2nd rev. ed. (New York: Schocken Books, 1988).

3 In the mid-1940s, the *Negro Digest* published a series of thought-provoking essays titled "My Most Humiliating Jim Crow Experience," in which prominent black writers, including Langston Hughes, Zora Neale Hurston, and Ann Petry, testified to their encounters with white racism. See, for example, Zora Neale Hurston, "My Most Humiliating Jim Crow Experience," *Negro Digest* 2 (June 1944): 25–26. See also Erving Goffman, *Stigma: Notes on the Management of Spoiled Identity* (Englewood Cliffs, N.J.: Prentice-Hall, 1963). See also Charles Ogletree, *The Presumption of Guilt: The Arrest of Henry Louis Gates Jr. and Race, Class and Crime in America* (New York: Palgrave Macmillan, 2010).

For a comprehensive and provocative portrait of despair and anger among middle-class black people confronting America's racial shortcomings, see Ellis Cose's path-breaking work, *The Rage of a Privileged Class* (New York: HarperCollins, 1993). Also, see Joe R. Feagin and Melvin P. Sikes, *Living with Racism: The Black Middle-Class Experience* (Boston: Beacon Press, 1994), and Andrew Hacker, *Two Nations: Black and White, Separate, Hostile, Unequal* (New York: Scribner, 1992). Also see Eduardo Bonilla-Silva, *Racism without Racists: Color-Blind Racism and the Persistence of Racial Inequality in the United States* (Lanham, Md.: Rowman & Littlefield, 2006).

4 For an illuminating historical perspective on how such policies worked for whites, see Ira Katznelson, *When Affirmative Action Was White: An Untold History of Racial Inequality in Twentieth-Century America* (New York: W. W. Norton, 2006).

5 See St. Clair Drake and Horace R. Cayton, *Black Metropolis: A Study of Negro Life in a Northern City* (1945; rev. ed., Chicago: University of Chicago Press, 1993); Allen H. Spear, *Black Chicago: The Making of a Negro Ghetto, 1890–1920* (Chicago: University of Chicago Press, 1967); Gilbert Osofksy, *Harlem: The Making of a Ghetto: Negro New York, 1890–1930* (New York: Harper & Row, 1965). For Philadelphia, see W. E. B. Du Bois, *The Philadelphia Negro: A Social Study* (1899; reprinted with a new introduction by Elijah Anderson, Philadelphia: University of Pennsylvania Press, 1995); Allen F. Davis and Mark H. Haller, eds., *The Peoples of Philadelphia: A History of Ethnic Groups and Lower-Class Life, 1790–1940* (Philadelphia: University of Pennsylvania Press, 1998). Aldon D. Morris, *The Origins of the Civil Rights Movement: Black Communities Organizing for Change* (New York: Free Press, 1984).

6 For a brilliant sociological analysis of the importance of split-second deci-

sions in everyday urban life, see Malcolm Gladwell, *Blink: The Power of Thinking Without Thinking* (New York: Little, Brown, 2005).

7 Everett C. Hughes, "Dilemmas and Contradictions of Status," *American Journal of Sociology* 50 (1945): 353–59. See also Howard S. Becker, *Outsiders: Studies in the Sociology of Deviance* (New York: Free Press, 1973); Elijah Anderson, *Streetwise: Race, Class, and Change in an Urban Community* (Chicago: University of Chicago Press, 1990).

8 See Herbert Blumer, "Race Prejudice as a Sense of Group Position," *Pacific Sociological Review* 1 (1958): 3–7. Ellis Cose makes this point as well. See his *Rage of a Privileged Class.*

9 For a phenomenological view of the "shock experience," see Alfred Schutz, *The Phenomenology of the Social World,* trans. George Walsh and Fredrick Lehnert (Evanston, Ill.: Northwestern University Press, 1967).

10 Such "little humiliations" are described by the psychologist Derald Wing Sue as "racial microagressions." Sue delineates three types of racial microaggressions: microinsults, microassaults, and microinvalidations. See Sue et al., "Racial Microaggressions in Everyday Life: Implications for Clinical Practice," *American Psychologist* 62, no. 4 (2007): 271–86. The term "racial microagression" was coined by the psychiatrist Chester M. Pierce in 1970.

11 See Harold Garfinkel, "Conditions of Successful Degradation Ceremonies," *American Journal of Sociology* 61 (1956): 420–24.

12 See Douglas S. Massey and Nancy A. Denton, *American Apartheid: Segregation and the Making of the Underclass* (Cambridge: Harvard University Press, 1993).

13 See Drake and Cayton, *Black Metropolis.*

14 See Goffman, *Stigma.*

15 See Everett C. Hughes, *The Sociological Eye: Selected Papers* (Chicago: Aldine-Atherton, 1971).

CHAPTER 9: CONCLUSION

1 On the history of racial and ethnic group relations in Philadelphia, see Matthew J. Countryman, *Up South: Civil Rights and Black Power in Philadelphia* (Philadelphia: University of Pennsylvania Press, 2006); Allen F. Davis and Mark H. Haller, eds., *The Peoples of Philadelphia: A History of Ethnic Groups and Lower-Class Life, 1790–1940* (Philadelphia: University of Pennsylvania Press, 1998); Theodore Hershberg, ed., *Philadelphia: Work, Space, Family, and Group Experience in the Nineteenth Century : Essays Toward an Interdisciplinary History of the City* (New York: Oxford University Press, 1981); Roger Lane, *Roots of Violence in Black Philadelphia, 1860–1900* (Cambridge: Harvard University Press, 1986); and Sam Bass Warner, *The Private City:*

Philadelphia in Three Periods of Its Growth (Philadelphia: University of Pennsylvania Press, 1968).

2 For the Brookings Institution report, see www.brookings.edu/reports/2003/11_livingcities_Philadelphia.aspx.

3 W. E. B. Du Bois, *The Philadelphia Negro: A Social Study* (1899; reprinted with a new introduction by Elijah Anderson, Philadelphia: University of Pennsylvania Press, 1995).

BIBLIOGRAPHY

Alexander, Jeffrey C. *The Civil Sphere*. New York: Oxford University Press, 2006.

Anderson, Elijah. "Against the Wall: Poor, Young, Black, and Male." In *Against the Wall: Poor, Young, Black, and Male*, edited by Anderson, 1–27. Philadelphia: University of Pennsylvania Press, 2008.

———. *Code of the Street: Decency, Violence, and the Moral Life of the Inner City*. New York: W. W. Norton, 1999.

———. *A Place on the Corner*. 2nd ed. Chicago: University of Chicago Press, 2003.

———. *Streetwise: Race, Class, and Change in an Urban Community*. Chicago: University of Chicago Press, 1990.

Appiah, Kwame Anthony. *Cosmopolitanism: Ethics in a World of Strangers*. New York: W. W. Norton, 2006.

Baudelaire, Charles. "The Painter of Modern Life." 1863. In *The Painter of Modern Life and Other Essays*, edited by Jonathan Mayne, translated by P. E. Chavret. New York: Phaidon, 1995.

Bearman, Peter S. *Doormen*. Chicago: University of Chicago Press, 2005.

Becker, Howard S. *Outsiders: Studies in the Sociology of Deviance*. New York: Free Press, 1973.

Berger, Peter L. *The Sacred Canopy: Elements of a Sociological Theory of Religion*. New York: Anchor Books, 1967.

Blumer, Herbert. "Race Prejudice as a Sense of Group Position." *Pacific Sociological Review* 1 (1958): 3–7.

———. *Symbolic Interactionism: Perspective and Method*. Englewood Cliffs, N.J.: Prentice-Hall, 1969.

Bonilla-Silva, Eduardo. *Racism without Racists: Color-Blind Racism and the Persistence of Racial Inequality in the United States.* Lanham, Md.: Rowman & Littlefield, 2006.

Cavan, Sherri. *Liquor License: An Ethnography of Bar Behavior.* Chicago: Aldine, 1966.

Collins, Randall. *Violence: A Micro-sociological Theory.* Princeton: Princeton University Press, 2008.

Cose, Ellis. *The Rage of a Privileged Class.* New York: HarperCollins, 1993.

Countryman, Matthew J. *Up South: Civil Rights and Black Power in Philadelphia.* Philadelphia: University of Pennsylvania Press, 2006.

Crenshaw, Kimberlé, Neil Gotanda, and Gary Peller. *Critical Race Theory: The Key Writings That Formed the Movement.* New York: New Press, 1995.

Davis, Allen F., and Mark H. Haller, eds. *The Peoples of Philadelphia: A History of Ethnic Groups and Lower-Class Life, 1790–1940.* Philadelphia: University of Pennsylvania Press, 1998.

Doyle, Bertram Wilbur. *The Etiquette of Race Relations in the South: A Study in Social Control.* 2nd revised edition. New York: Schocken Books, 1988.

Drake, St. Clair, and Horace R. Cayton. *Black Metropolis: A Study of Negro Life in a Northern City.* 1945. Revised edition, Chicago: University of Chicago Press, 1993.

Du Bois, W. E. B. *The Philadelphia Negro: A Social Study.* 1899. Reprinted with a new introduction by Elijah Anderson, Philadelphia: University of Pennsylvania Press, 1995.

———. *The Souls of Black Folk.* Chicago: A. C. McClung, 1903. Reprinted New York: Vintage Books, 1990.

Duneier, Mitchell. *Slim's Table: Race, Respectability, and Masculinity.* Chicago: University of Chicago Press, 1992.

Feagin, Joe R., and Melvin P. Sikes. *Living with Racism: The Black Middle-Class Experience.* Boston: Beacon Press, 1994.

Fischer, Claude S. "Toward a Subcultural Theory of Urbanism." *American Journal of Sociology* 80 (1975): 1319–41.

Frazier, E. Franklin. *Black Bourgeoisie.* New York: Free Press, 1957.

Gans, Herbert J. "Urbanism and Suburbanism as Ways of Life: A Reevaluation of Definitions." 1962. Reprinted in *People, Plans, and Policies: Essays on Poverty, Racism, and Other National Urban Problems,* 51–69. New York: Columbia University Press, 1994.

———. *The Urban Villagers: Group and Class in the Life of Italian-Americans.* Glencoe, Ill.: Free Press, 1962.

Garfinkel, Harold. "Conditions of Successful Degradation Ceremonies." *American Journal of Sociology* 61 (1956): 420–24.

Geertz, Clifford J. *Local Knowledge: Further Essays in Interpretive Anthropology.* New York: Basic Books, 1983.

Gladwell, Malcolm. *Blink: The Power of Thinking Without Thinking.* New York: Little, Brown, 2005.

———. *The Tipping Point.* Boston: Little, Brown, 2000.

Glazer, Nathan. *Affirmative Discrimination: Ethnic Inequality and Public Policy.* Cambridge: Harvard University Press, 1987.

Goffman, Erving. *The Presentation of Self in Everyday Life.* New York: Doubleday, 1959.

———. *Relations in Public: Microstudies of the Public Order.* New York: Basic Books, 1971.

———. *Stigma: Notes on the Management of Spoiled Identity.* Englewood Cliffs, N.J.: Prentice-Hall, 1963.

Hacker, Andrew. *Two Nations: Black and White, Separate, Hostile, Unequal.* New York: Scribner, 1992.

Hershberg, Theodore, edited by *Philadelphia: Work, Space, Family, and Group Experience in the Nineteenth Century: Essays Toward an Interdisciplinary History of the City.* New York: Oxford University Press, 1981.

Hughes, Everett C. "Dilemmas and Contradictions of Status." *American Journal of Sociology* 50 (1945): 353–59.

———. *The Sociological Eye: Selected Papers.* Chicago: Aldine-Atherton, 1971.

Hurston, Zora Neale. "My Most Humiliating Jim Crow Experience." *Negro Digest* 2 (June 1944): 25–26.

Jacobs, Jane. *The Death and Life of Great American Cities.* New York: Random House, 1961.

Jaynes, Gerald. "Immigration and the Social Construction of Otherness: 'Underclass' Stigma and Intergroup Relations." In *Not Just Black and White: Historical and Contemporary Perspectives on Immigration, Race, and Ethnicity in the United States,* edited by Nancy Foner and George M. Fredrickson, 100–116. New York: Russell Sage, 2004.

Katznelson, Ira. *When Affirmative Action Was White: An Untold History of Racial Inequality in Twentieth-Century America.* New York: W. W. Norton, 2006.

Kennedy, Randall. *Nigger: The Strange Career of a Troublesome Word.* New York: Random House, 2002.

Lacy, Karyn. *Blue-Chip Black: Race, Class, and Status in the New Black Middle Class.* Berkeley: University of California Press, 2007.

Landry, Bart. *The New Black Middle Class.* Berkeley: University of California Press, 1987.

Lane, Roger. *Roots of Violence in Black Philadelphia, 1860–1900.* Cambridge: Harvard University Press, 1986.

Lidz, Victor. "The Sense of Identity in Jewish-Christian Families." *Qualitative Sociology* 14, no. 1 (1991): 77–102.

Lofland, Lyn H. *A World of Strangers: Order and Action in Urban Public Space.* New York: Basic Books, 1973.

Loury, Glenn C. *The Anatomy of Racial Inequality.* Cambridge, MA: Harvard University Press, 2002.

Lynch, Kevin. *The Image of the City.* Cambridge: MIT Press, 1960.

Massey, Douglas S., and Nancy A. Denton. *American Apartheid: Segregation and the Making of the Underclass.* Cambridge: Harvard University Press, 1993.

Mead, George Herbert. *Mind, Self, and Society: From the Standpoint of a Social Behaviorist.* Chicago: University of Chicago Press, 1934.

Merton, Robert K. "Patterns of Influence: Local and Cosmopolitan Influentials." In *Social Theory and Social Structure*, 441–74. New York: Free Press, 1968.

Morris, Aldon D. *The Origins of the Civil Rights Movement: Black Communities Organizing for Change.* New York: Free Press, 1984.

Ogletree, Charles. *The Presumption of Guilt: The Arrest of Henry Louis Gates Jr. and Race, Class and Crime in America.* New York: Palgrave Macmillan, 2010.

Osofksy, Gilbert. *Harlem: The Making of a Ghetto: Negro New York, 1890–1930.* New York: Harper & Row, 1965.

Park, Robert E., Ernest W. Burgess, and Roderick D. McKenzie. *The City: Suggestions for Investigation of Human Behavior in the Urban Environment.* Chicago: University of Chicago Press, 1925.

Pattillo-McCoy, Mary. *Black Picket Fences: Privilege and Peril among the Black Middle Class.* Chicago: University of Chicago Press, 1999.

The Pew Charitable Trusts. *Philadelphia 2009: The State of the City.* Available online at www.pewtrusts.org/our_work_report_detail.aspx?id=50478 (accessed July 23, 2010).

———. *Philadelphia: The State of the City—A 2010 Update.* Available online at http://www.pewtrusts.org/our_work_report_detail.aspx?id=57931.

Richards, Leonard L. *"Gentlemen of Property and Standing": Anti-Abolition Mobs in Jacksonian America.* New York: Oxford University Press, 1970.

Ross, Jennie-Keith. "Social Borders: Definitions of Diversity." *Current Anthropology* 16, no. 1 (1975): 53–72.

Schutz, Alfred. *The Phenomenology of the Social World,* translated by George Walsh and Fredrick Lehnert. Evanston, Ill.: Northwestern University Press, 1967.

Sennett, Richard, and Jonathan Cobb. *The Hidden Injuries of Class.* New York: W. W. Norton, 1993.

Simmel, Georg. *On Individuality and Social Forms: Selected Writings,* edited by Donald Levine. Chicago: University of Chicago Press, 1971.

———. "The Metropolis and Mental Life." 1903. In *The Sociology of Georg Simmel*, edited by and translated by Kurt H. Wolff, 409–24. Glencoe, Ill.: Free Press, 1950.

Spear, Allan H. *Black Chicago: The Making of a Negro Ghetto, 1890–1920*. Chicago: University of Chicago Press, 1967.

Sue, Derald Wing, et al. "Racial Microaggressions in Everyday Life: Implications for Clinical Practice." *American Psychologist* 62, no. 4 (2007): 271–86.

Thomas, William I. *The Unadjusted Girl*. Boston: Little, Brown, 1923.

Tocqueville, Alexis de. *Democracy in America*. 1835–40. Edited by Oliver Zunz, translated by Arthur Goldhammer. New York: Library of America, 2004.

Urban Dictionary. Definition of "nigga moment." Available online at www .urbandictionary.com/define.php?term=nigga%20moment.

Warner, Sam Bass. *The Private City: Philadelphia in Three Periods of Its Growth*. Philadelphia: University of Pennsylvania Press, 1968.

Wasik, Bill. *And Then There's This: How Stories Live and Die in Viral Culture*. New York: Viking Press, 2009.

Weber, Max. "Objectivity in Social Science and Social Policy." 1904. In *The Methodology of the Social Sciences*, edited and translated by Edward A. Shils and Henry A. Finch. Glencoe, Ill.: Free Press, 1949.

Wilson, William Julius. *The Declining Significance of Race: Blacks and Changing American Institutions*. Chicago: University of Chicago Press, 1978.

———. *The Truly Disadvantaged: The Inner City, the Underclass, and Public Policy*. Chicago: University of Chicago Press, 1987.

Wirth, Louis. "Urbanism as a Way of Life." *American Journal of Sociology* 44, no. 1 (1938): 1–24.

Zukin, Sharon. *The Naked City: The Death and Life of Authentic Urban Places*. New York: Oxford University Press, 2009.

INDEX